Ted Schwarz is the author of approximately sixty books including the best selling *DeLorean* (written with John DeLorean) and the internationally successful *The Hillside Strangler*, a book on the Los Angeles, California, mass murders. He has written over 2000 articles for newspapers and magazines throughout the world. He has been an adjunct professor of journalism at Northern Arizona University and has taught writing in several cities throughout the United States. For the Peter Lawford biography Schwarz interviewed major entertainers and others who knew Lawford, his friends, and his family, in addition to working closely with his widow, Patricia Seaton.

D1649547

PETER LAWFORD

MIXING WITH MONROE, THE KENNEDYS, THE RAT PACK AND THE WHOLE DAMN CROWD

PATRICIA SEATON LAWFORD
with Ted Schwarz

Futura

A Futura Book

First published in Great Britain in 1988 by
Sidgwick & Jackson Limited

This Futura edition published in 1990

ISBN 0 7088 4481 2

Typeset by Selectmove Ltd London

Printed in Great Britain by
BPCC Hazell Books Ltd
Member of BPCC Ltd
Aylesbury, Bucks, England

Futura Publications
A division of
Macdonald & Co (Publishers) Ltd
66–73 Shoe Lane
London EC4P 4AB

A member of Maxwell Pergamon Publishing Corporation plc

For Daniel, who encouraged me and showed me that I could love again.
For P.K. who shares my pillow talk.
For Peter whose life gave me new life.

CONTENTS

Acknowledgements

To Gloria Luchenbill, with thanks for her many kindnesses and generous assistance.

To Seymour Grush, who provided the facilities of the Best Western Sunset Plaza Hotel as a base for the research for this book.

To Jackie Gayle, for his assistance both with interviews and with lodging.

To Lee Briggs of USA ComputerTech of Canoga Park, California, for providing the computer equipment for both authors of this book which enabled us to meet what would otherwise have been an impossible deadline.

To Kent Carroll, for his sensitivity as an editor, both to the often delicate subject matter and to my needs in trying to come to grips with what I have for so long suppressed.

To James Mason, who helped me meet deadlines and prodded me when I did not.

To Susan Hill, who was the first to believe in this book and who worked to shape it into a project of which I am extremely proud.

To Ted and Leslie Schwarz who were always there when I needed support.

To Princess Alia Ali Khan for her on-going friendship, support and assistance.

To Anthony Haas and Brian Morris whose love and support were invaluable both to Peter and myself.

And to P.K., Peabody and Sherman, who had to get into this book somewhere or I'd never hear the end of it.

1

The Early Years

The first time I met Peter Lawford it was the mid-1940s and he was already the hot new actor in town. My father was doing a radio show called Sealtest Village Store *with Joan Davis at NBC and it was live on the air. Peter was the guest star that week and had been fine at rehearsal. However, the show was about to air and he was late.*

I was a twelve- or thirteen-year-old kid and I remember being bored and wanting to get out of everyone's way because they were freaking out that Mr Peter Lawford was not arriving. I stood at the back of the building, looking out at the parking lot, thinking that maybe I'd see him first or something.

All of a sudden there was a honking and Peter pulled into the parking lot. He was driving an open-topped convertible filled with four girls, all of them in bathing suits. He had gotten caught in traffic coming from Malibu and didn't realize how late it was.

It was like watching Errol Flynn. Peter stopped the car in the middle of the lot, leaped over the side without opening the door, and started running towards the studio. He was very fit, well muscled and tanned, and was wearing a bathing suit, sweater and sandals. He ran down the hall, sending the pages flying, and went inside the studio, which had a live audience, and did the show that way.

Jack Haley, Jr, actor, producer, studio executive

Peter Lawford was born into controversy, foreshadowing a life in which his name would be linked with the alleged murder of Marilyn Monroe, the Kennedy White House, the era of burned out, drug-abusing movie stars, and even the beginning of the sun-and-surfing California beach bum era. Luck and natural good looks brought him a successful career in movies. The influence of his father-in-law, Joseph Kennedy, at one time reputed to be one of the wealthiest and most powerful men in the world, allegedly brought him a career in television. And his insecurity, self-doubt and dependence upon drugs and alcohol resulted in four wives, great debt and deep emotional pain.

May Aylen was living in India with her husband, Colonel Ernest Aylen, a member of the British forces commanded by General Sir Sydney Lawford, a handsome, regal man known behind his back as 'Swanky Syd'. The general was all military, one of the most highly decorated British soldiers in World War I, eventually knighted in the field. His world was one of power, influence and high position. When in dress uniform, his chest was covered with medals and battle ribbons, a swagger stick at his side. He delighted in the company of beautiful women, including the wife of Colonel Aylen, with whom he had an affair that would have remained discreet had May not become pregnant.

She explained to her husband that she was going to divorce him, for obvious reasons, but the colonel was a proud man who could not handle the emotional reality of knowing that the wife whom he loved was pregnant by the leader whom he most admired. Colonel Aylen summoned her to his office, meeting her at the door when she arrived. The first thing May noticed was his regal bearing, his full dress uniform and the military posture he adopted when he faced her. Then she saw that his feet were bare and that a shotgun was at his side. Without saying a word, the colonel angled the shotgun so the barrel was pointing towards his face. He slipped a toe onto the trigger, carefully balanced the weapon, then saluted May, almost simultaneously using his toe to fire the gun. His head exploded before her, blood, brains, and bits of skull splattering against the wall.

The trauma was so great that, when Peter was born at home with a nurse in attendance, it was a breech birth, his body weight low and the umbilical cord wrapped around his neck. He was named Peter Sydney Vaughn Aylen, the last link with the colonel whom he would never know. After his mother married the general he became Peter Sydney Lawford, the only name he would use throughout his life.

The shock may have started May's deterioration into mental illness. Certainly it accounted for the love-hate relationship with her son, which caused her constantly to look for ways to humiliate the boy.

May would never admit to the truth, despite the evidence from Peter's birth certificate, friends' statements and other documentation over the years. In her autobiography (*Bitch! – The Autobiography of Lady Lawford* as told to Buddy Galon), she tells the story that her first husband died without leaving her any money. She claims that he left it all to his girlfriend, a woman who was probably a figment of her imagination. The general was a friend of her father's who she claimed approached her only when she was in young widowhood. The marriage was allegedly as passionless as if it had been arranged, yet the truth was quite different:

Peter was an awful accident! I did everything to prevent such an accident ... including the cause of such accidents. After I married, I used to lie awake and make up excuses to my husband to keep from having to endure that horrible, messy, unsanitary thing that all husbands expect from their wives. If only the Bible had not said, 'Wives, submit yourselves unto your husbands.'

I can still remember slipping to the kitchen and getting uncooked meat which I rubbed against my nightdress. I was *always* having my period! But, oh, that horrible time when I really did not have my period. I rushed to Lord Evans to hear my fears confirmed – I was two-and-a-half months pregnant. Oh, God! Even too late for an abortion – of course, I don't believe

3

in that anyway — it's murder. I've never approved of abortion. Yet I never wanted Peter.

I can't stand babies! They run at both ends; they smell of sour milk and urine. I never saw Peter until he was washed and perfumed. Ugh! Peter was such a mistake! No, I don't think Peter knows he was an accident. It might hurt him if he knew. But I made the General promise that there would be no more babies – *ever*!

Peter was born on 7 September 1923 (May Lawford admitted to being married in 1924, not realizing that Peter's birth certificate was a public record that would reveal the truth). It was a time of relative peace for the British Empire and the world. World War I was over. The Russian Revolution had taken place. The general lived peacefully with his family in various countries; much of the time he and May would be on ships or staying in luxury hotels and apartments, citizens of the world with a son whose nationality was British yet whose first language, because of all these travels, became French.

The Lawfords were wealthy enough to afford both necessities and luxuries for Peter. Yet May was uncomfortable with the son who was the focal point for so much conflict and pain. He was kept relatively isolated from other children during those early years, and she avenged herself on him by dressing him as a girl in all the latest fashions. His family album contains photographs of one of the most adorable 'flappers' ever to be raised in the decade known as the Jazz Age and the Roaring Twenties. The horror of it is that the 'flapper' is actually Peter.

There were other indignities as well. Peter was not educated, though he did have nannies who cared for him, teaching him the basics of reading, writing and language. May, knowing that preventing Peter from learning would be considered wrong by her friends, created the myth that there were tutors travelling with them to educate their son. Peter later commented,

'The biggest mistake which I was to find out was that because of not going to school, I would feel inferior for a long time.' He felt himself to be a fraud, despite his sophistication, a brilliant mind and fluency in several languages, and this attitude contributed to his self-destructiveness in later years.

The importance of learning was not lost to Peter, though. He became a slow but avid reader, always keeping a dictionary close at hand. As an adult, he bragged that there was a period in his life when he took a dictionary to bed each night, teaching himself the meaning and proper use of two new words. In that way he was able to increase both his vocabulary and his understanding of the world around him.

When plain May Aylen became May, Lady Lawford, the wife of a man who walked with royalty, she had a great desire for public attention. This she achieved in the first instance by joining the British Empire Party, a right-wing movement receiving great exposure in the press. May became an active campaigner on behalf of their candidates, speaking frequently – though as much to get her name in the papers as to support a cause in which she believed. She carefully cut out all the articles in which her name appeared.

May's flamboyance also led her to become interested in the movies, still a new industry in Britain and the United States. One day the family went on a tour of a studio in Shepherd's Bush, then the heart of the British film industry. A movie called *Poor Old Bill* was being made there by director Monty Banks, the husband of Gracie Fields. The film was not going well. This was a time when child stars, such as America's Jackie Coogan, were popular, and the scene being shot – without much success – involved a little boy cutting a pair of trousers to fit his pet dog. Then he was to put the clothing over the dog's paws, add his father's glasses and get 'caught' by his irate parent. Everyone thought it could be achieved in one or two takes. The dog seemed cooperative, but the boy was unable to play his part right. Scene after scene was being ruined, and hundreds of feet of film wasted.

Finally Banks called for a break in the shooting while he tried to compose himself. He walked over to where the Lawfords had been watching and was introduced to the family. Banks looked at Peter and said, 'That's the kind of boy I need.' Peter was not impressed. In later years he remembered the occasion and felt that, had his parents been accompanied by a dog instead of a child, the director would have declared, 'That's the kind of dog I need.'

Suddenly, at seven, Peter was in his first movie. He was given a contract, a week's work and £7 for his efforts. Although not even Peter realized it then, he was also given a career.

The first surprise for Peter was how much he enjoyed the smell of the production studio. Stage actors frequently speak of the 'smell of the greasepaint' – that dressing-room mixture of sweat, make-up and cold cream. A different, yet distinctive smell was found on the old movie lots, reinforcing the fantasy world of the film maker. It was one that remained in the boy's consciousness; something he wanted to experience again.

Peter also enjoyed the separation from his mother. He had become extremely introverted, playing by himself or dominated by May. On the set, though she was present, the director was king. For one week and a total of five scenes, he was not a withdrawn little boy. Even when the director yelled at him the first day on the set, he felt as though he had broken through his mother's control.

Oddly, when Peter finally saw himself on the screen for the first time, he was embarrassed. 'I thought that I really looked like a bloody fool. I thought, "What am I doing up there?"' Yet despite all this, he had to admit it was fun. 'It was fun because it was different,' he said later. Then he asked his parents, 'Am I going to do another one?'

May Lawford was delighted with her son's interest. Jackie Coogan was a big child star whose proud mother was regularly interviewed by the press. If Peter became England's new child star, May would be a great celebrity. So she readily agreed to let Peter work later that year when Monty Banks called again.

At this time the London County Council decided that acting was not a healthy profession for children, who should really be in school during their formative years. Child stars in the United States were being given sleeping pills at night and stimulants in the morning in order to keep them working. They had tutors on the movie lots, yet it was obvious that the children were open to exploitation. The LCC did not want to repeat such horrors and thus enacted what came to be known as the 'Coogan Law', which ensured that for children working in films their schooling and their health would be given priority.

Peter, of course, was not receiving an education in the first place, but May could not admit this fact. However, she avoided embarrassment by claiming boredom with the film industry. Peter made his second movie, but there were no more after that.

The change in the law was not a serious disappointment for Peter himself. Instead of escaping his mother by making movies, he now did so by attending them. There were always Saturday shows for children, but Peter also went every day of the week that he was allowed to. Later he recalled: 'I think in a funny way I was probably hoping to see myself up there. The make believe [of movies] was like a game. It is hide-and-seek on a higher level. I mean I didn't sit down at age seven or eight and lay out my future, but it obviously had an effect. And when I was older, I started to get idols.'

There was one adult pastime to which the young Peter Lawford was introduced that did stay with him over the years. His teacher was the German nanny who lived with the family when they moved to Monte Carlo.

'In this arena I consider myself most fortunate,' Peter later wrote.

I did not learn about it on the streets, or from grubby little boys with hair in their palms, or from playing the popular game of 'Doctor!' I was, as I recall, about ten years old. We were in the south of France. My parents were away. ... This particular [tutor] was ... about thirty-five and, even I could tell at an early age that she was a sure number nine, on a scale for female beauty of one to ten.

One lovely day she suggested we take a picnic basket and go off into the country which was quite close by. 'What fun,' I said to myself and off we went.

Let me make it quite clear that up to now there had been no mention, even in jest, of anything pertaining to sex. We found this lovely spot in a meadow under a tree, there were some beautiful flowers growing wild all around us. We had our sandwiches and some fruit.

I was comfortably full and felt relaxed and happy. She was sitting against the tree with her eyes closed, when she gently put her arm around my shoulder and pulled me towards her saying, 'Rest your head in my lap.' There seemed to be nothing wrong with that so I complied.

In a few minutes I was half asleep when I felt her hand gently rubbing my stomach. The next thing I knew she had slipped inside my little short pants and was caressing my penis. My God, it felt good and, for some reason, most natural.

Meanwhile, with her other hand she had unbuttoned her blouse and was pulling my head towards her breasts. She told me I was such a good boy that she wanted me to kiss them. 'Will you?' she said, as she put her nipple in my mouth. In French she said, '*doucement*', gently. She was becoming aroused and made me suck them both while holding the back of my head. She wouldn't let me up.

Unbeknownst to me, because my eyes were closed, she had been playing with herself during all this and must have had her own climax because she suddenly rose up, flipped me on my back, my pants suddenly vanished and, she was eating me alive! Needless to say, with the erection I was sporting, my arrival couldn't have taken more than a minute and a half.

Well! In my life I never experienced such a feeling! To try and describe where my head went would be futile. I was to learn later on that that was the beginning of my sexual addiction. The opposite sex would be, was, and is still being chased. The season is always open.

Other picnics in the park followed this early initiation. Peter, his nanny and a woman friend of the nanny's would sit in the shade of a tree, eating lunch and mutually fondling one another. There were no threats, no violence, yet Peter sensed that if his mother found out there would be hell to pay.

Peter never told his parents what was happening with the nanny over the months they enjoyed each other. However, he did tell them about an uncle who tried to molest him sexually. Peter was staying with the uncle one night when he woke up to find a pillow being pushed over his head to silence him. The uncle was trying to suffocate the boy just enough to stop him resisting while he fondled him. Peter would never say whether or not he escaped unmolested, but he told his parents immediately and they banished the uncle from their home. That incident turned Peter against the idea of homosexual relationships, though, like most members of the movie colony, he was not biased against men and women who enjoyed their pleasures with consenting partners of the same sex.

When the nanny stopped working for the Lawfords, Peter was crushed. This was the first love of his life and he never wanted it to stop. He later claimed that every little boy should be introduced to sex in this manner, so pleasurable had it been for him. The following poem, written by the adult Peter, is an ode to the memory of those early sexual experiences.

Connaught Square

Connaught Square – a lazy square
Where gardens intertwine.
With privilege to play in
if born of social kind.

It's reaching chestnuts,
tailored lawns.
The bramble bushes,
so full of thorns.

Running through
with mirthful glee.
Herbaceous borders
tall as me

The rush of traffic
on the fringe.
The whirring sprinklers
on a binge.

The famous tree
from whence I fell.
Which I avoid
like holy hell.

The grocer boy would
like to play.
Not aloud [sic] he's black
they say.

Then my nanny
I loved her skirt.
An early start
for such a squirt.

Diaper changes
on the hour.

With penises about
to flower.

A crack of thunder
makes us flee.
My mother screaming
time for tea.

Nanny takes me
by the hand.
I visualize
a wedding band.

My fondest memories
my exclusive lair.
I shall always
remember Connaught Square.

The close relationship with the nanny was so similar to that between mother and child that the sex
acts caused emotional problems similar to those which
can result from incest. Peter came to fear intimacy
yet to desire frequent sexual relations, preferring the
impersonal approaches of *ménage à trois* and oral sex
with as many different partners as possible. When
he eventually reached Hollywood, his name would be
linked with the wilder women of the 1940s – Lana
Turner, Judy Garland, Nancy Davis and numerous
others.

Even as Peter aged, his sexual predilections remained
the same. I was the fourth woman to be married to
him, and I came into his life when heavy drug use
had made him almost impotent. He was incapable of
having intercourse and his rare orgasms came through
prolonged oral sex, usually with two partners.

I remember a time in Los Angeles when Peter sent
me out shopping for some things he said he needed.
I had just purchased a couple of beautiful new negligees, and in my bathroom was an array of expensive
cosmetics as well as a new bottle of Joy perfume. When

I returned, I discovered two girls in the bathroom, each wearing one of those new negligees, smelling of my perfume and applying my make-up. As I watched, they leaped onto the bed and began fooling with Peter's cock. I was irate, but if Peter was shocked or embarrassed he never said so. He merely expressed annoyance with what he called my 'common Catholic upbringing'.

Looking back on Peter's past and our relationship, I can understand how the childhood sexual experiences influenced him, especially when he lost his sex drive through heavy drug use. Yet I am equally surprised that I loved him so much and myself so little that I accepted his desires in our relationship. For six and a half years, I had only oral sex with Peter, sometimes alone and sometimes with another woman whom he wanted to watch with me before bringing us both to orgasm. Finally I sought regular intercourse outside our relationship, having a series of affairs with various celebrities we knew. But that life was years away for Peter. As he moved into adolescence he firmly believed that his early sexual experiences had been among the happiest times of his life.

There was also tragedy during those early years, accidents that physically would scar Peter for life. The first, and the least visible, came when he was only three years old. His parents were spending the winter in Monte Carlo where Peter was cared for by a rather incompetent nanny. The woman liked to bath Peter in the kitchen, in a large sink next to a double burner device for making coffee.

The nanny would bath Peter, rub him down, then hold him over the hot burner to dry his back. Usually the rub-down made Peter easy to handle. However, one day he was still slippery from the soapy water and slid from her grasp – he fell on to the hot coffee maker and was badly burnt. May, hearing the screams, rushed in, fired the woman on the spot, then looked to see what could be done to help Peter.

The second injury occurred several years later in a small town in France. Peter, playing with some other children in his parents' rented bungalow, was near a french window when he tripped. 'To save myself,' he later recalled, 'I stuck my hand out and went through it. The mistake I made was in pulling back. That's when the damage was done.' Peter's artery began gushing blood. 'I looked down and the flap was laid back, and I could see bone, muscle, everything. . . . But my first reaction was, "Give me a Band-Aid".' He went over to the bathroom basin, applied a Band-Aid and decided that nobody would ever know what had happened. 'But then self-preservation and instinct told me, "That ain't going to handle it", so I started to run because I started to feel a little queasy.'

Peter was in danger of dying, though he did not realize it. Modern open heart surgery is routinely accomplished with blood loss of less than a pint. By the time he reached professional help, he had lost over two pints.

The child raced to the *concierge*'s desk, then sat on the floor, too weak to move. As he recalled it, 'The *concierge* said, "What are you doing bleeding on my carpet?"' It was teatime and bloodstained carpet would look unappetizing to the guests of the posh hotel in the grounds of which the family had their bungalow. Embarrassed, Peter mumbled an apology. Only then did the *concierge* realize that the child was in a serious condition.

He shouted for a doctor. A man on the fifth floor leaned over the railing in response and, seeing what was happening, raced downstairs, removed his tie and made a tourniquet to stop the bleeding.

Moments later General Lawford appeared and said, 'Good God, what did you do?' Peter explained, then said that it was lucky it wasn't his left arm since he was left-handed. Meanwhile he was carried to the hotel bus to be transported to the local clinic.

If the general was calm, his mother was even more so at first. She looked at her son and said, 'Peter, couldn't you have done it in the springtime?' Her reasoning was unclear, though the question seemed to make sense to her. May showed no fear, no emotion, as they drove to get help.

The injury was so severe that the doctor at the clinic wanted to amputate. Lady Lawford very quietly explained, 'You don't have my permission to cut his arm off. You will do the best you can and try to save the arm, and we will see what happens.' But the doctor was very insistent. Finally, exasperated, Lady Lawford looked at the man indignantly and said, in perfect French, 'Fuck off.' A second doctor came in, took Peter to hospital and stitched him together.

The repair was relatively successful despite the warnings of the first doctor. All the nerves had been severed, an injury that was not treatable until after new surgical techniques were discovered during World War II. Yet despite that, gangrene did not set in and Peter eventually had approximately 75 per cent use of the arm. Only his hand was twisted and withered, an embarrassment he kept hidden in a pocket most of the time. When he did use it, it was much like a hook into which he inserted a cigarette, a glass or anything else. Oddly, should he forget a cigarette was in that hand, he would not feel the pain when the lighted end burned his flesh. Instead, he would suddenly grasp his shoulder in agony, that being the first place where his nerves were sensitive to pain.

If there was ever a time when Peter felt any closeness to his mother, it was during this period. Her fight to save his arm revealed the most emotion and caring he had ever experienced from her. His only other vivid memory of his mother's toughness that he would mention in later life came when the family was staying in a hotel in France. May was alone in their upper-floor suite when she heard a burglar at the balcony window. May calmly went to where the general kept his service revolver, made certain it was loaded, then returned to the window the burglar was forcing open. She aimed

14

and fired; the bullet killed him instantly and the impact threw him back off the balcony, careening to the ground. She eventually went downstairs and explained to the French police what had happened. There was no emotion – not fear, nor anger, nor remorse. A man was trying to break into her room, and the only proper response was to kill him. It was all so very simple that she could not understand why there was any fuss.

During the recovery period Peter got injured yet again. Standard nursing treatment included using stoneware hot water bottles packed around the ankles to keep the body warm. Boiling water was placed inside them, and then they were wrapped in towels so as to reduce the heat to a bearable temperature. The nurse wrapped one badly and the full heat of the bottle was placed against Peter's feet, causing third degree burns and blisters. The severed nerves in his arm had prevented his serious injury from hurting him, but now the 'treatment' was causing him severe pain.

Peter's right hand started to atrophy, which the doctor counteracted by physically forcing it open during one of the post-surgical check-ups. The pain was intense, and Peter nearly passed out. Yet it saved him for acting. The hand would never again be quite so disfigured. He was taught how to grasp a tennis ball to keep the hand as supple as possible, though it never had any strength.

Peter was always quite close to his father. He trusted the older man completely, a fact that saved Peter's life when they were travelling in Ceylon (now Sri Lanka). One evening, after Peter had got ready for bed, the general, wearing a side arm as was his habit, walked into his son's bedroom to say goodnight. The boy had pulled back the covers and was sitting on the bed when his father said, 'Peter, don't move.' Then he drew his service revolver and fired into the mattress until the gun was empty. When Peter looked to see what had happened, there was a dead snake next to him. It was a Russell's viper, one of the deadliest snakes in the world.

There were fairly frequent trips to the United States during the next few years, especially to Hawaii, California and, later, Florida. May Lawford suffered from arthritis, and the doctor had also said that the warmer climate would help Peter's hand and arm to heal.

Prior to the accident, a military career was a foregone conclusion for Peter. He would have had a commission in the Guards, and then gone on to a life that would take him to whatever heights his talents allowed. The only person who had objected to these career plans was Peter, who was relieved when he realized that the accident would give him the freedom to pursue acting without hostility from his family.

May Lawford made the adjustment quite easily, but was then surprised by the way she was treated as she tried to help her son. When Peter was about eleven the family was cruising on the *Mariposa* just off Hawaii. Cruise ships were popular at the time, and actors and actresses frequently used them to relax between film projects. One such actor spotted the Lawfords and appeared impressed with May and the general. He told them to come to his home for lunch when they reached Hawaii, an invitation May thought was serious. As Peter explained:

> We were staying at the Ambassador Hotel and she called his house a couple of times, but he never called back, so that was my first smell of 'Let's have lunch next week.' He really meant, 'Don't call me; I'll call you.'
>
> She said those movie people are uncouth, don't answer telephone calls, and it got her so pissed off that we got on the next boat and went to the Panama Canal.

From the Panama Canal the Lawfords went to New York, where another culture shock was waiting. Peter, though no longer dressed as a girl, was still being dressed as a little boy. He frequently wore short trousers and white socks, both considered grave social errors by the pre-puberty set. As they walked down a

16

Manhattan street, '. . . suddenly a rock lands at my feet from across the street. "Hey, white socks!" And there was a near riot. I react right away. . . . Instinct. . . . Somebody threw a rock at me and I threw it back. My parents were trying to get me out of there. I was into it. Ten to one with these kids against me. They would have eaten me alive.'

The Lawfords managed to get Peter back to the hotel room. May's attitude was that Americans didn't know how to dress children. The general, on the other hand, was pleased with his son for fighting back. 'Good work,' he whispered. Then he convinced May that perhaps it was time for Peter to be dressed like older American boys.

The one area where Peter was able to be active without ridicule from other kids or problems with his mother was athletics. Henry Lawford, Sir Sydney's brother, had been a champion tennis player who won the first Wimbledon tournament. Peter became so skilled that when the family moved permanently to the United States, Peter gained a place on the Davis Cup team. However, he was not allowed to compete in the finals because participants had to be citizens of the country they represented, and Peter was at that time still a British subject.

I remember one time when Peter and I were in London and he decided to show me the club house at Wimbledon. As much as Peter was hurt by being dressed differently from other children when he was growing up, as an adult he came to believe that a man had 'style' by the way he held himself, not because of what he wore. He knew that you could look just as elegant in faded jeans and a T-shirt as you could in a tuxedo – if you had the style to carry it off. Peter did, dressing to please himself. However, when we arrived at Wimbledon it was made very clear that Peter's causal clothing was not appropriate.

Peter would not tolerate being kept out of the club. He explained who he was as an actor and in relation to the Kennedy family. He stood up to the pompous attitude he was facing and we got inside, much to the disgust of the official who agreed to show us the portraits of past champions. As we climbed the stairs we passed pictures of such recent stars as Connors and Borg. The man became haughtier as he read us each name. Then, at the top, he looked down at Peter and commented, 'And that, sir, is the gentleman who won the very first Wimbledon championship, H. F. Lawford. ...' Suddenly he looked at Peter again, realizing for the first time that the man in front of him might have some connection with this revered player. Peter just smiled and said, 'Yes, I know.'

Peter's first film after his hand became deformed was a movie called *Lord Jeff*, starring Freddie Bartholomew. Peter was one of several boys who supposedly attended a naval academy. They wore sailor suits and Peter got to say such inspired dialogue as 'Yes, sir.' He received less camera attention than in his first movie. However, it did rekindle his interest in being an actor.

The movies and the constant travel ended in 1939. On 3 September, Great Britain was officially at war with Germany. The Lawfords were in New York when the Irving Trust Company, the bank where his father kept some of his funds, informed him that all accounts were frozen in England. The cash he had in the United States, plus what possessions he retained, would be all he could have if he stayed in America.

General Lawford had come to the United States with enough wealth to have allowed the family to weather the war years despite most of their holdings being in England. However, he had made some bad investments, including becoming involved with an outlandish scheme to use sugar beet plants in the construction of model homes. The general had no business sense, though he thought he had enough money to be able to absorb the losses. The war proved him wrong.

The family decided against going back to England. The general was retired and quite elderly. May, though much younger, had no fondness for Britain and needed a warmer climate. And Peter, because of their way in which he had been raised, was a citizen of the world. He had no particular ties with any country, had neither the interest nor the physical ability to go to war, and hoped for a career in the film industry.

What Peter did not know until later was that his father had lost everything he had in England. It is uncertain whether his assets were destroyed during the blitz or whether the holdings he had were used as collateral for his many bad investments. Whatever the situation, without Peter's financial support at this time the Lawfords would have been impoverished.

There were several options, including taking the train to California. But the cheapest approach seemed to be selling what they could, buying a second-hand Lincoln and driving to Florida where they had friends. The climate would be better and they could survive financially.

Florida was yet to be fully developed, even the major cities being relatively small and housing inexpensive. The general borrowed money from friends and rented a small house at the end of West Palm Beach. It was an unfashionable area, but the cost of living was cheap.

Peter cared little about the loss of the family fortune. He got himself a job parking cars for $25 a week at a lot in Miami. It was in an area that contained clubs, stores and businesses. Many of the customers paid by the month and Peter was assigned to act as manager, collecting the rents and overseeing what took place. Two other young men, whose names were Frank and Ham, also worked at the lot. They were both black, one an extrovert, the other rather quiet, and both were friendly with Peter.

This was a period when racial segregation was normal in the southern states and it was not unusual to see drinking fountains with signs marked 'White' and 'Coloured'. Many restaurants were required by law to use separate dishes for blacks and whites – in those

19

circumstances where blacks were allowed to be served at all. Violence against blacks was not uncommon, yet Peter was unaware of this. Having been raised throughout the world, he had become friendly with people of all races and never given anyone's colour a second thought. The three of them ate lunch together, played 'pigeon' poker in which the dealer would cheat if not watched closely, and generally had a good time.

What Peter did not know was that several of the long-term, regular customers were racist. They found the sight of a white boy being friendly with 'niggers' offensive. Eventually they complained to the man who had given Peter the job, a man who – ironically – was Jewish and had been subjected to bigotry himself.

The man was gentle with Peter. He tried to explain the social climate in the United States. Then he said that when the three of them were together, it didn't look as though anyone was working, even though Peter explained that one of them jumped up to help whenever a car came into the lot. Finally the man simply had to tell Peter to stop being so friendly with the blacks because he had had complaints from people who might take their business elsewhere. There was no threat to fire Peter. There was also no threat against the other employees. However, the man did summon up the courage to explain to all three that their actions did not look good to the customers, something Peter was forced to accept.

Peter stayed at the parking lot for two years, enjoyed the money he was making, which he later estimated was probably $9 a week more than the job should have paid. The man who hired him was apparently trying to help the Lawfords any way he could. The only problem with the man's intentions was Peter's love for poker and his two new friends. He knew they cheated. He knew that he was a poor player even in an honest game. Yet he loved his new friends and delighted in the games, during which he lost most of his earnings.

Oddly, there was one extremely rich man who occasionally used the lot and tipped well for service – 25 cents instead of the usual dime. The man's name was Joseph Kennedy and he was known to the attendants as a 'heavy cat'. He was considered extremely friendly, always stopping to talk with anyone, no matter how humble that person's position. Later Peter learned that Joe Kennedy had been the major reason why he had been told to avoid his new friends. 'It doesn't look good to see the niggers sitting under the tree with the white boy,' the older man was alleged to have complained. But the attitude in Florida and other parts of the south was such that the issue would inevitably have been raised one way or another.

Despite Peter's job and the money his father had borrowed, family life was becoming increasingly grim. He had only received a small fee for *Lord Jeff*, and that money was spent. He had not impressed anyone enough to be offered further parts. The Lawfords still followed such conventions as teatime, but they now had to watch their spending, learning to shop around for the lowest prices.

Finally, by chance, the daughter of a family friend told Peter that she felt nothing was happening in Miami. She was planning to drive out to California, where she knew someone connected with the movie business. If Peter wanted to go with her, she would introduce him.

Peter had never lost his delight at making movies and readily agreed, staying with the girl's family after they arrived. General and Lady Lawford followed soon afterwards, taking a small apartment on Ophir Drive while Peter found work as a movie theatre usher. What they did not know was that all of their lives were about to change in ways that would involve some of the most prominent entertainers, power brokers and politicians in the United States.

2

New Stars, Old Moguls

Of course we shall have sex. As long as we have men and women in the world, we'll have sex. And I approve of it. We'll have sex in motion pictures, and I want it there.

But it will be normal, real beautiful sex – the sex that is common to the people in the audience, to me and to you. A man and a woman are in love with one another. That's sex and it's beautiful.

Louis B. Mayer

Peter Lawford owed his Hollywood career to World War II. He arrived in California a handsome kid whose greatest desire in life was to ride the waves on a surfboard. He was wild, delighting in the sun, the beach and every willing girl he could find. He had no training as an actor, no special skills that electrified a room the moment he entered it. He was just a newly poor kid with an English accent and a desire to break into the movies. Except for his accent and looks, he was no different from hundreds of other young men and women who flocked to California in an effort to be discovered. At least not until the war began.

Peter's first job was as an usher at the Village Theater in Westwood. Knowing that he had to work, yet not wanting to push himself too hard, he began altering the job to suit his temperament. First he was asked to put up on the marquee the letters spelling out the names of the new shows. The task involved using a ladder and a letter-holding device that Peter hated. He told Richard Anderson, an usher at the Bruin Theater across the street (and later an actor in his own right), that putting up the letters was impossible because of his shrivelled hand. It wasn't true, but Anderson was convinced and Peter paid him to do the task.

Peter also did not see why his friends should have to pay to see the movies. He began sneaking them through the back exit, supplying both himself and his friends with sweets. Eventually his generosity was discovered and Peter was fired. But he had already managed to get occasional parts in films. There was no money for a car so Peter attended auditions by streetcar. Many were 'cattle calls' where anybody could appear. Others were more specific, a limited number of actors being asked to appear, so that just the chance to audition meant he was a step ahead of many of his rivals for the same parts.

The part Peter played in *Mrs Miniver*, a film starring Greer Garson, was more important than he realized. He had an almost meaningless role, his total speaking performance being the one line: 'The Germans are coming!' The best young male part in the film belonged to Richard Ney. He played Greer Garson's son (and later married Garson), but many people in the film industry confused Peter and Ney, thinking that Peter had played the son. Ney was so good that producers who heard of the performance but had not seen the film auditioned Peter by mistake.

The story of *Mrs Miniver* began with the discovery of some newspaper articles by Jan Struther, a British mother of three who was trying to explain what it was like to endure the German blitz. She told of life in the shelters, the fear, the efforts to survive and carry on as normal an existence as possible, and brilliantly captured the lives of everyday people caught up in extraordinary circumstances. The articles were then successfully published in book form and bought for Metro-Goldwyn-Mayer.

At this time the White House was interested in bringing America into the war with Germany and encouraged any project that would help Americans understand the Battle of Britain. Also, before the picture could go into production Japan bombed Pearl Harbor, making a film relating to war all the more likely to succeed.

The movie was extremely powerful despite numerous changes in the script, including Garson's insistence upon wearing a sexy negligee during a bedroom scene where a plain flannel nightgown would have been more appropriate. When Franklin Roosevelt saw an early print at the White House, he asked Louis B. Mayer to rush the film into the theatres instead of waiting for the usual publicity build-up. He felt that it would show American women what their British counterparts were being forced to endure. Winston Churchill applauded the release, sending Mayer a message that read, '*Mrs Miniver*' is propaganda worth a hundred battleships.

The film went on to earn Greer Garson an Oscar as best actress of 1942. Other awards included Best Picture and honours for the director, supporting actress Teresa Wright, the cinematographer and the scenarists. Peter gained by association with such greatness – not just because people confused him with Richard Ney.

The war helped Peter in other ways, too. First there was the genuineness of his accent. The British were heroes before America entered World War II because they were standing alone against Hitler; once the USA was in the war, they were Allies. Thus many films required English actors – but they were in extremely short supply. Anyone with a genuine British accent who was not in the war was pressed into films. Many movies had one or two British actors and numerous Americans trying desperately to produce believable English accents.

Another element that boosted Peter's career was the fact that he was not in the army, and therefore available for work, because of his hand injury. Other actors who were 4-F (the classification for men who were physically unfit) or too old also found a chance for stardom that had previously been denied. After all, the real stars were gone. Clark Gable had enlisted after his wife of twenty-two months, Carole Lombard, was killed in Nevada when the plane carrying her on a tour to sell war bonds crashed. James Stewart and Robert Montgomery entered the services, as did Mickey Rooney and numerous others.

At first Louis B. Mayer at MGM took these departures angrily, feeling that the patriotic duty of Hollywood was to make movies. However, after Pearl Harbor he fired Lew Ayres for refusing to serve. Ayres, star of the popular *Dr Kildare* series, declared himself to be a conscientious objector. He was quoted as saying, 'I'll praise the Lord, but I'll be damned if I'll pass the ammunition.'

Only older stars or those with health problems, such as Spencer Tracy and Walter Pidgeon, remained. New blood, no matter how inexperienced, was desperately needed. A handsome, young man with a British accent seemed made in heaven for Mayer. In reality, the two would clash almost violently.

To understand the conflict between the young Peter Lawford and the ageing L. B. Mayer, it is important to understand how the studios were run in the early days. There had been scandals, of course, and some of the studio heads were known for their excesses. Harry Cohn, for example, ran a studio where it was rumoured that you could not be nurtured into becoming a great star under his tutelage unless you had sex with the producer. This edict existed for all actors, male and female. Likewise, some of the stars were known for their excesses. They were rich, hero-worshipped, able to have any man, woman, physical or sensual pleasure they desired. But in general the men who ran the studios had high standards that could not be broken without retribution against the people involved. This attitude would eventually damage Peter in his relationship with Louis B. Mayer. The attitude of management becomes much more understandable when you know a little of the history of MGM and of its most powerful head.

Louis B. Mayer was born into poverty, in 1882 or 1885 – he was never sure which – in a small Russian town suffering a devastating famine. Jacob Mayer, Louis' father, worked in a menial trade but was a scholarly man who revered the traditional Jewish lifestyle that stressed the religious life. His wife, Sarah, was a natural entertainer. She liked to tell old stories, to sing folk songs and holy music, and she encouraged her children to use their imagination in an effort to grow as individuals.

By 1888 Jacob had managed to save the $30 steerage passage to the New World for each member of his family. They arrived in New York, stayed long enough for Sarah Mayer to have two more sons, then moved to Canada which seemed to offer greater opportunities.

Louis understood the importance of hard work and making money, leaving school shortly after his twelfth birthday in order to work in his father's scrap metal business. By the time he was fourteen, the sign in front of his father's shop read 'J. Mayer & Son'.

By 1900 Mayer & Son were the north-eastern representatives of a national salvaging operation, which enabled Louis to travel throughout New England. He loved Boston and moved there in 1904, settling in a boarding house in the South End, a Jewish ghetto. There he met Margaret Shenberg, the daughter of a synagogue cantor, and married her a few months later.

Mayer attempted to enter the scrap business in New York but was wiped out by the recession that affected many small businesses in 1906–7. Then he began working at a nickelodeon called the Hub on Dover Street. The business fascinated him and he made an effort to learn all that he could about it.

The entertainment was crude by modern standards, comprising short silent dramas and scenes of everyday events. However, tickets were cheap and the films could be understood by everyone, even the large immigrant population. It was one of the few businesses that prospered when times were bad, and in due course he invested in a theatre of his own called the Gem, in Haverhill, Massachusetts.

Mayer prospered, buying several more theatres and showing programmes that included such live entertainers as Harry Houdini, the famous magician and escape artist. Then he added vaudeville acts, showing the films at the end as 'chasers', the signal for the audience to leave. He also experimented with different forms of entertainment. In March 1912 he arranged for Alice Neilsen and the Boston Opera Company to perform *Madame Butterfly* for one day in Haverhill. Later the Boston Symphony Orchestra would appear, and all performances were sell-outs.

But Mayer wanted to do more in the entertainment business than just have theatres. His genius idea was to divide up the film industry into three parts: exhibitors, distributors and producers. The producers were in the best position in some ways, because they controlled the length and type of product available. The distributors also had great power, determining the prices to be charged. The exhibitors were the last in control, having to settle for whatever product was available at whatever rental rates were asked.

He now formed the Louis B. Mayer Film Company, which started by buying the rights to three-reel comedies starring Stan Lupino, a British music-hall comedian. Then he agreed to handle the work of a partnership run by former glove manufacturer Samuel Goldfish, Jesse Lasky, an ex-vaudeville player, and Cecil Blount De Mille, a playwright and actor of little repute. Together they ran the Jesse Lasky Feature Film Company, which planned to copy an idea of Adolph Zukor's and film Broadway plays. The first two films, *The Squaw Man*, directed by De Mille, and *Brewster's Millions*, were rather poor. However the latter was extremely popular with the public and made everyone quite a bit of money.

Mayer's financial base for future operations came from *The Birth of a Nation*, D. W. Griffith's film that was sold by region throughout the United States. Mayer formed a separate company, Master Photoplays, which paid $50,000 plus 10 per cent of the net profits for the right to show the picture. The four-man partnership cleared $600,000 profit, and Mayer's share ensured that he could expand.

It was in 1907 that film companies first started moving west. The city of Los Angeles actively pursued them, stressing the quality and consistency of the weather. Great amounts of light were critical when working with the relatively insensitive films of the day; variations in scenery were needed for different pictures; and the weather had to be generally mild. From the promotional material sent by the city California seemed like another Eden. In 1918 Mayer joined the exodus from the east.

During this period other companies were forming which would be influential in Mayer's life. Samuel Goldfish joined up with the Selwyn brothers, Edgar and Archibald, to form Goldwyn Pictures Corporation. (Eventually the name would be adopted by Goldfish as his own.) Goldfish put up the working capital and the Selwyn brothers put up the motion picture rights to the numerous highly successful plays they had produced on Broadway.

Goldfish was a marketing man who understood how to reach the public, and he pioneered the kind of advertising that is familiar today. His first effort was a series of full-page advertisements in the *Saturday Evening Post*, then one of the largest and most popular American family magazines. It was extremely high-class and not normally associated with the film industry, so Goldfish's ads emphasized quality. His company offered 'Pictures Built upon the Strong Foundation of Intelligence and Refinement'. This was also the time when the trademark of the Goldwyn company was first used: a lion resting in profile and framed with a flowing loop of film bearing the motto '*Ars Gratia Artis*', Latin for 'Art Is Beholden to the Artists'.

The same year that Mayer went to California, Goldwyn too travelled west, leasing the Culver City studio of Triangle Productions. The various companies were positioning themselves for an important merger, though of course none of them realized that at the time.

Culver City lies between Los Angeles and the seaside community of Venice. Its creator, Harry Culver, a real estate agent, erected a hotel and then offered free land to any movie studio that wanted to go into business there. The area had already been used for a number of one-reel westerns and the movie companies were familiar with the location and the sunlight. They were happy to get the free land, just as Culver was delighted to have the actors and support personnel start to build homes and develop the area.

While all these business manoeuvrings were taking place, Mayer was developing his unique style of that management-by-emotionalism that would eventually bring him into conflict with Peter Lawford, a man yet to be born. His sentimentality, though exaggerated, was genuine. Mayer would cry at films whose heroine came from a poor, honest, hard-working background, her family exploited by the rich. Such a woman would profess that love was the answer to all problems, then prove it by marrying one of the wealthy men in the story.

The other aspect of his emotionalism was carefully controlled and designed for show. For years, whenever he had an argument with one of his stars – an argument the star just might win – he would suddenly faint.

The period of 'unconsciousness' would last long enough to strike terror into the heart of the other person. Then Florence Browning, Mayer's secretary,

29

would come rushing in, throw cold water in his face and 'revive' him. He would mutter, 'Where am I?', be helped to his feet, and continue the discussion with his opponent well under control.

It was on 17 April 1924 that the merger that would affect so many stars of the 1940s took place. Loew's Inc. purchased Goldwyn Pictures Corporation, then merged it with Metro to form Metro-Goldwyn Pictures. Subsequently Louis B. Mayer and his partners in what was known as 'the Mayer group' were brought in to manage the operations. Mayer was named vice-president and general manager at a salary of $1,500 a week. His partner, Irving Thalberg, became second vice-president and supervisor of production at $650 a week, and his other partner, Robert Rubin, was company secretary at $600 per week. Mayer insisted upon having a separate identity from the company and eventually decided that the pictures would bear the credit: 'Produced by Metro-Goldwyn-Mayer'. From that point forward, the MGM trademark would be the most important in the industry.

Mayer began to mould an image for the studio based on strict moral codes and pragmatism. He believed in the family and respected sex only in the context of life-time commitment, a fact noted in many of his films. At the same time, he had great power and influence and liked to maintain it by currying favour with politicians and other power brokers.

For example, the Goldwyn group had distributed all releases made by Cosmopolitan Pictures, owned by newspaper magnate William Randolph Hearst. The company was little more than a vehicle for market-ing productions involving his mistress, actress Marion Davies. She would have done well on her own, but not nearly so well as with the backing of Hearst. Mayer, who enjoyed the company of Hearst and Davies, took over the distribution contract. But MGM's sales personnel rebelled because the pictures, such as *The Red Mill* and *Zander the Great*, were far below MGM standards.

Mayer's defence was quite a performance by Mayer. First he stressed the 'bottom line'. The Marion Davies pictures all made money. He did not mention that they made far less money than MGM originals. Then he went on to tell a story designed to avoid the reality of the philandering Hearst. He spoke of George Hearst, a Missouri native who, as a young man, had made his way across the rugged, little-explored west to California where he found success in the mining business. George Hearst went on to influence the future of the state and the nation when he was elected to the Senate. William Randolph Hearst was George Hearst's son, Mayer explained, as though that somehow made everything clear. Finally, with tears in his eyes and a quivering voice, he said, 'This is the point I wish to impress upon you gentlemen here today. We live in a land of opportunity. God bless America! Does that answer your question?' It didn't, but none of the staff had the nerve to repeat the question. Louis B. Mayer had spoken.

During the 1930s Mayer strove to bring the finest stars and the best 'family' pictures to Hollywood. Helen Hayes won an Academy award for *The Sin of Madelon Claudet,* an MGM film which had lured her from her successful New York stage career. Alfred Lunt and his wife, Lynn Fontanne, the biggest names on Broadway, were brought out west for *The Guardsman.* However, Fontanne proved an embarrassment – when a scene called for her to be in a bathtub, she stripped naked. Other actresses wore clothing that disappeared beneath the water, but the Lunts said that they had to 'feel what they were doing', which shocked the crew since the movie was a family picture. Gradually the feeling grew that all the major stars of Hollywood were MGM stars – Lionel and John Barrymore, Jean Harlow, Wallace Beery, Marie Dressler, Clark Gable, Joan Crawford . . . on and on went the list. Then there were the writers and directors, people such as Richard Rodgers and Lorenz Hart, Herman Mankiewicz, George Cukor and David Selznick. Even the children brought to the lot became legend. Mickey Rooney, Judy Garland, Jackie Cooper, Freddie Bartholomew and, in the 1940s, a young girl named Elizabeth Taylor all began or found their greatest success at MGM.

By the time Peter moved to California, Mayer presided not just over a studio but over what he thought of as his family. He was their supporter, confidant, provider, mentor, caretaker and teacher. He created schools on the lot to teach not only basic subjects to the children but also such special skills as fencing, dancing, singing, acting and everything else you needed to know to be a success. There were voice coaches, acting coaches, doctors, nurses and dentists. MGM was small town America where you could be born, raised, eat, sleep, perform and die without going far from the lot if you just followed the Mayer ideals.

Even what would later become scandals were innocent in those early days. In the 1940s, the dispensing of drugs was a loving act by the naïve, paternalistic studio. Drug addicts, those who were using such things as heroin, were not actors. They were life's losers, the ghetto poor who were perceived as having neither brains nor a future.

There was stress on the lot each day. A child might be learning to sing, dance and act, taking school lessons and appearing in pictures. The day was long and intense, and sleeping could be difficult. Thus it made perfect sense for the loving parent, Louis B. Mayer, to see that his medical staff provided 'his children' with pills to help them go to sleep. Of course, many of them became so relaxed from the drugs that they also had to have stimulants to keep them going. Thus they fell into a cycle of pills to sleep, pills to stay awake, good food, good training and salaries that exceeded those of the average adult. What more could a loving father offer?

Later this lifestyle would be seen as exploitative, as indeed the LCC had already realized when Peter Lawford was a child actor in London. People would discover that taking such drugs more than two or three times could

32

be addictive and deadly. But at this time the studios' actions were in keeping with what were considered the loving, moral and ethical attitudes of a studio head who truly cared for the people who worked for him.

Mayer may have been a moralist and a bit of a prude, but he understood the human failings of his stars and did not hesitate to address them. Lana Turner, who would play a brief, tempestuous role in Peter's life, went about with a group of young stars that included Mickey Rooney, Linda Darnell, Jackie Cooper and Betty Grable. They would go to parties, dance, cruise the drive-ins, roller-skate on Sunset Boulevard and have seemingly endless series of affairs which received a lot of attention in the press. In her book *Lana*, Lana Turner commented:

> Eventually Louis B. Mayer himself took notice. He summoned me to his office, along with my mother. In an emotional, disappointed tone he told me that keeping late hours and making the papers were risking my wonderful future. He actually had tears in his eyes at one point, so I started crying too. Then he jumped up and shouted, 'The only thing you're interested in is . . .' and he pointed to his crotch.
>
> Outraged, my mother rose from her seat. 'How dare you, Mr Mayer! In front of my daughter!'
>
> Then, grabbing me by the arm she marched me out of his office. After that I did try to slow down for a while.

Sam Marx, a story editor and producer for MGM for more than thirty years, explained in an interview: 'Without doubt, Mayer tried to guide the private lives of the people. It was for the good of the company. It was for the good of them themselves. You won't find a still anywhere in the history of MGM in those days that shows a person drinking liquor, standing in a bar. Only in a production still. Never in a publicity still. I know for a fact that he advised some of the younger people whether they should marry or not.

'When Peter showed up in 1941 or thereabouts, MGM was still riding the tremendous heights that Irving Thalberg had taken them to. When Irving died in 1936, Mayer had only hopes of keeping up those triumphant years and it wasn't always successful.

'I don't think that L.B. paid much attention to the writing. But that didn't alter the fact that he did keep a voice in the selection of the stories. He turned down many stories that were against his own moral code. We were all trying to make those. He didn't want them.'

3

Tinseltown at War

After 'Two Girls And A Sailor', Van Johnson and I did so many war movies together that the studio joke was that no one would ever know how many missions Van had flown over my dressing room.

June Allyson

The importance of Hollywood's war effort is much greater than most people realize. Peter Lawford's life and career were shaped by the war and the enlistment of so many of Hollywood's male stars. Yet what took place in the industry, and the effect of the propaganda not only on the nation but also on the men who made that propaganda, would shape the leadership almost forty years later.

The reality of World War II was that the Americans were unprepared. The Japanese had made plans to travel further inland but were certain that the Americans had extensive coastal defences. The truth was that there was only one anti-aircraft weapon along the coast of California. Then, as America joined the war effort, almost every battle was lost. The soldiers were under-trained, under-armed and dying both in combat and in training, a national scandal that was not publicly discussed.

In Hollywood, things were quite different. Americans had more money and leisure than ever before. The recession of the thirties had ended with almost full employment, brought about by the war industries.

Movies were the most popular form of entertainment, and Hollywood was anxious to provide for this demand. At the same time, the film industry recognized the importance of boosting morale and encouraging a positive attitude to the war.

Mrs Miniver was the first of many films that told the story of the war years from the British viewpoint. Other movies focused on American women waiting for soldiers who might never return, and on battles against the Germans and Japanese. Comedies ridiculed the enemy: the Three Stooges took on Hitler and secret Nazi spies in America, while Bugs Bunny single-handedly disrupted the leaders in Tokyo.

Interviews with men and women who were a part of MGM's operations during World War II show the intensity of feeling that existed within the industry. Peter Lawford was both made a star and viewed with suspicion by those who were unaware of his handicap. They knew he was British, and he 'claimed' to be the son of a general, so why hadn't he returned to his native land? Was he making movies to avoid his responsibilities? A retired MGM producer who only learned of Peter's physical disability more than forty years after first working with the actor, was somewhat mollified by the news. However, the residual bias could be heard in his voice when he said, 'But I've always thought that he would have tried to avoid the war if he had been able to fight.'

Other actors who avoided the war threw themselves into the propaganda machine to such a degree that the fantasy of Hollywood became their reality. No one better personifies the blend of fiction and truth that surrounded Peter during the war years than Ronald Reagan, a man for whom myth became history and eventually influenced the way in which he tried to run the United States.

One of Reagan's favourite stories about heroism was an incident he claimed occurred during World War II, and which he told frequently over the years as he moved from acting to politics. It concerned a B-17 bomber pilot, who, desperate to save his men, ordered the crew to bail out after the plane had been so badly hit that it was bound to crash. This they did with the exception of a wounded belly gunner who could not move. The youth began crying when the crew left the plane and the pilot, moved to compassion, said, 'Never mind, son, we'll ride it down together.'

Often the story would leave Reagan near tears, his voice choked as he recalled the dramatic scene. The only problem was that the story came from a movie he had seen, not from real life. Had Reagan used a little logic he would ave realized that, had the incident actually occurred, the only men how would have known about it would have died in the crash of the B-17.

Reagan's military career was typical of the way Hollywood created its own war and history. Bad eyesight kept him from active service. The Reagan war effort was the making of movies such as *International Squadron, Secret Service of the Air, Desperate Journey, Murder in the Air, This Is the Army, Rear Gunner*, and *Mr Gardenia Jones*, as well as various training films. The Army Air Corps assigned him to the Hal Roach Studio in Culver City, only ten miles from Warner Brothers, the studio where Reagan had done most of his early work. He was thus able to live at home, a fact that was kept from the fans.

The Hal Roach Studio was where many actors and technicians fought the war, and so it was dubbed 'Fort Wacky'. It produced training films and documentaries, and also trained combat camera units. For the latter it was necessary to re-create the sights the gunners would see when they attacked Japan. The film experts took old stock footage of Japan, then edited it until it looked as though it was being viewed through a gunsight. Much of this faked footage was also used as 'newsreels' to show the American public their soldiers' heroism in the Far East.

Ronald Reagan and his then wife, Jane Wyman, were not big stars in Hollywood in 1940 when they first began making a comfortable living there ($500 per week each). However, by the time Reagan entered the military he was financially one of the more successful actors, his latest contract giving him $3,000 per week. Thus the publicity departments wanted to turn Reagan into a war hero, gaining respect for him even while he 'fought the enemy' in nearby Culver City. Stories were released that were as fanciful as his subsequent memories.

Some of the stories released to fan magazines such as *Modern Screen* and *Photoplay* gave Reagan motivation for 'going to war'. In July 1942 *Modern Screen* told of Jane Wyman seeing 'Ronnie's sick face bent over a picture of the small swollen bodies of children starved to death in Poland. "This," said the war-hating Reagan between set lips, "would make it a pleasure to kill."' The magazines also discussed Jane Wyman's loneliness. She would look for her man and he was not there. She was left with her baby, another woman sacrificing her happiness for the war effort. The fact that Reagan slept at home each night was ignored. There would be references to Reagan being 'on leave' to explain why he was appearing in a particular place at a particular time. In reality, his war work might take him to the Disney studio to narrate an animated film on the war, or to Fort Wacky for his regular work.

The studio public relations arm did everything possible to boost the image of the stars, regardless of reality. For example, when Reagan's second wife, Nancy Davis, arrived in Hollywood after the war, her career was carefully orchestrated. She had had supporting roles on the New York stage and was not considered a particularly skilled actress, though Dore Schary, the producer of the film *The Next Voice You Hear*, in which she was introduced, had great hopes for her future. Her goal was to be an actress, her avocation was to have a good time. She was rather wild, the delight of a number of men and the lover of the alcoholic actor Robert Walker who died tragically in his early thirties.

38

'I remember when three or four of us walked into Bob Walker's house and saw a naked Nancy Davis standing there, looking shocked at being caught like that. She grabbed a towel and ran into the bathroom,' said a long-time friend of Peter's, recalling an incident that remained in his mind after Nancy had become the First Lady. She was single at the time and there was nothing wrong with the situation – only embarrassment at the memory after her life changed radically. He explained that his son had become friends with Ron Reagan, Jr, and he always had the feeling that Nancy was afraid he would reveal the incident.

It is clear from the fan magazines and publicity releases that Nancy Davis was known to have been dating men such as Walker. However, by the time she was engaged the studio made certain her virginity had been restored. An effort was made to give the impression that she had been working so hard on her career that she had hardly any time for men until Ronald Reagan came along. Care was also taken to avoid mentioning his divorce from Jane Wyman at the time. The deeply loving relationship between Ronald Reagan and Nancy Davis Reagan has never been questioned, but the Hollywood reality of their lives before they fell in love differed greatly from the truth.

4

Sex and Stardom

*If I had as many affairs as they say, I would now be speaking
to you from inside a jar at the Harvard Medical School.*
Frank Sinatra

Peter Lawford had no interest in the war or in the
pseudo-soldiers like Reagan. He wanted to surf, play
volleyball and chase women. In fact, Peter created
the surfing craze that swept the nation in the late
1940s and gave the fun-in-the-sun image to parts of
southern California. He was not the first person to
ride a surfboard, nor was he anywhere near the most
skilled, but he was the first actor to be photographed
enjoying the activity as part of MGM's publicity campaign.

Peter also pursued the interests first aroused by his
nanny. He met Lana Turner when they were both trying to break into movies, though she became successful
before he did. Lana was seemingly as wild as Peter and
the two of them hit it off almost immediately.

Peter never made a film with Lana Turner, though
their affair was so intense that they became engaged
to be married. This situation made his mother furious.
With Peter's upbringing, she felt he needed to be involved with women of position and breeding such as
Princess Margaret and Sharman Douglas, the daughter of an American ambassador. Unfortunately for his
mother, Peter preferred the company of the young
actresses he was meeting in Hollywood.

Sir Sydney also enjoyed meeting Peter's new friends, especially Lana. The actress owned a Lincoln Continental in which she would pick up Peter for their dates. Although Peter had begun making money in films, he felt that he should use his early good fortune to buy his parents a house on Sunset Boulevard in Brentwood. Sir Sydney immediately made a garden, a hobby he kept up until his death. This required regular watering of the plants, something he always managed to time for the moment when Lana would be driving by. Sometimes Lana would pick Peter up late when she got out of the studio – ten or eleven o'clock at night was not uncommon. But no matter what time it might be, there was his father, out watering the garden so that he could see the beautiful blonde in her blue Lincoln convertible driving up to the house. One incident stayed in Peter's mind for many years. One day Lana came by as usual but his father became so excited at seeing her that he tripped over the hose and fell into the bushes.

One afternoon, Peter had to meet Lana at the railroad station, a romantic scene that seemed to be part of some movie. They would be marrying shortly, and he was expecting her to rush into his arms. Instead, she not only did not show up but sent word that she had run off with the new love of her life, an Arab actor named Terhan Bey.

Peter was furious. He found some publicity stills from a movie called *Lost in a Harem* which starred comedians Bud Abbott and Lou Costello, as well as his friends Marilyn Maxwell and actor John Conte. The pictures showed men in Arab costume and he carefully took a crayon and recaptioned them in order to ridicule Lana's new lover. He called the man 'Turban' Bey and entitled one photo of Abbott in costume 'Turban Bey's father, Oi Bey'. Another, showing Lou Costello in costume, was captioned 'Turban Bey's mother, Elly Bey'. The action was typical of Peter. He was deeply hurt, but he took out his anger through humour.

Despite Peter's actions, I suspect that he missed the sex that included the maid as much as or more than he missed the relationship with Lana. He was seeing other women the entire time that he was engaged, a fact that upset her and may have caused her to do what she did.

The major extra relationship during the time Peter was engaged to Lana was with his close friend Judy Garland, and it caused great strife between the two women. Judy was jealous of Lana's appearance, while Lana was jealous of Judy's abilities as an entertainer.

The dates with Judy Garland were humorous considering the reputation for wildness that Peter had at the time. They were pals more than lovers, though sex together was a common way for them to end the evening. The sex was not serious – just fun that they both enjoyed. Peter told me that every date with Judy Garland followed a similar pattern. They would have take-away Chinese food, which they adored and would eat from the carton. Then they would go bowling, a sport they both loved yet neither could handle.

Judy and Peter could not use any one bowling alley consistently because, despite their star status, they regularly got thrown out. Judy was worse then Peter because she never learned how to throw the ball correctly. She would lob it into the air with an underhand toss that might be aimed anywhere. Frequently her ball went two or three lanes over, rolling into someone else's pins or smashing the protective barrier that was lowered while the pin boys reset the pins. She thought that you scored when the ball went down your own lane, and that you had a gutter ball only if it went down someone else's lane. Peter had a little more sense but could not bowl effectively with his left hand, the only one that functioned normally. Instead he would wedge his deformed right hand into the holes, make a proper approach, then hope the fingers would function well enough to release the ball. Usually they didn't, and the ball either shot out with a sudden 'pop' like a cork from a child's toy gun, or pulled Peter down the lane with the momentum. Only after he fell to the floor would the ball roll free, a fact that greatly upset the bowling alley owners.

Eventually Judy married Sid Luft, to whom Peter introduced her. As was usual for them, they insisted that Sid accompany them to the various bowling alleys, an experience he tried not to repeat after he married Judy.

Lady Lawford had no illusions about what was happening in Peter's personal life. Her husband was a philanderer. She had been wild. And now her son was heavily involved with Lana Turner, a women she could not stand, while the general encouraged the affair. May wanted to gain revenge against the two of them, which led to a rift between Peter and his boss, as well as, later, a split with his mother.

Acting on the sly, Lady Lawford made an appointment to see L. B. Mayer. Her performance in Mayer's office could easily have won the woman an Academy Award. She acted the part of someone who was embarrassed, worried and seeking help from a man who would understand all and be able to solve all.

As near as the conversation could be reconstructed in later years, Lady May told the studio head that she wanted him to keep a private matter secret. When he assured her that he would, she explained that Peter preferred men in bed. Mayer was neither angered nor shocked by the revelation. He explained that he would handle the matter and told May not to worry. Then he summoned Peter to his office.

Peter held Mayer in disdain. He did not like the idea of being moulded in the MGM image. He refused to conform to the MGM dress code – an unwritten, unspoken but well-understood guide to how stars should dress. In fact, he drew Mayer's ire on more than one occasion when the studio head discovered that Peter was not appearing properly dressed during filming. For example, if Peter had to be in formal attire for a particular scene, but knew that none of the camera angles would take in his feet, he would remove the fancy leather shoes he had been given and switch into black velvet slippers. The slippers were considered quite proper throughout Europe, where Peter had been raised. It was not a rebellious act, just Peter acting like Peter. But Mayer was annoyed.

Peggy Lynch, a Metro featured player interviewed by Kitty Kelly for *Elizabeth Taylor, The Last Star*, explained the system best. She said:

> Publicity people formed us in those days. They really shaped our persona, our psyche, our selves. They chose the image they felt would be best for us; they would fine us and take the money from our paychecks if we did not live up to that studio image. I was supposed to be the girl-next-door type and act as a wedge against June Allyson not to let her get out of line, the same way Kim Novak was later supposed to keep Rita Hayworth in check. If I went to the store in a man's shirt hanging out of a pair of jeans, like we did in those days, I'd be fined. That was considered detrimental to the star system. As a pretty princess type, Elizabeth was never once fined by Publicity because her mother kept her dressed perfectly at all times.

Now there was serious reason to talk with Peter. Mayer invited the young man to his office, which was designed so that the desk was raised and gave him an added illusion of power. He explained to Peter that he understood about his problem. He said that there were other man on the lot with the same sexual preference. He would provide Peter with shots of male hormone to help him. It was a quiet matter that would go no further.

Peter told me that he was furious and said, 'Mr Mayer, I don't know where this rumour's come from but it's completely false. How would I be with Lana Turner if I preferred men?'

According to Peter, Mayer replied, 'I can't tell you where it came from, Peter, but I am insisting that you get these injections. We have several people who are doing it.'

Peter said, 'Do you want to tell me who they are?'

'No,' Mayer reportedly said. 'I'm not at liberty to tell that to you.'

'Then who is the person behind this so I can straighten it out with them?'

'I cannot tell you.'

'Fine. Then I'm walking out of this office now and I'm never doing another picture on this lot if that's what you want. I'll get a contract with Paramount or Warner Brothers. I don't care about your studio and this is the last time I'll ever see your office, Mr Mayer!'

Peter's reaction apparently combined the right amount of indignity and respect, despite the anger. Peter was not fired, though Mayer's days were numbered at the studio and Dore Schary eventually took his place. However, a year later Peter learned that it was his mother who had been the source of the information about Peter's supposed sex preferences. From then on, Peter hated the woman. He also tried to get his father to move out of the house so the two of them could share bachelor's quarters somewhere. But Sir Sydney did not go along with the idea, either because he truly loved his wife or because he was comfortably set in his ways.

Some of Peter's later troubles did start during those early years at MGM. When Peter was dying of a cross-addiction to alcohol and other drugs, he wrote that:

I began on a small level around the age of twenty-one. In those days drugs were not 'in' with that age group, though I had heard that Sherlock Holmes was into them, it did not impress or make me curious enough to investigate them – thank God!

The progression with booze seemed quite natural, except for some horrendous hangovers there were no real problems caused by alcohol until about four years ago when my sweet liver turned on me [This was written approximately six years before his death on Christmas Eve 1984].

I was never a 'problem drinker' as such. Only to myself and eventually to my health. I was never one of those unfortunate people who had a history of auto crashes, police problems, staying away from home or family for days at a time, bar fights, you name it! I was very lucky and, at the risk of sounding like a snob (which I am not), I learned to drink like a gentleman.

The nature of the drinking that Peter did while under contract with MGM was in the line of active partying. Peter liked good times, yet never missed work or was a problem for his directors.

Peter's first film with the young Elizabeth Taylor was *The White Cliffs of Dover*, in which she starred with Roddy McDowall. Although Elizabeth was considerably younger than Peter, they eventually became close friends. The fact she had been born in England, though to American parents, provided a link with his own origins.

Elizabeth had joined MGM, after some forgettable appearances in Universal movies, for *Lassie Come Home*. The movie was successful enough for sequels to be planned, including *Son of Lassie* which also starred Peter. 'I cringe when I tell you of the title,' said Sam Marx, the producer. 'It was the way we called pictures in those days. We didn't think to call it "Lassie II, III, IV, V". We just called it *Son of Lassie*. "Son of" became a general term. You had *Son of Dracula,* and I once had the suggestion to call one movie *Son of a Bitch*, which I think they should have considered.'

The White Cliffs of Dover was another of the wartime pictures meant to encourage Anglo-American unity. It's a dramatic story starring Irene Dunne as an American who marries a prominent Englishman just before World War I. They have a son, but her husband is killed in the war and she chooses to stay in England, a country she loves. Then, at the end of the picture, Roddy McDowall, who plays that son, is killed in World War II. Elizabeth Taylor's role was a minor part, that of a neighbour's child who has a crush on McDowall. There is a brief moment at the end of the picture where Roddy and Elizabeth go up a hill and are transformed into adults – Peter Lawford and June Lockhart.

As Elizabeth reached adolescence, she recognized what all the girls had seen in Peter and developed an intense crush on him. This concerned Sara Taylor, who had no illusions about either her daughter's emotions or Peter's reputation with young women. She told Peter that she was aware of Elizabeth's feelings and ordered him to take it easy on her daughter. Elizabeth was to become one of the few women with whom he had a close and valued friendship that never involved bed.

There may, however, have been another reason why Peter was never linked romantically with Elizabeth during those early years. He later told me that she was a sexual turn-off to him because she had fat thighs.

Interestingly Elizabeth was later sexually linked with Peter's son, Christopher, who looks exactly as his father did at that age. Although there were supposed witnesses to this liaison, a relationship reported in at least one of the many books written about Elizabeth, her long-time friend and former lover, Henry Wynberg, claims that the story is completely false. She never discussed such a relationship with him, and he also stresses that Elizabeth has always dated men of her own age or older. The idea that she would get involved with a boy young enough to be her own son, even one as handsome as Christopher, is completely out of character, according to Wynberg.

Peter's lifestyle during this period was typical of the way he wanted it to be like for the rest of his life. He was a major movie star because of the opportunities the war years had brought him in Hollywood. His family position was such that he had socialized with royalty. He was as much at ease with heads of state and leaders of major corporations as he was with ordinary people who did not have 'names' or titles or positions of power.

One of Peter's closest friends from 1947 on was Joe Naar, a football player studying at UCLA who met Peter through mutual friends. Peter took his new friend on one of the MGM tours

Touring the country on behalf of the studio, the war effort and/or the film industry was a common experience during the 1940s. Films may have been the major form of entertainment for most Americans, but the MGM publicity department did not take the audiences for granted. They arranged for stars such as June Allyson, Janet Leigh and Peter Lawford, and sometimes studio executives too, to travel to major cities for local film premieres. The stars would give a talk to the audience and perform, often doing a song and dance number, then leave the stage so the film could be run. San Marx went on one such tour to upper New York State. 'When I came home,' he recalled, 'my son used to tell his classmates, "My father's been out begging people to go to the movies."'

Joe Naar talked about the multi-city tour in the East on which he accompanied Peter and Janet Leigh to help sell their movie *Red Danube*. 'Peter was dating Janet Leigh at the time,' said Naar. 'I was still in college and it was all new to me and I didn't know anything about anything. . . . Before the movie opened, they would get up on stage and they would have Peter Sabistan planted in the audience and they'd throw a joke at him so Peter [Lawford] could look good on stage. Sabistan was a planted heckler. That was his trick. Peter [Lawford] then, with Janet, would do some sort of a show. He was a song and dance man. He would entertain the people for fifteen minutes and say hello. He would sing a song or dance and answer questions. Janet would do something.' Sabistan was a surfing buddy who, later, was sleeping in Peter's bed when Peter and Pat Kennedy came home from their honeymoon. The incident caused a rift in their relationship because Peter found this offensive.

'But my job was to set up parties,' continues Naar. 'I'd get the pretty girls and have some fun. I was supposed to be "learning the business" because after I graduated, I was going to get into the business, some way, some how.' In reality, Joe simply made certain that they all had a good time.

Mayer had no illusions about how little Naar was doing on the road. However, he felt that this was the ultimate vindication of Peter's manhood and delighted in the knowledge that a football player was travelling with him. In fact, at one point he had the MGM publicity department arrange for an article to appear in one of the movie fan magazines. By-lined by Joe Naar, it told of the relationship between the UCLA football player and the actor. It was an extremely positive story, excellent for Peter's image, yet Naar knew nothing about it until it appeared. 'There was word out that Peter might have been homosexual because he knew Van Johnson and Keenan Wynn,' said Naar. 'I have no idea if they were or not, though Van Johnson might have been. Peter couldn't have been more heterosexual. All we did was chase ladies in those days.'

Peter also acted as a mentor for Naar during those early years. He taught him how to dress, how to talk, and how to deal with the great stars of the day. 'Peter would take me and tell me to say to Mr Berle, if I met him, "Don't call him Milton. Call him Mr Berle until he gives you approval to say call me Milt. You call him Mr Berle. Anybody older than you, you show them respect."

'He would tell me what fork to use when we had dinner with people who were important, and they always were. He would tell me what clothes to wear. He would tell me anything and everything that made me and my life more important. Anything good that's happened to me I owe to Peter Lawford.'

Interestingly, Joe Naar's friendship with Peter in the forties was a little like Peter's friendship with the members of the Clan in the early 1960s. Naar felt out of place, not certain what he was doing being a part of the glamorous life of an MGM movie star. Likewise, comedian Joey Bishop would later comment that Peter seemed to be a little out of place when working on stage with Joey, Frank Sinatra, Sammy Davis, Jr and Dean Martin. Yet Naar was completely accepted by Peter, just as Peter would be by the Clan.

Peter was experiencing true stardom during that period, though Naar was naïve about his friend's success. 'I had no idea how people looked at him and thought of him when I met him. They looked at him the way they looked at Richard Burton. They followed him. He was handsome. He attracted people everywhere.

'His hero was Fred Astaire. I didn't particularly like Fred Astaire but Peter liked his style. Peter was the first to wear sandals without socks. He was the first to wear a tie instead of a belt around his waist. He claims he got it from Fred Astaire. I found out later that everybody else gives Peter credit for most of the style.'

There was a tragedy during this period. Charlie, the friend who had introduced Peter and Joe, was a handsome man who eventually was separated from his wife, a woman he loved but to whom he was not always faithful. After the separation Peter seemed to increase his friendship with Molly, who had been hurt by her husband's affairs. Whether or not they had an affair, Charlie believed the two were seeing each other more than they should. He still loved his wife, despite their problems. When the Korean War started, Charlie told a mutual friend that he was going to re-enlist in the Marines and get killed. He was declared a hero for single-handedly attacking an enemy machine-gun nest, committing suicide in a way what would save others. Peter probably never knew what happened to Charlie. Certainly there was no reason for him to feel responsible for the apparent suicide. Yet in a sense this event foreshadowed the tragic end of Peter's relationship with Marilyn Monroe.

The other important aspect of those MGM years was Peter's meeting with Frank Sinatra, described later because it is so closely connected to his relationship with John F. Kennedy. There was nothing about Sinatra that should have made him a major entertainer. Even his friends saw little more to him than a skinny kid with big ears from Hoboken, New Jersey. His speech was atrocious, the street slang of the uneducated hustler. Yet his approach to singing was flawless, the words clearly enunciated. Even before he had fully mastered his voice, he had developed a style that gave each woman in the audience the impression that he was singing specifically to her.

The high point in Sinatra's early career came in May 1941. He was twenty-five and had been named the top band vocalist by *Billboard* magazine. The same year he received the honour of being *Downbeat* magazine's most popular male vocalist. For the previous six years the winner had been Bing Crosby. The two singers' rivalry would become extremely important more than twenty years later. Yet even in this early period, the differences between Sinatra and Crosby were clear to gossip columnists. Typical of the way the two men were discussed in print was a poem by Larry Siegel, later a major comedy writer, published by Earl Wilson, for years one of the most respected Broadway and Hollywood columnists in America.

> Oh dear, what can Sinatra be?
> A hanging curl, two dreamy eyes.
> Looks that swirl to distant skies,
> The unconscious girl sits and sighs.
> A quivering lip
> Blaring lovesick rhyme,
> Her insides flip in double time.

A slender frame with sagging knees
Yet garnering fame with uncanny ease
The stricken dame pants the breeze.

Eyes of blue, two hands alike
Stretching forth true
Lovingly to strike
Close to you? No, his mike.

Although this lank's
The latest thing
He'll never outrank the 'groaning' king
You take Frank, I'll take Bing.

Sinatra, like Peter Lawford, was 4-F (physically un-fit) for military service, due to a punctured eardrum caused by a series of mastoid operations as a child. In 1942 he decided to spread his wings. He had been singing with the Tommy Dorsey band, had been in-volved with two minor movies and had made over eighty recordings. But he could make more money on his own, and he also wanted to establish a unique identity. Obsessed with success, he worked hard both on his performing and on generating publicity. He pushed to appear in important columns such as Walter Winchell's. He made certain his records were sent to important shows such as the Lucky Strike *Hit Parade*. He took radio disc jockeys out to restaurants, knowing that air play was vital for his future. He courted report-ers and anyone else who could do him some good. The approach Sinatra used seems normal today, but in the 1940s such a concentrated effort was unknown.

The timing for Sinatra to go on his own was as good as that for Peter's arrival in Hollywood. America was at war and people had money to spend. Movie theatres still had acts playing with the films, mostly big bands and famous singers such as Jimmy Dorsey, Helen O'Connell, Glenn Miller, Benny Goodman and Peggy Lee. It was time when a young kid (Sinatra was twenty-seven by then but had the looks of a much younger man) could make appearances where houses were full and the back-up bands were as strong as the ones he had known in the past.

Sinatra also had the help of George Evans, a press agent whose client list included many of the most famous entertainers in the business. Evans paid girls to mob Sinatra, shouting: 'Oh, Frankie! Oh, Frankie!' They would faint at key moments, yell, squeal, and talk to him during songs. He also organized events such as Frank Sinatra Day, and contests called Why I Like Frank Sinatra and I Swoon for Sinatra.

When Sinatra went to Hollywood to begin making movies such as *Anchors Aweigh* with Gene Kelly, his first important film, he discovered a very different world. In Hollywood the columnists could make or break you. They would also do anything for a story, something their 'spies' knew and utilized. Typical was the way in which columnists anticipated marriages. They would pay waiters to see which female stars were regularly going out with which men. Then they would tip the women in the dressing rooms, the powder rooms and other intimate places. As soon as these people reported that a single movie star, dating one man regularly, had missed two periods, the gossip columnist would announce a sudden engagement, probably elopement, or some other euphemism that would tell the public that the woman was pregnant. Some of the readers understood the code and delighted in such insider knowledge. Other fans had no conception of the hidden messages – delighting, instead, in the sudden intensity of the romantic life of their favourite stars.

Sinatra quickly got to know some of the Hollywood celebrities such as Toots Shor and restaurateur Mike 'Prince' Romanoff, which led to his first exposure to political power and influence. Shor, friendly with Robert Hannegan, the Democratic National Committee Chairman, was a guest at the White House for tea with President Franklin Roosevelt. He took comic

Rags Ragland and Sinatra with him. Roosevelt was intrigued with Sinatra because he knew his reputation. However, he was not impressed, commenting to Marvin McIntyre, his secretary, 'Mac, imagine this guy making them swoon. He would never have made them swoon in our day, right?'

The celebrities were, however, extremely impressed at meeting Roosevelt. Toots Shor later explained to Earl Wilson: 'I was nervous. I kept thinking, "A bum can go in and see the President. A crooner, a restaurant guy and a burlesque comic can go call on the Prez!" I kept eating cake to keep myself busy. It was damned good cake. I wish I could get the recipe for my joint [Shor too owned a restaurant]. Sinatra did a Sinatra. He fainted.'

Sinatra did not faint, but he did decide to become active in Democratic politics. New York Governor Thomas E. Dewey was campaigning for President in 1948. Since Sinatra supported Harry Truman against Dewey, he deliberately went to the entrance of the Waldorf Astoria Hotel when Dewey was scheduled to be there. The crowd that had arrived to see Dewey was much more interested in Sinatra's glamour and ignored the Governor.

Sinatra's support of Truman did not save him later from a similar embarrassment to Dewey's. Both the President and Sinatra were eating, separately, at Toots Shor's. A crowd had gathered outside and, when Truman left the restaurant first, they surged forward. Then, recognizing that it was 'only' the President, they moved back, disgustedly commenting, 'We wanted Frankie.'

Two other important events were taking place in Sinatra's life in Hollywood. One was his growing friendship with Marilyn Maxwell during a a period when his first marriage was breaking up, at the same time that he signed a $1.5 million contract with MGM. The other was his becoming involved with Phil Silvers, who was playing out a contract at the Copacabana after Rags

Ragland had died. Sinatra agreed to be Silvers' new stooge.

After a little warming up Silvers, who had a voice like a man gargling with sandpaper, got Sinatra up from the audience and gave him a singing lesson. Sinatra could never seem to learn to do it correctly, so the disgusted Silvers would finally slap Sinatra for his stupidity before sending him back to his seat. Sinatra did not take a bow, having been thoroughly chastised for his inability to learn. When the show was over and the two men took their bows, the crowd went wild. Sinatra had learned an important lesson – adding comedy to a nightclub act – a lesson that would be remembered when he eventually performed with Sammy Davis, Dean Martin, Joey Bishop and Peter Lawford – the infamous Clan.

5

Hollywood Friends

Everybody kisses everybody else in this crummy business all the time. It's the kissiest business in the world. You have to keep kissing people when you're penned up and working together the way we are. If people making a movie didn't keep kissing, they'd be at each other's throats.

Ava Gardner

In a novel a hero can lay ten girls and marry a virgin for a finish. In a movie, this is not allowed. The hero, as well as the heroine, has to be a virgin. The villain can lay anybody he wants, have as much fun as he wants cheating and stealing, getting rich and whipping the servants. But you have to shoot him in the end. When he falls with a bullet in his forehead, it is advisable that he clutch at the Gobelin tapestry on the library wall and bring it down over his head like a symbolic shroud. Also, covered by such a tapestry, the actor does not have to hold his breath while he is being photographed as a dead man.

Herman Mankiewicz

A sex symbol becomes a thing. I hate being a thing.

Marilyn Monroe

The years between the end of World War II and the time when Peter became involved with the Kennedys were enjoyable ones for him. Older male stars were returning to the industry from the war but Peter was still in demand. He had money, he had friends and he wanted to have fun. Joe Naar, his closest friend during this period, described what he was like.

'The beach was a huge part of our lives. Peter was glued to the beach every second he wasn't working. He was a super volleyball player. He taught me to play volleyball. He was a board surfer and tried to teach me how to board surf,' explained Naar. 'Everybody in our crowd did everything he did. He was the star of State Beach.

'In and amongst all of this there were a lot of parties. I went to Arthur Loew's house one night and Gene Kelly was there with Dean Martin and Jerry Lewis. Elizabeth Taylor was about fourteen or fifteen, with those purple violet eyes that were so gorgeous, and they were trying to get her to say the word "fuck", and they couldn't.

'Arthur had a strange sense of humour. He'd go to her and say, "Say intercourse". So she'd say "Intercourse". Say this. Say that. Now say "Fuck".

'She had a crush on Peter. In those days you'd see Elizabeth on the beach. She'd be waiting for Peter, looking for him.'

This was the crush of which Peter never took advantage, respecting both Elizabeth's age and her mother's wishes. He was involved with more mature women, as Joe Naar recalls.

'I picked up Ava Gardner to take her to the beach because Peter couldn't. He had to go to the studio. "Pick her up, will you?" he said.

'Ava Gardner, for Christ's sake! I was still in college. I told my friends in college and they didn't believe it. *I* didn't believe it. They *did* believe it was Elizabeth Taylor because she didn't look that good. Ava in a bathing suit was still smoky and smouldery. But if you had seen Elizabeth in a bathing suit you'd have said, "Gee, I'm a little bit disappointed".'

Peter also became friendly with Marilyn Monroe during this period. She was a woman whose life Peter could understand. As a child Marilyn had been abused to a degree that troubled her throughout her life. She was not particularly well educated, yet, like Peter, she had a brilliant mind. Her interests ranged from the study of anatomy to Sigmund Freud's *Interpretation of Dreams*.

Marilyn was at this stage an aspiring actress, emotionally disturbed, extremely attractive and willing to do anything to succeed in films. She was desperate for male approval, her numerous lovers and husbands and her several abortions all attesting to this fact. She wanted attention any way she could get it, and told one interviewer this story of her childhood:

> The wish for attention had something to do, I think, with my trouble in church on Sundays. No sooner was I in the pew with the organ playing and everybody singing a hymn than the impulse would come to me to take off all my clothes. I wanted desperately to stand up naked for God and everyone else to see. I had to clench my teeth and sit on my hands to keep myself from undressing. ... I even had dreams about it. In the dreams I entered the church wearing a hoop skirt with nothing under it. The people would be lying on their backs in the church aisle, and I would step over them, and they would look up at me.

There was at least one partner of the same sex, though Marilyn was not a lesbian. The relationship was with Natasha Lytess, the head drama coach at Columbia, and it took place in 1948. Marilyn always had the attitude that no sex was wrong if there was love involved. She also understood that other women felt things that she did not. Sometimes she questioned whether or not she was 'frigid'. At other times she recognized that she was attracted to well-built women and wondered if she was lesbian. Eventually she decided that she was not, that one experience with another woman probably being her last as well.

Marilyn also knew how to create a personal history that would enable her to get away with what was then considered outrageous behaviour. Apparently she willingly posed naked for a photographer. Then, when the photograph was purchased by Hugh Hefner in 1953 for a calender that would be part of this new magazine *Playboy*, she took a reporter into her confidence and admitted that she was the subject. Marilyn claimed she decided to pose for the photograph because she had been without food or work for so long. It was a good story, touching story, and Marilyn had certainly known hard times in the manner of so many aspiring actresses. Telling it to a nationally syndicated writer would bring her greater attention.

There were other tricks as well. Marilyn was known for her walk, a movement that made her back end almost as famous as her face and bustline. Yet the truth is that she cut a quarter of an inch off one of her shoe heels. It was not enough to be noticed by a passer-by, but just enough to make it impossible to walk evenly. There would be a little dip that would cause her rear end to wiggle.

Marilyn also believed in physical fitness. She ran for her health and her looks long before that was popular, and followed a fitness regimen that brought her into contact with the athletic Peter. He was intrigued by her, sensitive to the pain she often hid, and asked her for a date. Although they liked each other enormously and remained friends throughout her life, her sexual attraction for him did not even last the evening. Peter told me that when he arrived at her house she said she needed more time to get ready. Lateness, he was to learn, was a classic Monroe trait, and that evening's delay lasted an hour. However, it was not the lateness that bothered Peter.

Marilyn had a dog that was not house-trained. Everywhere Peter looked in the living room, small piles, some fresh and some at least a day or two old, were in evidence. Marilyn was apparently oblivious to this. Peter spent that hour clearing up the mess. The idea of going to bed with Marilyn disgusted him.

Peter and Joe Naar double-dated that night, Joe taking a woman named Barbara Darrow. Peter had been so disgusted by the state of Marilyn's house that 'he said to me, will you take Marilyn home? I'll take Barbara. He was so pissed off, that's the only date they had,' Naar related.

Naar, a Jew, also met Peter's parents. 'His mother would say things to me like, "So you're getting into television? Will you look at my set, it needs fixing." She was kind of an anti-Semite back then. And Peter would say, "Would you shut up, mother? He's trying to get into television as an *agent*." She was kind of the chorus girl wife of the general. She looked and acted and talked like it, I thought.'

Naar was delighted with the general, though. His family, too, was from England, so he brought his father to meet General Lawford. The two men got along extremely well but May was disgusted and made her feelings clear to everyone.

'I must say that Peter handled his mother's attitudes extremely well, though,' said Naar. 'He'd walk out and be close to tears because of what she would say. But he'd just put it out of his head. He never apologized of her. He gave everyone the credit of knowing that he wasn't that way. Of course his father was a very, very genuine, very classy man and that's who he loved dearly.'

Joe began working at William Morris as a junior agent who was assigned to take care of Peter. His skills as an agent were based on his experiences as a street fighter and football player. He was not accustomed to verbal finesse, no matter what Peter taught him. The result was a rather humorous confrontation, at least in retrospect.

'Peter was doing a show that had a very bad producer on it,' Naar recalled. 'He was very angry with Peter who wanted a script change and I ended up, I thought, defending Peter – I had a fist fight with this producer, Alex Gottlieb. They just about fired me because of that. I felt so loyal to Peter, almost like a bodyguard. Part of my history was as a fighter in the Navy and as a street fighter. I was good with my hands and had a sort of reputation, so I figured myself as a boxer. So I went too far as a stupid jerk agent, and this jerk tried to throw me off the set.'

Though Peter acted the part of a playboy during this period, he was also gaining a reputation as a consummate professional. This was most obvious in the way he became involved with Jack Lemmon.

'Peter was a terrific guy at an important time for me,' Lemmon explained. 'And I think out of his good nature, period, not because he felt, "Oh, I'll help this kid because he's getting his feet wet and he doesn't know." He was just basically a hell of a nice guy.'

Lemmon's early career was in New York. He had acted in live television and on Broadway. 'I was doing a Broadway play which was a flop, but the actors got very good notices and the Hollywood producers were looking for someone to play opposite Judy Holliday in *It Should Happen to You*. They were looking for two men, and Peter had one of the parts.

'I was not only fresh from Broadway, the only time I had seen a movie camera was when I did one little army short years before. I did a hell of a lot of live television but that really is closer to theatre. And on that little box your eyes aren't three feet wide as they are on a movie screen.

'I'd be going up and down and George Cukor kept telling me at the end of every take, "Oh, that's wonderful. But let's do just one more. Less, Jack, less."

'Finally, after about two weeks of this, I screamed at him, which is uncharacteristic – I didn't realize what I was saying – I said, "Are you trying to tell me not to act at *all*?"

'And he said, "Oh, yes. God, yes." And crossed himself.

'I was playing to a theatre. What he was really trying to say – and he was a marvellous director – was bring it down. Just feel it and think it, but you don't have to be as big [of voice].

'I laughed, and so did everyone else. Peter was on the set and he was very sweet. He came over and he squeezed my elbow – I remember this very vividly – and he whispered to me, "You don't *have* to!"'

Lemmon continued, 'Peter really was very, very helpful, and so was Judy. Working with the two of them, and with George Cukor as the director, was such a wonderful experience that I switched my whole life plan. I had no intention of coming out to Hollywood. I was going to stay in New York, doing theatre as much as I could, and I had it in my contract with Columbia that I could do four shows on Broadway in the next seven years or more as long as I tacked the two pictures a year on the end. But the experience was so terrific, working with them, that a year later I bought a little house and I've stayed here ever since.

'Another thing that I will always remember – it sounds like a scene from some of the early movies I used to do, the wild comedies in the early days with Columbia – was when my former wife and I tried to drive out here with our little dog, Duffy.

'The movers were supposed to meet us at a certain time with the furniture. We got out here finally, absolute wrecks. The car broke down. The dog ate up all the seats. We were sitting on newspapers. It was a terrible, terrible cross-country trip for about five or six days. And when we got here there were no movers. The house was totally empty. We couldn't even stay there.

'It was now late afternoon and we didn't know what to do. But I remembered a little country type of restaurant which was only minutes away. And I said, "Well, let's get something to eat." I thought we could go to a motel or something and I was looking to see if I had enough money for that before I could get into Columbia the next day and try to get an advance.

'We walked into the restaurant and it was as if I saw Jesus. There was Peter. So we sat with him and told him the story. He just smiled and said, "Follow me." He brought us back to his house and got sheets. He got a mattress. He got blankets. He brought a couple of lights. He was even starting to put food into boxes for us until I stopped him and said, "Oh, we can get to a market." Then he drove back with us and helped us set everything up. It was terribly important to me at the time, that kindness. He was always a terrific guy.

'I remember the very first day when we were reading the script for that movie with George on the sound stage. "God, that's a marvellous script, isn't it? The parts are so good," I said to Peter. And Peter just smiled and said, "Yours sure is!" Mine was the lead, so to speak. It was the better of the two male parts and it had a little more depth than Peter's. But he said it with a smile, then proceeded to make me to lunch and we had a ball.

'That was a problem. There was a certain limitation – because of the accent and everything else – on the parts that Peter could play. If he had had an American accent, he might have had God knows what other parts in his career.'

Lemmon discussed Peter's professionalism on the set of *It Should Happen to You*. 'Peter was there, letter perfect and with it. And he was very much like Judy. If anything was bothering him personally, you damn well never knew it. That's a difficult thing to do. Professionally, Peter was tops, and that I admired immensely because I've always prided myself on being professional – if there's something bothering you, God damn it, put the blinders on, leave it at home, do your work! Try to keep everything else out, no matter how tough it is.'

Off the set, Peter stayed with the cast, sometimes playing word games with Judy Holliday ('She was anything but the dumb blonde she played so often and so well,' said Lemmon), sometimes running through a scene if that seemed necessary. There would also be jokes or 'laughing over the antics of some crazy grip,' Lemmon explained. 'That's another reason I was attracted to him, because he was bright. You can't be a great actor unless you are bright. You can be a screwed-up emotional mess, but you have to be bright.

'And the other thing that I loved is that Peter always had a great sense of humour and he was marvellous in comedy. He was always laughing, giggling, saying things or doing things. ... What that does is keep a bubble on the set. That was one happy set with Judy and Peter, and I love to work that way, too. We had fun.

'I don't care if it's Virginia Woolf or Tolstoy's *Power of Darkness*, you've got to have that bubble of energy, fun and joy in your work. Peter had that. Peter was a total pro, but he had had a ton of experience by the time I worked with him.'

6

Marriage to a Kennedy, Friendship with Sinatra

My dear Jack,

Just a line to let you know how things are going here. A lot of the same that you left behind – Bureaucracy bullshit and a President [Ronald Reagan] who can taste that second term in office so badly that he has created this false economy in which we are existing – and the poor people are believing it! I can't wait for the deficit to start falling in on him and his 'kitchen' group! And that's where they belong.

Enough of that dreary stuff. I have managed to drink myself into the BFC [Betty Ford Center]. My liver drove me down and here we are – it's a very pretty Stalag 17 which is supposed to help one back to the world of sobriety. I must say they do their best and I'm sure it's helped me. You, my friend, would hate it – not a pretty girl within miles and, every time you turn around, you trip over someone's ego or someone expressing an authoritarian spasm (here they call it therapy). . . .

I know you're having a good time. You always do. Are you Pres. of anything? A garden club or bowling team perhaps! You must be running something, knowing you. Jackie is terrific – Spent a lot of time with her at Sydney's wedding.

How are Marilyn, Bobby, [unreadable]? Give them my love. If you should run into Steve McQueen or Vic Morrow, give them my best.

Well that's about it for now. Believe me, you are sorely missed here and around the world if I may say so.

All the kids send their love. Let us hear from you soon.

Take care of you–

Love, Peter.

Peter Lawford to his former brother-in-law, John F. Kennedy, written while undergoing treatment for alcohol and drug addiction at the Betty Ford Center in Rancho Mirage, California many years after John F. Kennedy's death.

The Kennedy family rose to regional prominence under P. J. Kennedy, father of Joe and grandfather of Jack, Bobby and the rest, who was a Boston politician. The connections he forged made the Kennedys extremely influential in both their community and the state of Massachusetts. But Joe decided that he did not want to be in politics himself, and chose to make his living in the business world. While at Harvard he and a friend purchased a tour bus and took groups of people on guided visits to historic sites. The men cleared a profit of $10,000, a tremendous sum back in 1912.

Kennedy put those early earnings into real estate, then came to realize that bankers were always in the middle of any business venture. He decided that becoming a banker would not only enable him to amass personal wealth, it would also give him access to other people's money. By 1914, the year he married, he had manoeuvred his way into the presidency of the Columbia Trust Company.

Joe Kennedy now began to master both the stock market and the ways in which it was possible to take control of companies through the manipulation of their stock. He was becoming a man of the world, a power broker who was not yet thirty when World War I ended and international business was becoming a reality for many Americans.

Joe Kennedy's business acumen was best instanced during Prohibition. He had both the money and the storage facilities to buy up thousands of bottles of whisky in anticipation of Prohibition. He was also able to work through pharmacies which had licences to dispense alcohol by prescription. Since doctors wrote prescriptions fairly freely, his legitimately purchased alcohol had a ready market. During Prohibition physicians were no more likely to consider liquor 'medicinal' than they are today. But it was this stockpile that put Joe Kennedy ahead of the game, guaranteeing himself large profits.

Joe's young bride, Rose, would prove to be both his greatest advocate and his most difficult emotional attachment. She was torn between the desire for independence sought by many highly intelligent, independent women of her day, and her strict Irish Catholic upbringing. Rose was clever, and had gained a place at Wellesley College, an institution dedicated to providing women with the same academic standards of higher learning as were available to men – a rarity at that time. But she had also been raised to think that marriage was the ultimate achievement for a woman.

Rose was also taught that sex, no matter how enjoyable, was meant for procreation. The teachings of the Catholic Church in fact never spoke against sex as pleasure, nor did most Church leaders feel that sex should not be frequently enjoyed between married couples. However, many nuns taught young girls in their care that sex was for the purpose of having babies. To continue sex during pregnancy, or after there was no longer a desire to have children, was sinful. Thus Rose would eventually be torn between the strict teachings of the nuns and her spirit that demanded knowledge, excellence and the sharing of all life's adventures with her husband.

In the end, the strictness of her upbringing would dominate, and she settled for the traditional role of housewife while her husband travelled the nation and the world. Absent from home, his domestic sex life limited by his wife's beliefs, Joe Kennedy would have a series of affairs that became well known to his children.

Oddly, all the Kennedy women seem to have been drawn to womanizing husbands. Rose's father was notorious for his affairs. Jacqueline Bouvier, who became the wife of Jack Kennedy, had a father who was both an alcoholic and womanizer. In fact 'Black Jack Bouvier', as he was known, had an affair with another woman during his honeymoon with Jackie's mother. The Kennedy women were deeply hurt by these infidelities, yet they had observed their own fathers and perceived such situations as 'normal' and, in many instances, to be tolerated.

John Fitzgerald Kennedy was typical of most of Joe and Rose's publicly active children. He was aggressive in pursuit of his goals, yet he had more style than substance, a reality that was not a concern by the time he set his sights on entering the White House in the late 1950s.

Jack Kennedy, the Massachusetts Senator with a glamorous wife, was little more than an adolescent in his personal life. He was unable to commit himself emotionally to any woman, and his marriage was in name only. Much of his leisure time was spent in pursuit of the pleasures of the flesh, and he was rumoured to have said that he was not done with a woman until he had had her three different ways. Regardless of the truth of that remark, interviews with former Secret Service agents, White House staff members and friends reveal that he had sex with as many as two different women a day.

By contrast his younger brother Bobby was an odd combination of moralist, pragmatist and extremely aggressive politician. He had worked for Senator Joseph McCarthy when he was destroying reputations through slander and defamation of character. Later Bobby became an advocate of many of the people and groups he had previously attacked. He had been neutral at best on the issue of civil rights until, as US Attorney General, he realized that his future would be determined, in part, if he was perceived as a strong advocate for minorities. He was also the only one of the Kennedy men who believed in monogamy, interpreting his Catholic training literally.

Although there would be rumours of Bobby Kennedy's infidelity, Peter frequently told me that they were not true. He stated, often with some surprise, that the only time Bobby was ever involved with a woman other than his wife was during a brief, rather intense affair with Claudine Longet, then married to entertainer Andy Williams, a close friend of Bobby's wife Ethel. The accuracy of Peter's remarks was later confirmed by William Sullivan, third in command of the FBI under J. Edgar Hoover. In his book *The Bureau: My Thirty Years in Hoover's FBI,* Sullivan stated:

> Although Hoover was desperately trying to catch Bobby Kennedy red-handed at anything, he never did. Kennedy was almost a Puritan. We used to watch him at parties, where he would order one glass of scotch and still be sipping from the same glass two hours later. The stories about Bobby Kennedy and Marilyn Monroe were just stories. The original story was invented by a so-called journalist, a right-wing zealot who had a history of spinning wild yarns. It spread like wildfire, of course, and J. Edgar Hoover was right there, gleefully fanning the flames.

Peter said that in most instances where Bobby was linked to some woman, it was because of Jack. The woman would be having an affair that had become blatant enough for Bobby to feel it might compromise the White House. He took upon himself the role of convincing the woman that it was time to leave his brother alone.

Peter never discussed the reasons why Jack Kennedy was so determined to have sex without commitment, perhaps because this was a lifestyle he too enjoyed at the time. In Peter's case, much of the blame may be attributed to the way he was raised. Kennedy was probably influenced by the lifestyle of his father.

Joe Kennedy and his son Jack shared a delight in affairs with the most famous movie stars of their day. Long before Peter helped his brother-in-law secretly meet and seduce Marilyn Monroe, Joe Kennedy was having an affair with Gloria Swanson. At the time Joe was active as a producer in the film industry and Gloria was making a break from the studio-controlled star system. She turned down a million-dollar contract, only the third or fourth such contract ever awarded in the fledgling film industry, in order to gain more control over her own pictures. This fascinated the businessman side of Joe Kennedy almost as much as her beauty triggered his lust.

The difference between Kennedy father and son was in the way they handled the moral dilemma of marriage and affairs. Jack Kennedy never gave any indication that he was in the least bothered by his actions. Joe Kennedy, on the other hand, was extremely troubled. Towards the end of 1929 he arranged for Gloria Swanson to receive a visit from Boston's William Cardinal O'Connell, who explained that each time she saw Joe Kennedy she became an occasion of sin for him. In *Swanson on Swanson* she wrote:

> He told me that Joe had spoken about our relationship with some of the highest representatives of the Catholic Church. Since there was no possibility of dissolving his marriage under church law, he had sought official permission to live apart from his wife and maintain a second household with me. That was impossible, the cardinal explained. Furthermore, he went on, as one of the most prominent Catholic laymen in America, Mr Kennedy was exposing himself to scandal every time he so much as appeared in public with me.

Swanson told the Cardinal that if the relationship was a problem for Kennedy, then it was up to him to do something about it, not her.

Despite this apparent guilt, Joe Kennedy flaunted his sexual activities in front of his wife and children.

He regularly called the girls that Jack dated, often taking them to dinner and questioning them about their personal lives. He also told them about Gloria Swanson.

In her memoirs, *Times to Remember*, Rose Kennedy spoke of Gloria, giving an insight not only into her acceptance of the situation but also into the influence the affair may have had on Patricia Kennedy, one of her daughters. Pat Kennedy would eventually become Peter's first wife, tolerating not only his periodic affairs but also the fact that her brother Jack regularly had sex with other women in the Lawfords' California home. I have no idea if Peter wanted his wives before me to engage in *ménages à trois* or whether that was something he decided to try when his sex drive was waning from all the drugs and alcohol. But the infidelity of both Jack and Peter was so blatant that it was hard for me to understand how it was tolerated until I read Rose's book. Remember that this was written about a period in her life when the Kennedy/Swanson affair was common knowledge in America. They were photographed together and regularly mentioned as an obvious gossip column 'item'. Rose commented:

Gloria Swanson was our house guest for a couple of days in Bronxville and brought along her small daughter, who was about the age of our Pat, who was about ten. The two got along well together, and Pat took her down to show her the Bronxville public school and meet her classmates and perhaps show off a little, as she did by introducing her as 'Gloria Swanson's daughter'. Nobody believed her. They all just grinned, thinking it was a joke. After all, Gloria Swanson was, to them, practically a supernatural being, so she wouldn't be in Bronxville and wouldn't have a daughter, and Pat was just doing some silly spoofing. I can't recall the exact details but I do remember how completely indignant Pat was when she and Gloria's little girl came home and told us.

Rose Kennedy also talked of Joe's trips abroad, including one to Paris with Gloria when her marriage was falling apart. There was a closeness to Joe that most women would not tolerate, but which Rose accepted. Her only comment was about the 'competition' in general, not any specific affairs.

> During Joe's years in the movie industry he was surrounded daily by some of the most beautiful women in the world, dressed in beautiful clothes. Obviously, I couldn't compete in natural beauty, but I could make the most of what I had by keeping my figure trim, my complexion good, my grooming perfect, and by always wearing clothes that were interesting and becoming. And so, with Joe's endorsement, I began spending more time and more money on clothes. Eventually, I began landing on some lists of 'Best Dressed Women'.

There were also stories of the way Kennedy reacted to his daughters' friends. Female friends of his daughters who were staying at the family compound on Cape Cod found that Joe liked to kiss them goodnight. His actions were more in keeping with a teenager on the make than with a father and respected business leader.

By the time Peter met Joe Kennedy's daughter Patricia, Jack Kennedy was radically different from his father. He suffered no guilt over his actions and his affairs, which were far more numerous than the old man's. Jack's attitudes to life seemed to match those of his favourite fictional hero, James Bond. If Ronald Reagan had his presidency coloured by the war films he made during the 1940s, Kennedy was influenced by the image of the casual sex, machine-like brutality and cold sophistication of Bond. The intensity with which he worked, his casual affairs, and his fascination with elite military units that led him to create the Green Berets are all emblematic of that influence.

Kennedy may have been a swinger, but the women who were willing to talk about his prowess in bed never considered him much of a lover. Marilyn Monroe, who at one time expected to marry Jack Kennedy, laughingly explained to columnist Jim Bacon that there was never any foreplay. He would enter, satisfy himself and return to work. The woman adapted or remained unsatisfied.

Peter first met Jack Kennedy around 1945, at Gary Cooper's house. Kennedy had just been released from the military, a war hero whose PT boat had been shot out from under him. He was still undergoing therapy for his back injury, weighed only 130 pounds and had none of the vigour of his later years, yet Peter liked him instantly. 'My immediate reaction was that there was no bullshit with him. He was very straightforward and had a marvellous sense of humour. I knew there was a force in the room when I shook his hand. I felt that he was a rather extraordinary fellow.'

The seriousness of Kennedy's back injury was kept from public awareness even more carefully than was Franklin Roosevelt's inability to walk. Peter told me that a medical attendant followed Jack everywhere carrying a syringe filled with a cortisone-type drug, because Kennedy could suddenly find himself unable to move and in great pain. The only way he could continue would be with the help of an immediate injection, and Peter said that it was not unusual to see the woman jab the needle right through Kennedy's suit.

Perhaps Kennedy's seemingly destructive way of handling his disability – numerous affairs, rather violent touch football games and so on – were somewhat immature. But Peter and I both admired the way the man did not let himself live the life of a cripple despite being in almost constant pain. No matter what else might be said of him, when it came to facing personal adversity he showed remarkable courage.

Kennedy was also impressed with Peter, if only because he was an actor. 'He had an affinity for Hollywood and its personalities that I think came from his father,' said Peter. 'He would read weekly *Variety* voraciously. After he was President, he would sometimes ring up and tell me what the grosses were on *Ocean's Eleven*, etc. He was that kind of fellow.'

Peter met Jack's sister Eunice, later Eunice Shriver, back in 1949 when he was on a promotion tour in Washington, DC for *Red Danube*. Typical of the time, the movie had an anti-Soviet theme. Whether through a sense of humour or because she had not seen the picture, Eunice took Peter to a cocktail party at the Russian embassy. A couple of the Russians had seen the film and began making nasty remarks about it. Peter, rather frightened, quietly told Eunice that they had better leave.

Peter had seen Eunice occasionally after that, and in 1952, at the Republican Convention, he met her sister Pat, who would become his first wife. Peter had become friends with a number of wealthy, influential Eastern business leaders including Henry Ford, who was a delegate to the Convention. Peter joined Ford as an observer, having the same curiosity about the event as the Kennedy sisters.

Peter and Pat began talking, each intrigued by the other. Then, later that year, Peter's father died while Pat was on a world tour. She took the trouble to send him a note of sympathy, a gesture that deeply moved Peter, who later wrote: 'One night we were having dinner in LA and we started talking about love and marriage. I told her I thought I was falling in love with her, and that maybe she might consider making it permanent. She said, "How's April for you!" Obviously we shared dreams of a marvellous, happy life together.'

Joe Kennedy was not happy about his daughter's decision. He told Peter: 'I don't like the British. I don't like actors. And I don't like men who wear red socks.' When I asked Peter what he did about his future father-in-law's statement he merely smiled and said, 'I stopped wearing red socks.'

There was no sex before the marriage. Peter respected Pat Kennedy and did not force the issue.

Peter and Pat were married, despite Joe Kennedy's objections, on 25 April 1954. The smart New York society wedding, followed by a honeymoon in Hawaii, befitted their status as the son of a retired British general and the daughter of a former Ambassador to the Court of St James. Hollywood stars, minor royalty, jet-setters and the glitterati came to toast this attractive couple.

However, Peter did not remain faithful after the marriage, eventually having such a serious affair with actress Lee Remick that there was a chance Peter would leave Pat. At one point he talked with his brother-in-law, Jack Kennedy, about the fact that the marriage had fallen apart. But it was 1962 and Peter knew that a divorce within the Kennedy family would result in a bad press that could affect the re-election. Because the affair was so serious, he was unusually closed-mouth about it. Lee Remick was going through her own personal hell. Her husband had been in an accident that left him brain damaged. He became a shell of a man, eventually dying from his injuries. She nursed him constantly, but became extremely lonely, desiring companionship.

Peter was fun, empathetic with her plight, and estranged from Pat Kennedy by then, even though they still gave the impression of being a happy couple. They fell quite deeply in love, yet Lee could not leave her husband. She felt that she owed him her staying with him until he died, even though they could no longer communicate, have sex, or lead any semblance of a normal life. She told Peter not to divorce Pat, because she had to stay with her husband through his dying days. By the time Lee's husband died, enough had changed between she and Peter that the affair was over.

The first few years were relatively happy, despite Peter's philandering. Pat had conquered a handsome British movie star with whom she was deeply in love, and Peter had gained not only a wife but a family, the one thing he had always lacked.

7

Young Blue Eyes, and the Move to Television

You may get the impression that the gentleman in question was a total ogre. Far from it. I meant, just because he punched a few defenceless girls, broke a few cameras belonging to news photographers in the line of duty, instigated the roughing-up of a couple of parking lot boys who were guilty of that unpardonable faux pas in the world of status, that his car was not prominently first in line outside the old Romanoff's Restaurant, or probably the most infamous of all, by having one of his illiterate, but blindly-loyal, goons bury a six-inch cut glass ashtray into the head of a man sitting in the booth next to him sitting in the Polo Lounge of the Beverly Hills Hotel, who he happened to overhear made a mildly derogatory remark about him. I gather that, to this day, the unfortunate gentleman is still not himself, due to some form of brain damage. So you can plainly see, he's not all bad.

Peter Lawford on Frank Sinatra

I make a prediction. Frank [Sinatra] is through. A year from now [1948] you won't hear anything about him.

He'll be dead professionally. I've been around the country looking and listening. They're not going to see his pictures. They're not buying his records. They don't care for Frank Sinatra any more!

George Evans, publicist, speaking to columnist
Earl Wilson,
From *Sinatra: An Unauthorised Biography*

Pat Lawford was fascinated with Hollywood and anxious to meet some of the celebrities with whom Peter had been friends. Among the first was Frank Sinatra, a name Peter would rather she had not mentioned. 'Boy, did you come to the wrong window!' he told her, for reasons that will soon become clear.

The Sinatra relationship went back to the early years at MGM, described in Chapter 4. Sinatra had just been signed by the studio after extremely successful performances at the Paramount Theater and the La Bomba nightclub in New York. Both men were friends of Marilyn Maxwell and she introduced them during an extremely boring dinner – a 'command performance' for MGM actors under contract. Any time L.B. Mayer wanted to honour a friend, he would invite many of the contract players as a way of impressing him. This party was for Henry Ford II. Fortunately, Marilyn, Frank and Peter were seated together and could delight in making nasty remarks about the people Peter called the 'ass kissers, sycophants, court-jesters, and a plethora of terminal egos'. None of the three would ever be a part of the Hollywood 'establishment', and a Mayer command performance was the ideal time for them to made facetious remarks about everyone present.

Marilyn Maxwell knew about the problems of Hollywood. She had been married to actor John Conte, from whom she was getting a divorce. Sinatra had been dating her, despite the fact that he was then married to Nancy.

Peter was fascinated by Sinatra. He later commented,

I would be lying through my teeth if I said I was not more than a little curious and interested to meet this somewhat frail and gaunt young man who obviously had the power in his God-given lungs, and a built-in, smouldering, quiet mystique to cause continents of women of all shapes and sizes to have to change their pants (they wore them in those days) more than once a day, listening to his woeful, sensual, and doubtless scratched 78s.

Peter discovered that Sinatra had a delightful sense of humour and no self-importance. Only later would he find that Sinatra was extremely volatile, quick to anger if he felt he was slighted. Peter once commented, 'I will always think of him as the lovable landmine – something no sturdy American household should be without.'

Yet for all the facetious remarks, for all the bitterness that would afflict Peter in later years, he genuinely liked Sinatra. In the 1940s, when the friendship was young, they went to parties together and Peter met the elite among songwriters, playwrights and conductors. He came to know Sammy Cahn, Jimmy Van Heusen, Jule Styne, Axel Stordahl and numerous others. Peter and Frank opened new avenues of the entertainment world to each other.

In 1947 Peter, Frank, Jimmy Durante and Kathryn Grayson made *It Happened in Brooklyn*. It was one of Sinatra's first films and he was still rather nervous. He had known great success as a nightclub and big band singer, but he was not yet at home on the movie set. The result was the side of Sinatra that Peter respected to his death. 'He took direction beautifully, listened, contributed, and was generally extremely professional about the whole operation. In other words, he was a joy to work with, which surprised everyone from the prop man to L.B. Mayer because of his reputation, which preceded him, of his being difficult to get along with.'

Oddly, Kitty Kelley, in her biography of Sinatra, *His Way*, quotes MGM production memos from this period that indicated that Sinatra was frequently late for work or off the set without permission. There is no reason to question the authenticity of those memos. However, considering how much Peter felt hurt by Sinatra in later years, if Sinatra's actions had ever caused a problem on the set Peter would undoubtedly have mentioned it. I can only assume, therefore, that Sinatra's relationships during the filming were much like Peter's. People like

Sam Marx attacked Peter's actions during the filming of such shows as *The Thin Man* series. Yet the directors and actors who worked with Peter and agreed to be interviewed for this book considered him cooperative, highly professional and a delight to work with on the set. Perhaps Sinatra was the same way – a delight for his immediate colleagues and a pain in the butt of the top brass.

This was not to say that Frank's 'other side' would not be present when he and Peter worked together. Peter explained that,

> as the years went by, and he mastered his craft in a myriad of movies and several very good performances, this, unfortunately, was all to change. By the time we did *Ocean's Eleven,* a property I found many years later, he had reached the point where he would tear handfuls of pages out of script and allow the director only one take of a scene, unless there was a technical difficulty of some kind. I remember once the sound man kept complaining about an unusual number of low-flying airplanes which he was picking up through his earphones, and which were consequently being heard on the track. Well, after about the fourth take, which was unheard of for Frank, he said, 'AW, fuck it! Everyone knows they're airplanes.' Indeed! But flying through a bathroom? Which was where the sequence was being shot.

The relationship with Sinatra was a close one up until an incident with Ava Gardner, Sinatra's ex-wife, was blown out of proportion by gossip columnist Louella Parsons. That incident followed an earlier, humiliating experience for Sinatra at the hands of his then wife.

Sinatra and Ava Gardner were in the Plaza Hotel, having an argument in their suite. She ignored his advances and he announced that he was going to commit suicide. He took a gun, locked himself in the bathroom and fired a round.

Ava Gardner was not fooled by Sinatra's dramatics.

She knew that whatever he had done, it would not be shooting himself. She assumed that he expected her to come rushing to his side, pounding on the door, begging for a second chance. He would then throw open the lock and she would sob gratefully at the sight of his being alive. The incident would probably end in bed and Sinatra would get his way. The only problem with the scenario was that Frank had not reckoned with Ava Gardner.

Instead of rushing to Frank's side, Mrs Sinatra calmly left the suite, took the lift to the lobby and walked up to the front desk. 'Mr Sinatra has shot himself,' she said, casually. 'You'd better call an ambulance.' When the police and ambulance crew arrived they found an irate, thoroughly embarrassed Sinatra pacing back and forth in his suite.

The Sinatra/Ava Gardner marriage was over when Peter met her for a drink in Frascati's, a bar and restaurant on Wilshire Boulevard in Hollywood. Ava was with her business manager, a fact the Parsons column happened to omit.

As Peter later explained,

Ava and I embraced and, as it is with so many true friends, we simply resumed our conversation where we'd left off two years before, but with one exception: no mention was made of Frank. She knew we were friends and we all knew the marriage ended badly. No point in causing pain. Ava had to conduct business with her manager over dinner, and so I promised to grab a bite at another table and then join her for an after-dinner drink. . . .

We chatted and laughed, recalling some of the antics of the Metro years, and then we said goodnight. Ava went home one way, and I went home another. And that should have been that.

It would have been, too, except that Louella Parsons, whose spies were everywhere and were generally inaccurate, announced, in a nice big headline – 'AVA'S FIRST DATE BACK IN THE U.S. IS PETER LAWFORD'

– the day after we were together. The day after that, at about 3 a.m. in the morning, the phone rang.

'Peter?'

I recognized the voice instantly, even though I was still half asleep.

'What the fuck are you doing going out with Ava? You want both of your legs broken?'

It was a threat I'd heard before. I immediately launched into an explanation, figuring the truth would set me free. I never got past the word 'but', but I did manage to utter it about three times during Frank's tirade.

'I don't want to hear that shit,' he shouted every time I tried to speak. then he hung up.

Much later that morning I began calling around, trying to find him. I finally tracked him down in New York where he was staying with Jimmy Van Heusen.

Jimmy got on the phone and said Frank wasn't around just then.

'You know what happened?' I asked Jimmy.

'Oh, don't worry, Peter. You've been around long enough to know he'll get over it.'

'But nothing happened,' I insisted.

'Just let him calm down. It'll blow over.'

It finally did blow over – seven years later. When it happened, Frank was at the nadir of his career. He hadn't yet made *From Here to Eternity*, and the crooning was not going well. His recovery, of course, was spectacular and, by the time we became friends again, he was back on top and I was married to Patricia Kennedy.

The Lawfords had been married four years when they were invited to dinner at Rocky and Gary Cooper's home. Peter was working on the Jimmy Durante show, but expected to get home in time to take Pat. However, an accident on the set delayed him and he had asked Pat to drive over alone, making excuses for him if the time grew too late for him to go.

By the time Peter had had a minor burn treated at the infirmary and could get to the Coopers' home, dinner was over. The women were going into the drawing room and the men were having brandy in a different part of the house.

Peter went straight to the drawing room without stopping to see Cooper. He was concerned that Pat might be worried and he wanted to show her the bandaged hand so she could see he was not badly hurt.

'Guess what?' She said to him. 'I've got bigger news than you've got.'

He asked her what her news was and she said, 'I just had dinner with Frank Sinatra. He's very charming.'

When they met up, Peter and Frank began talking as though there had never been an argument. They avoided the past, talking about a film they might make called *Ocean's Eleven*. It would be filmed in Las Vegas and the property had been purchased by Peter for $10,000. Frank wanted to include Dean Martin and Sammy Davis, Jr, and Peter felt that Lewis Milestone should direct. Both men agreed to begin putting all the elements in place.

Not long after this meeting, Frank decided to join Pat and Peter on a trip to Rome. Ava Gardener was living there and Sinatra thought he might be able to see her – in fact she did not allow him to do so. However, despite Sinatra's personal frustration, the relationship with Peter blossomed. As Peter later explained: 'In those days I was still drinking, so we stayed up all night and I'll never forget the next morning. It was very early and the sun was shining, really beautiful. Frank looked at me, bleary-eyed, and said, "Charlie, I'm sorry." All I said to him was, "I am, too." It was such a waste of time, but it was so hard for Frank Sinatra to say he was sorry.' Charlie, incidentally, was a nickname based on 'Charlie the Seal' whose identity never has been determined. However, the name evolved because of the smoker's cough Peter had which Sinatra felt made him sound like a seal 'barking'. Eventually everybody in the clan seemed to call everybody else 'Charlie' at one time or another, the nickname even getting to Shirley MacLaine.

Despite the reconciliation, the 'dark side' of Sinatra reared its head again on New Year's Eve, 1958. The Lawfords had become so friendly with Frank that the singer kept a room in his home for them where Peter and Pat stored some of their clothing. It seemed a good idea for the Lawfords, Sinatra and two other friends, Robert Wagner and his wife, Natalie Wood, to drive to Sinatra's home for the holiday.

Sinatra and the two couples were in Beverly Hills for the New Year, attending a private party held by restaurateur Mike Romanoff. They were all in formal clothing, though without top coats, when the weather turned unusually cold. The temperature dropped into the forties, the wind came up and Pat and Natalie became extremely uncomfortable. The Lawfords and the Wagners decided that what they really wanted to do after the party was to go to bed as quickly as possible. They would drive to Frank's home in the desert the following morning. As Peter explained,

I was a close enough friend to know that Frank, once he's got his mind made up and his plans made, didn't like to deviate from his chosen course. (Somewhat reminiscent of a dynamite truck travelling down the road. Fine until it hit a pothole.) It was a character trait we shared, and so I approached our suggestion [to wait until morning] carefully, making sure it made sense and was understood as a majority opinion, one that I hoped would appeal to his chivalrous nature. After all, the girls were cold and worried.

Frank froze, glared from one of us to the next. 'Okay. Well, I'm going [to drive to the desert].' And with that he turned and walked out of Romanoff's. The rest of us went home to our warm beds.

'He'll get over it,' I said to Natalie, Pat and R.J. [Robert Wagner]. 'I'll call him in the morning before we all leave.'

What happened next formed an odd pattern that Sinatra repeated whenever he was angry with Peter and Pat. When Peter called the house the next morning to alert Sinatra that all of them were still coming, he talked to George Jacobs, Frank's butler. Jacobs explained that Sinatra had arrived about 5 a.m. and gone to bed just after 6. However, the butler's voice sounded odd and, when pushed by Peter, he said, 'I guess Mr Sinatra's really pissed off about something.'

'How so, George?' Peter asked him.

'He came in and had a couple of drinks. Then he went into the room where you and Mrs Lawford stay and took all of your clothes out of the closet.'

'What'd he do with them, George?' Peter asked him.

'Tried to make a bonfire out of them out by the pool. When the fire wouldn't get going, he threw everything into the pool.'

Peter was shocked, then amused. He also realized that the gathering would not take place. 'Don't worry, George,' Peter said. 'Everything will be all right. Just tell him when he gets up that we won't be coming down today.'

'I fished the clothes out this morning,' added George. 'I'm afraid they're ruined.'

Pat was amused by Sinatra's immaturity, but Peter was annoyed that he had lost a favourite pair of jeans. 'We'll age another pair,' Pat said. 'Just make sure you don't take them down to Frank's.'

During this period, Peter was working in television. He first had a short-lived series called *Dear Phoebe*, the story of a male journalist hired to act as Phoebe, the female writer of an agony column. The second series was *The Thin Man*, adapted from the book by Dashiel Hammett that had already been developed into half a dozed MGM movies starring William Powell and Myrna Loy. Peter was paired with Phyllis Kirk, an attractive brunette who, because of her current position with

CBS, refused to be interviewed for this book. Others who were on the set talked about those days: apparently she was the subject of a number of hostile remarks and practical jokes.

Peter intensely disliked Phyllis Kirk, though many who worked with her found her a total professional and an extremely friendly woman. She was slightly handicapped – a degenerative illness had affected her muscles so that her way of walking was a little awkward. She never spoke of it and had learned to hide her problem, though her walk was just odd enough to seem stylized. She did not want sympathy or special working conditions, which caused those few who knew her well to be impressed with her courage.

Sam Marx recalled:

I was executive producer of MGM Television during its very first years and we had decided to do *The Thin Man*. I was seeking a good kind of replica of William Powell because he had made such a smash hit in the part of Nick. I was pretty close to a couple of other actors who we were going to give the nod to when I got a call from Eddie Mannix who was the tough, rough, Irish studio manager who said, 'We've got your Nick for *The Thin Man*, Peter Lawford.' At that time, Peter was the brother-in-law of President Kennedy. And I have no doubt that Joe Kennedy, who had pulled many strings and was a friend of Mannix, had simply got Peter the job.

I had no voice in it. I won't say that I would have been against it. He was young, good-looking still – 1950-something – and we were going to have Phyllis Kirk play Nora. I would say that they were going to make a good team.

The Thin Man must have been cast before September 1957, when the series began, and Jack Kennedy was not elected President until November 1960. People's memories are not always perfect. But Jack did not need to be President for him or the powerful Joe to have helped Pat Kennedy's husband with his career.

The hostility from Peter was a problem because of the nature of the characters. Peter and Phyllis played Nick and Nora Charles, a couple who had become wealthy New York sophisticates as a result of her inheritance. 'Peter,' said Sam Marx, 'had the gall to come to me one time in his typical abrasive way and say, "Why am I tied to the hip with this dame? Get rid of her. Kill her off and I'll hold the show."' John Newland, one of several directors for the series, also recalled this animosity:

'They [the Nick and Nora Charles characters] were intimately related and there were many times when they should have been shown in bed together. He never really touched her. And I never knew why he hated her because she was good, she was never unprofessional. Possibly the advance of Ms Kirk's own increasingly debilitating illness was disturbing enough to make Peter, selfishly, troubled about his own lesser handicap.

'Peter was one of the most enjoyable men that I have ever known. He was droll, witty, charming, gracious, very intelligent, very well read, and a very good actor.

'Everybody who worked with him loved him. Except Phyllis Kirk, and she did her best. She was embarrassed that he did not like her. She did not dislike him.

'His adroitness at getting away from her physically was really something to see. Like Fred Astaire, dancing. He'd find things to do that went around her, over her, it was manic almost. It had no sense to it at all. Everybody knew it, including Phyllis.

'I don't know why it wasn't totally mortifying. I guess because she handled it so well. She handled it in such a wonderful, emotional fashion.

'At first, when I was exposed to it, I was dumbfounded as to how to handle it because he said, "Johnny, I'm never going to lay a hand on her, on that girl."

'I said, "Why?"

'And he said, "I'm not going to do it. It's right here in my contract." Sure enough there's a codicil saying that at no time should Mr Lawford be required to make love or do anything physical with Phyllis Kirk.'

Peter also hated the three terriers that played the part of the dog, Asta. The dogs were highly strung and Peter complained that they would wet on him without warning and, seemingly, without reason. On many occasions Peter handled both the dog problem and his hostility towards Phyllis by simply placing Asta in her arms. That way he would not have to hold either of them.

Sam Marx thought that Peter did not play the character tone to the spirit of Dashiel Hammett. 'Peter under no circumstances would follow in the path of William Powell who played it the way Hammett wrote it,' he said, 'an impeccable, smooth, charming, and a very witty kind of man. And the relationship between Nick and Nora in the original *Thin Man* we used to do through character touches without even hanging on them. You know, of course, the marvellous scene where Nick is half loaded at a bar and Nora walks in and says to the bartender, "How many has he had, Joe?" And Joe says, "Six." And she says, "Set 'em up!"

'And there's a scene in which they're having a spat, or she says to him that they might get killed and he has to be on guard because he's going into a dangerous place. And he says, "Well, you won't be a widow long. Not with your money."

'Now that was the spirit of the original Nick and Nora. But Peter went completely opposite. He was content to wear a soiled sweater. He had no particular feeling for character.

'I could see it beginning to go down the drain because he was so adamantly in charge himself. My office was maybe twenty-five yards away from him. Every week, when the scripts came in, he only read his part, I'm convinced. If he didn't think it was big enough or if he didn't like what he was going to do, he didn't call me. I was the executive producer. Peter would call his father, Joe Kennedy, in Florida and say, "Daddy-in-law,

I don't like next week's script." Daddy-in-law would call Joe Vogel, who was President of MGM in New York. Joe Vogel would then call Bud Berry, who was in charge of sales, distribution and everything else, and was actually President of MGM TV in New York. Then Bud Berry would call me, twenty-five yards away from Peter Lawford, to say, "Peter doesn't like next week's script." And that went on all the time.'

Sam Marx talked about other incidents of conflict with Peter during the filming. "Phyllis Kirk was well aware that there were deficiencies in the series and we often talked about it. And then I made a suggestion. One of the most respected directors at MGM, a dear friend of mine, was curious about the workings of television and I knew it. So I went to see him in his office and I asked if he would mind coming down and talking with me, with Ben Star, the producer, with Peter, with Phyllis, and with the director at that time Don Weiss, with the idea of discussing the characters of Nick and Nora Charles. It never occurred to me that anybody would not like George Cukor to come down and do it. But Peter flatly refused to allow it. When I said he had no choice, he said, "Yes, I do. The minute Mr Cukor walks on this set, I walk off." And he did. And he took Don Weiss with him. I never spoke to Don Weiss again, and that was the beginning of my ongoing hostility towards Peter Lawford. It was utterly insane, in my estimation, and Phyllis joins me in that, I'm sure – not to be willing to listen to a man of that calibre talking about only things that can be to your own benefit and best interest. When you've got a recalcitrant leading man who stands back and says, "My brother-in-law is President of the United States and you're not going to tell me what I'm going to do," you're finished.'

Still speaking of *The Thin Man* series, Marx said, 'Phyllis was a very liberal-minded lady and men like Mort Sahl, who was kind of a rebellious comic against the establishment, and some of the Negroes who were prominent in those days, were friends of hers and would come on the set. I used to get ridiculous phone calls in my office from some prop man on the picture: "Miss Kirk has just taken a black man into her dressing room and you've got to come down and open up that door or there'll be trouble down there." I didn't go down, but I talked it over with Phyllis and she finally – somewhat unhappily – agreed that rather than provoke trouble on the set she wouldn't do it again. But it was totally innocent. She was just a bit ahead of the time.

'Later on Peter hung around with the Rat Pack and became friends with Sammy Davis, so I won't even hint of any racism with him because I don't believe he had it.

'What I do think is that Peter sauntered through, at that time, feeling a sense of tremendous importance because of his marriage and letting everybody know it. He then owned, through Patricia Lawford, the house that Louis B. Mayer had once owned on Santa Monica beach, another great sign of success.' The records I have from Peter indicated in fact that he paid the bills on the house from his own earnings, not from the money inherited by Pat.

John Newland countered some of Sam Marx's hostility by adding, 'One of the sweet anecdotes I remember about him is, after we had finished *The Thin Man* and *One Step Beyond* [a series Newland helped create] was sold, he sent me a big case of champagne.

'We were making one of the episodes on the MGM lot, the back lot. And another Metro shoot was right next door to our set, or the outdoor part of it was. Peter was working on this picture with Sinatra – it was a war picture of some sort.

'Peter appeared on the top of a knoll and said, "Johnny." And I said, "Hi, Peter."

'He said, "Frank wants me to tell you something. Could you be a little quieter over on this set?"

'I said, "Tell Frank to go fuck himself, Peter." Then I forgot all about it.

'About half an hour later I'm directing when suddenly the crew starts looking the other way and it's very quiet. I look around, and on the same mound is Peter standing with Sinatra. And Sinatra says, "John, I got your message." It was a paralysing moment of how powerful that man Sinatra is. It was a delivery of total charm and humour.'

8

Politics and the Clan

I was spilling more than Dean Martin drinks.

Peter Lawford

Sinatra was to provide an important link in the show-business connection that helped Jack Kennedy succeed in his campaign for President. Unlike Peter, whose interest in politics was not particularly intense before he married into the Kennedy family, Sinatra had been involved ever since the day when he met Franklin Roosevelt with Toots Shor.

Roosevelt had been criticized for spending time with Sinatra. Republicans accused Roosevelt of ignoring the death and danger in Germany by entertaining so controversial a figure – yet the few minutes that he spent with the singer hardly represented a national crisis or a dereliction of duty. Still, Sinatra was un-doubtedly annoyed with the reaction and pleased with the President. He donated $5,000 to the Roosevelt re-election campaign and made recordings on behalf of the Democratic National Committee.

'I'd just like to tell you what a great guy Roosevelt is,' he was quoted as saying. 'I was a little stunned when I stood alongside him. I thought, here's the greatest guy alive today and here's a little guy from Hoboken shaking his hand. He knows about everything – even my racket.'

There was a later period when Sinatra commented

about his speech at a Madison Square Garden political rally.

> I said I was for Roosevelt because he was good for me. He was good for me and for my kids and my country, so he must be good for all the other ordinary guys and their kids. When I was through, I felt like a football player coming off the field – weak and dizzy and excited and everybody coming over to shake hands or pat me on the back. I'm not ashamed to say it – I felt proud.

As a dedicated Democrat it was natural for Sinatra to support Senator John Kennedy when he decided to run against Richard Nixon for President in the 1960 election. The fact that the singer was friendly with the Lawfords added to the appeal, but Sinatra already had a strong interest in politics of many years' duration. His support was all the more memorable because he mobilized showbusiness figures in a way that had never been seen before.

Around the time that Peter, Sinatra, Sammy Davis, Joey Bishop and Dean Martin were making the film *Ocean's Eleven,* in the late fifties Sinatra was instrumental in forming a different kind of showbusiness group. One of the most publicized sets of entertainers of their day, they were called the Clan and misnamed the Rat Pack. By the early 1950's they'd become something of a fixture.

The real Rat Pack, as long-time Hollywood personalities state with great vehemence, was the Holmby Hills Rat Pack set up by Humphrey Bogart and Lauren Bacall. Frank, who lived in the area, was a part of this group. They also included Judy Garland during the period when she was married to Sid Luft, Nathaniel Benchley, David Niven, agent Irving 'Swifty' Lazar, restaurant owner Mike Romanoff and a couple of others. Bogart commented that the group was created 'for the relief of boredom and the perpetuation of independence. We admire ourselves and don't care for anyone else.' They found the Rat Pack a delightful way to justify drinking, bad jokes and late nights.

Oddly, the Holmby Hills Rat Pack was severely criticized by other entertainers. Many resented their liberal attitudes which made them supporters of the Democrats (and also suspect because of the McCarthy hearings investigating Communists and Communist sympathizers, as well as anyone who might hint of harbouring such thoughts). The fact that the Rat Pack came to an end in 1956 after Bogart's throat cancer was diagnosed was of no concern to the public. The Holmby Hills Rat Pack was dead; long live the Clan, who became the new Rat Pack.

There were other differences between the two groups. The original Rat Pack had been a private group and their antics had been personal. Typical of Sinatra's humour was arranging to have a plasterer go to Lazar's apartment when the agent was at work. The plasterer covered over the entrance to Lazar's closet, so that when Swifty returned home he would be unable to get to his clothing. The Clan's practical jokes, on the other hand, were usually played out for an audience, even if that audience consisted of the cast and crew of a film in production. It was also less creative — fire crackers, for instance, were released on the set of *Ocean's Eleven*.

Ocean's Eleven was the story of a group of World War II veterans who decided to rob several Las Vegas casinos simultaneously. They cut off the electricity and successfully take the money. The script was so good and the idea so workable at that time that Jack Warner joked that he didn't want to make the movie, he wanted to pull the job.

Because the movie was actually filmed in Las Vegas several of the men were able to obtain jobs performing at the Sands Hotel each night. The experience was described by Joey Bishop, the writer who created the comedy that was far funnier and more sophisticated than the practical jokes. He was discussing the night-club act, a medium in which Peter, despite a love for performing and some experience on stage, was not very sophisticated. His world was film, and this created a minor problem.

'Originally we were supposed to draw straws. The one with the shorter straw was supposed to perform that night [while working on the film set during the day]. I drew it, pre-arranged, the first night, but the guys jumped up on stage and that's when we started to have so much fun. But the people were under the impression that there was only going to be one each night.

'The joke around – and it was a terrible joke – was, the loser at the crap tables says, "With my luck, I'll go see the show and Peter Lawford will be the headliner."

'Peter was a little ill at ease. Working with Durante [Peter also did a nightclub act with Jimmy Durante], you're playing straight. But here you're on stage with three guys, two who could sing very well. The third guy sings great, does impressions and dances, and I did comedy. There was no identification with Peter Lawford.

'Everybody had an attitude in the act except Peter. I remember I told Dean one night, "Pick up Sammy Davis in your arms and say, 'I want to thank the B'nai B'rith for this trophy.'" Sammy was black and Jewish, so he had an attitude.

'I had an attitude that was one of not belonging. I remember one time – I don't know where I had the nerve – I told Frank, "Stop singing and tell people about the good work the Mafia does." I don't know why. I used to address him as "the exhausted one – I mean, the exalted one".'

I remember years ago someone called Richard Gehman wrote a book called *The Rat Pack*. In chapter 4 the first line that he wrote was: 'The only guy who can tell Sinatra off and get away with it is Joey Bishop.' He neglected to say 'humorously'.

'Those were the kinds of things I did,' Joey continued. 'I was the underdog who had nothing to lose. I was the guy who never fought more than a four-rounder that decides he's going to fight for a title. And then he uses all of the false bravado to get him into the ring.

'As a matter of fact, it worked so well we did a number called "The Birth of the Blues" and I did the bridge – "From the whippoorwill". I have no voice at all. I explained that only Jewish dogs can hear me. "From the whippoorwill, high on the hill . . ." and that's as far as I got before they chased me off. The audience actually stamped their feet, saying, "We want Joey back!" And I'd come out as though I didn't care to come back on that stage.

'They still quoted an opening line I did at the Copacabana after Sinatra won his Academy Award for *From Here to Eternity*. You couldn't get in the place. It was his first time back in New York. I was a nobody in '53, '54 – maybe did a few guest appearances. But I said, "I can't believe the size of this crowd. I hope his following shows up." That made me. The one line! I can't explain it, but it was almost as though there were lines that produced it. I remember coming out and getting on one knee and saying, "Thank goodness. Now all I have to do is kiss his ring."

'What was great about Peter or Frank or Sammy or Dean was that, whatever line I thought of at the spur of the moment, they never questioned it. Peter never questioned it. One time when Dean was singing – we always wore tuxedos – I said to the others, "I think it would be very funny if we all three took off our pants, folded them neatly over our arms, and walked across stage behind Dean while he's singing and pretend we're discussing business." It was one of the biggest laughs! Another night Frank, Peter and Dean were pretty high out there. So I said, "This is a show business first. The stage is stationary but the performers are revolving!"

'Peter was very gracious to me. Even though I was the least known of the group, I was treated as an equal and that always felt good to me.' Frank, Joey said, was quite adamant about this.

'I remember one time in Miami Beach, we were going down to the Fontainebleau doing Elvis Presley's first show out of the army. Everybody had a suite on the fifteenth floor, but they gave me a room on the seventh floor. Frank didn't know that, so he said to Peter, "Run down the hall and get Joey. I want to rehearse something."

'So Peter said, "Joey's not on the fifteenth floor. He's on the seventh floor."

'Frank said, "What's he doing on the seventh floor?"

'Peter said, "They gave him a room."

'So Frank called up and said, "If Joey Bishop is not in a suite on the fifteenth floor within five minutes, there'll be no show tonight."

'I don't know this. I'm in my room, writing some material. Six bellhops come running in. They don't take out my clothes. They take out the drawers in it with the hangers and everything. I think the place is on fire!'

Joey recalled his first meeting with Jack Kennedy, arranged by Peter.

'I remember one time when I got a call from Peter. He said, "I want you to come down to Malibu." He had a home down there. "I just signed with the best manager and I want you to sign with him, too," he told me.

'So I said, "I have a manager."

'He said, "Joey, this is your chance of a lifetime. Listen to me and do like I'm telling you."

'So I said, "Okay." And I went down there.'

'When I came by the house Peter was there with Pat. There was no sign of any manager. Peter said, "He's in the ocean now." I didn't know it was John Kennedy. . . .' When Joey found out, 'I was kind of flattered. It was exciting for me.'

Asked if Kennedy could handle his career, Joey commented facetiously, 'No, I need a bigger person. Someone I could take care of. Managers are good if you can provide for them, not if they can provide for you.'

Kennedy's involvement with the Clan meant more at the time than people understand today. Sammy Davis was a black man who was daring to live in a white man's world. Racial hatred was still intense then, and top black entertainers were relegated to ghetto theatres such as the Apollo in Harlem. In the 1960s many a major black star was actually in his or her decline, not having been allowed to perform before mixed audiences during the many years they were at the peak of their talent.

Prejudice was so great that, when Peter and the others went gambling, Peter had to take Sammy's money and play for him as Sammy directed. No black man was allowed to be involved with the casino action. It was a combination of bigoted paternalism and irrational fear, yet whatever the reality the result was great pain and daily humiliation. Men with less inner strength than Sammy were often broken in spirit to such a degree that their talents were stillborn. The first time they tried to break through the meaningless colour bar, they were so emotionally hurt that they gave up showbusiness entirely.

Peter had come to accept the reality of racial prejudice, hating it and not fully comprehending how it had evolved. He simply accepted Sammy as he would anyone else, disregarding so superficial a matter as the colour of his skin, yet playing along with the charade of gambling for him. It was the only way they could function while in Las Vegas.

Jack Kennedy's involvement with them meant risking hostility in the South. He was not an advocate of civil rights. He was not a man who had ever had to confront the racial issue in his home state of Massachusetts. If anything, he might have been for the status quo at that time. The act of being seen with Sammy and the other members of the Clan could have cost him critical votes in the South at the time of the 1960 election, yet he did not seem to care. It was a circumstance that spoke well for his character at a time when other men might have avoided the entire issue in order to have the greatest possible chance of winning.

Jack Kennedy became a part of the showbusiness world after Peter married his sister Pat. He had for a long time been involved with Hollywood women, including stars such as Gene Tierney, and in 1954, after Peter's marriage, he was doing well enough to buy Louis B. Mayer's house in Santa Monica. It became a playground for Kennedy, who conducted many affairs in a bedroom next to that of his sister and brother-in-law. Because of his injured back, Kennedy also enjoyed making love with women in the large bathtub that was a feature of his bathroom.

Kennedy liked Sinatra, and all three men like similar women. Peter would fix Kennedy up with showgirls and others – Justice Department files indicate that Kennedy's suite in the Sands Hotel in Las Vegas had almost a swinging door for the beautiful women who worked in the area.

Members of the Clan and other showbusiness people, orchestrated by Sinatra, were active in the Kennedy campaign. Sinatra proved especially important in New Jersey, his home state and an important one for the election. The late 1950s was a time when the industrial north-east still dominated the nation's population. Anyone who could help deliver votes in such an area was important to the campaign.

Kennedy, of course, loved showbusiness, so many of its stars were happy to reciprocate and turn out to support him. He delighted in the entertainment world and was that best of all individuals for a performer – a good audience. During the filming of *Ocean's Eleven* Kennedy had stopped by the Sands to catch the Clan's nightclub act. There were numerous jokes at Kennedy's expense and their own. Sammy Davis was to become Ambassador to Israel and Sinatra was to become Ambassador to Italy, but Joey Bishop's request was more modest – he just didn't want to be drafted by the army again.

Later, other stars would tell jokes during Kennedy fund-raisers when the Senator was present. In one instance, the comedian Joe E. Lewis said that he had been out on the town until the early hours of the morning wearing a Kennedy badge. 'Where's the badge now?' asked the Senator.

Lewis responded, deadpan, 'Oh, I'm sober now.'

Joey Bishop stated that after the election the Clan would all be given 'legitimate' roles in the Cabinet. Dean Martin would be Secretary of the Cabinet – the Liquor Cabinet – and Sinatra would handle international affairs, as well as all other affairs, including his own.

Some entertainers believed in the potential of the youthful Kennedy, a striking contrast to the ageing Eisenhower. They felt that he had the best chance to improve international relations. Others delighted in the fact that he gave their industry so much attention. And still others, all of them women, combined ideological interest with the fascination that Kennedy's charismatic sexuality held for them.

During the interviews for this book, many female friends of Peter's, all of them television and/or motion picture stars, said they had photographs of themselves with the late President. In several instances they were known to have shared his hotel room as well as his rally platform. Yet these were all women who became involved primarily because they believed in him as a presidential candidate. The sexual relationship was merely a bonus. They also did not brag about it, considering the relationship personal, private and, surprisingly, in some instances unique. By contrast women delighted in discussing a date or a sexual fling they had had with Peter, often inventing parties which did not check out. The latter wanted to brag about having had sex with a handsome movie star. Kennedy's women often seemed to feel that their relationship was special, even though they were coldly referred to by friends as 'another of Jack's fucks'.

Jack Kennedy embraced Hollywood, but rumours behind the scenes indicated something quite different. One story had it that Kennedy actually disliked Sinatra, considering the singer a friend of Peter's and Pat's, not of his. Another said that Sammy Davis was an embarrassment because the entertainer was planning to marry a woman who happened to be white. There were even stories that Joe Kennedy was trying to end the entertainment world relationships his son had developed to ensure that the election would be won. Yet none of the rumours was true.

What was not discussed, and it was to play an important role in Peter's life, was the attitude of Bobby Kennedy during this period. Bobby was the ruthless brother, the one driven by causes and the desire for personal power. He was pragmatic, tackling the Teamsters' Union and its president, Jimmy Hoffa, only after being shown by friends that a major cause would help him with his career. He had been with Joseph McCarthy, a potential blight on his record despite the fact that his work had been sincere and valid and his reports accurate. With the publication of his book, *The Enemy Within*, he established himself as a foe of organized crime.

Bobby was also a moralist who worked hard both to slow down his brother's womanizing and to keep it from becoming common knowledge. The stories of Bobby sharing women with Jack make fascinating reading. They are also fabrications. Bobby was a zealot in the areas that mattered to him, and there would be a price that Peter would have to pay.

After Jack Kennedy won the election in 1960 many people gave Frank Sinatra great credit for the turnout of voters in the north-east. They felt that Sinatra's role had won states as effectively as the Senator's own efforts, perhaps even more so. This led to comedy

100

routines such as the one in which Don Rickles commented: 'Kennedy's boss – that's Frank Sinatra – said to Kennedy, "Jack, Baby, you see? It turned out just like I told you it would. Listen, Jack, Baby – now about Italy. . . ."'

Sinatra's world was primarily that of nightclubs, which had a bad reputation as far as most politicians were concerned. Peter performed, both with Jimmy Durante and with the Clan, but club work was only a minor part of his career. Thus he was considered relatively untainted by the people who ran such places, many of whom had ties with organized crime. Sinatra's friends were of ten accused of being either members of the Mafia or involved with underworld activities. Even someone who was completely honourable, such as Jack Entratter who ran the Sands, had a brother who had been murdered just after Prohibition when gangsters were jockeying for power in new businesses.

No matter what else they might be, many of Sinatra's friends were colourful characters. So long as they were not convicted criminals, the charges against them remained unproven allegations. Yet the reality of their business activities was well known in the Justice Department and, when Bobby Kennedy became Attorney General, he was determined to avoid having his brother's name connected with gangsters. If this meant breaking the Sinatra relationship, then that is what he would do.

Oddly, there were occasions when Bobby Kennedy was in Las Vegas, at least one of those times to meet Chicago mob boss Sam Giancana who was using the name 'Mr Match'. Joe Naar was present with Peter and Bobby at one such meeting, though the reasons were unclear to Naar who has no knowledge of what might have taken place behind the scenes. The most likely connection was Judith Campbell, a girlfriend of Sinatra, Giancana and Jack Kennedy during the late 1950s and early 1960s. She allegedly served as a go-between when Jack Kennedy was seriously considering either overthrowing or murdering Cuban leader Fidel Castro.

Campbell was used by Kennedy, yet she found him to be jealous as well. She later commented, 'Jack knew all about Sam and me, and we used to discuss him. He was angry about my seeing him. He had all the normal reactions that would take place between two people that cared for each other. Yes, he was jealous.'

But be that as it may, what mattered for Peter was the hostility between Bobby and Sinatra, a hostility that would later result in an incident that deeply hurt Peter. All of this took place after the election, though. During the campaign, Sinatra did whatever he was allowed to do. Strong concern was expressed about his image being connected with that of Kennedy. However, Sinatra was used in subtle ways, including having him sing a Sammy Cahn reworked version of the song 'High Hopes', with verses such as:

> K-E-double-N-E-D-Y,
> Jack's the nation's favourite guy.
> Everyone wants to back Jack,
> Jack is on the right track.
> And he's got HIGH HOPES
> High apple-pie-in-the-sky hopes.

The record was installed in jukeboxes in West Virginia, then a Kennedy aid paid the tavern owners $20 each to play the record as much as possible.

During this period another Sinatra controversy emerged. He was involved in the production of *The Execution of Private Slovik*, the story of the only American soldier to be executed for desertion in World War II. It was a problematical production, especially since the orders to kill Slovik had come directly from General Eisenhower. While Eisenhower was serving out his last few months in office as President, the movie drew attention to what many felt was a blight on his career. The film could be considered an attack against the administration, indirectly having a negative effect on Richard Nixon, Kennedy's opponent and the then Vice-President. Eisenhower was probably the best-loved president in American history at that time. He was the general who had won World War II in the eyes of most Americans. He was the grandfather to the nation. The facts of the movie were potentially a problem because the public did not want a hero criticized. People who were hostile to the Republican Party in general and planning to support Kennedy over Nixon still did not want their hero criticized. There was a chance that the movie would cause people to turn against the bearers of bad news and show their support for Eisenhower by voting for his vice-president when Nixon ran for office.

More serious was the situation with the screenwriter. His having been tainted as a Communist created a problem of guilt by association. This 'logic' went: Maltz is a Communist desired by Sinatra. Therefore Sinatra is a closet Communist anxious to support the Communist cause. Since Sinatra supports Jack Kennedy, Jack Kennedy must be espousing the Communist line. Ironic though all this may seem, there was a kind of logic.

To make things worse, Sinatra hired Albert Maltz, a member of what were known as the Hollywood Ten – writers who had been blacklisted for Communist sympathies at the time that the House Un-American Activities Committee (HUAC) had investigated Hollywood. Maltz refused to answer any questions and was sent to jail.

The story of Sinatra hiring Maltz was released on 21 March 1960, and the reaction was much rougher than anyone anticipated considering that twelve years had passed since his blacklisting. The *New York Post* declared Sinatra a hero for having the courage to stand up against secret blacklists and groups such as HUAC which had created terror in America. The *New York*

Mirror, on the other hand, decided that Sinatra had hired 'an unrepentant enemy of the country', and the *Los Angeles Examiner* was horrified that the movie could become a vehicle for Communist propaganda.

Then came corporate pressure. General Motors threatened to cancel advertising, and other companies followed suit. Leaders of the Catholic Church, strongly aware that Kennedy was the first Catholic politician to have a chance to become President, urged Joe Kennedy to disassociate the family from the singer.

Sinatra fought back. He took full-page advertisements in the press stating that he believed in the Bill of Rights, which gave him the legal authority to hire anyone he wanted. He claimed that Maltz was the best possible writer for the script.

In the end, there was too much pressure from all sides. Peter Lawford and Jack Kennedy were essentially innocent bystanders, carrying on the business of a presidential campaign as well as Peter's regular work in television and the movies. Peter never expressed concern, nor did he feel any need to take a stand either for or against Sinatra. But the companies and people involved were intensely partisan, putting pressure against Maltz in a way that no other writer had experienced since the days of McCarthy. It was an obscene blight on Hollywood, the Writers' Guild, the Producers' Guild, the Directors' Guild and other organizations.

Finally, Sinatra agreed to pay Maltz the agreed $75,000 fee for the screenplay, then to replace him with another writer. While many unfamiliar with the era or the intensity of the attack have used the incident to exemplify Sinatra's alleged weakness, it is doubtful that anyone else in Hollywood would have gone even as far as he did. Sinatra was finally forced to issue a statement that was applauded by all, though the situation which forced it to be made was soundly attacked by the publications that had supported him all along.

In view of the reaction of my family, my friends, and the American public, I have instructed my attorneys to make a settlement with Albert Maltz and to inform him that he will not write the screenplay for *The Execution of Private Slovik*.

I had thought the major consideration was whether or not the resulting script would be in the best interests of the United States. Since my conversations with Mr Maltz had indicated that he has an affirmative, pro-American approach to the story, and since I felt fully capable as producer of enforcing such standards, I have defended my hiring of Mr Maltz.

But the American public has indicated it feels the morality of hiring Albert Maltz is the more crucial matter, and I will accept the majority opinion.

Sinatra was sensitive to the potential impact of what he had done once he realized the intense emotions that had surrounded his earlier announcement. As a result, he kept a low profile until the July 1960 Democratic National Convention in Los Angeles, at which he helped stage a fund-raising dinner at the Beverly Hilton Hotel. He was able to bring out 2,800 people including numerous stars, some of whom would be romantically linked with Kennedy, and all of whom paid $100 for the dinner. The only sour note came during the singing of 'The Star Spangled Banner', when delegates from Mississippi, then a heavily segregated state, booed Sammy Davis, Jr.

Sinatra's problems did not estrange him from the Kennedy family, as some reports indicate. During the Convention Joe and Rose Kennedy stayed at the Beverly Hills home of Marion Davies. Sinatra was over there frequently, occasionally acting as bartender for the politicians, advisers and others who dropped by.

The only mistake in having entertainers as a major part of the Convention lay in not realizing that some might not censor their material. This was a problem with Mort Sahl, a man who delighted in making jokes at anyone's expense. The Clan had only heard

Sahl's anti-Eisenhower jokes. They knew he talked of Eisenhower riding to the White House on a white horse. His punchline told that, after four years, the horse was still there but the rider was gone. But the humour Sahl brought to the Convention spared no one. 'We've finally got a choice,' he said, 'the choice between the lesser of two evils. Nixon wants to sell the country, and Kennedy wants to buy it.' Sinatra was angry and Peter was embarrassed.

Election night was passed in Massachusetts, where the Kennedys gathered at Bobby's home. The voting was close, one of the closest-run elections in history. Had Nixon taken Texas and Illinois, states that he barely lost, Kennedy would not have been President. But the closeness did not matter. John Kennedy was President and Peter Lawford had gained both the status and the enmity that came from being his brother-in-law.

9

They Called It Camelot

I used to always cover J.F.K. when he came west to Palm Springs. We knew all about his girlfriends, but the press in those days was a little different than they are now. Everything changed after Watergate. We always looked upon Kennedy's affairs with girls as a hobby, just like Eisenhower's golf. And then when Nixon came and did to the country what Kennedy was doing to the girls, it made it different.

Hollywood columnist and author

There had never been a President quite like John Kennedy. Young, aggressive, handsome, a war hero crippled beyond what the public knew, a drug addict, a womanizer, and fascinated by showbusiness to such a degree that his hobbies sometimes seemed to interfere with his position as head of state. He was the kind of man you felt you could invite to your home for a touch football game and a can of beer. Yet there was also a sense of inner toughness giving the impression that, if someone backed you to the wall, he was a man you would want fighting by your side.

The addiction Kennedy experienced had nothing to do with the pain he constantly endured in his back. Determined to be strong and physically fit, he received what he thought were vitamin injections from Dr Max Jacobson, whose patients included many highly respected celebrities such as composer Alan Jay Lerner and singers Andy Williams and Eddie Fisher. Jacobson was given the nickname 'Dr Feelgood' because of people's reaction to his treatments. Kennedy and the others came to feel that it would be difficult for them to get through their hectic schedules without those vitamins. They were often dependent upon them, which seemed unusual – vitamins are not addictive and there are no withdrawal symptoms when you stop getting extra vitamins, whether by injection or by tablet. Finally it was discovered that Jacobson was actually injecting methamphetamine – the addict's highly coveted 'speed'.

Fortunately the addiction did not damage Kennedy's mind, nor did it affect his zest for life, including the film industry. Kennedy's interest in and awareness of the entertainment industry after he became President amazed Joe Naar. 'We'd sit down at a table together, maybe there'd be twelve of us there – Billy Wilder, Angie Dickinson, Frank Sinatra, Janet Leigh, myself, Peter and a few others.

He'd look at Angie and say, 'In the second act of that picture, it would have been funnier if you'd have done so-and-so.'

'And he'd say, "I saw your picture, Billy, and I hope they gave you a chance to do what you want to do." He had something personal to say to everyone in the room. He had that ability to make you feel important.'

Peter confirmed Joe's recollections. 'He was always ringing up – and I'm not trying to make myself a big man by saying the President was always ringing me up, because I'm sure he was always ringing up a lot of people.' The President wanted to know what was happening, 'who was making it with whom, what pretty new girls were on the scene. His interest was everywhere. He'd ring up and say, "What's going on? What about so-and-so? Is she really that pretty?" Imagine, even with all the things he had to worry about.'

Nowhere was the showbusiness interest more obvious than at the Inaugural Gala. Peter and Frank Sinatra were in charge of putting the event together.

Sinatra worked the telephone, using his influence to bring entertainers from all over the world. He pulled strings to give Frederic March time off from shooting a film. Ella Fitzgerald would be flying in from Australia. Leonard Bernstein would be on hand, along with Gene Kelly, arriving from Switzerland. Eleanor Roosevelt, widow of the late President, comedian Joey Bishop, poet Carl Sandburg, singer Nat King Cole, entertainers Jimmy Durante and George Jessel ... the list seemed to continue forever, a who's who of showbusiness and the arts. The gala was meant to raise money as well – to bring Kennedy into office without outstanding debts. By the time they were done, Peter reported a profit of $1.9 million.

There were rumours of a curious incident that is said to have taken place in the New York hotel where Peter, Frank and other entertainers were organizing the Gala. According to a statement Peter made to me, confirmed by others to the co-writer of this book, a famous performer – who obviously cannot be named since no indictment has been made – was enjoying the favours of some women, one of whom was a prostitute. Bodyguards and hangers-on were present, and they were not pleased to see the prostitute drink excessively.

Eventually she began fawning over the performer in question, spilling her drink and carrying on in a disgusting manner. The performer, not realizing how his orders would be taken, told a member of his entourage to get rid of her. The man did so, allegedly killing her, then arranging to have her body dumped far enough away from the hotel that there would be no connection with the performer or with the Kennedy people.

People involved with New York City law enforcement confirm that a known prostitute was found dead at this time, though there was nothing to indicate that she was in any way connected with the incident described. The hotel catered for the rich and famous, who often require privacy. There are a number of ways to enter and leave it without being spotted. Finally, the alleged killer had a history of violence. Peter was afraid of the man and was furious because such an incident could have greatly damaged Kennedy's image, even though the President-elect was hundreds of miles away at the time and never knew anything about it.

So much connected with that period is only conjecture, misrepresentation or rumour that I would normally hesitate to give the story much credibility. Only the fact that Peter was there when the woman was drunk, heard the orders given and was convinced that the murder later took place has made me mention it.

The other problem connected with the Gala was a natural one – snow. That night saw one of the worst blizzards that Washington, DC had ever encountered. By 6 p.m. most cab drivers had gone home for the night. Rented limousines were stuck somewhere between their pick-up points and the armoury, where the Gala was being held. Master of ceremonies Joey Bishop looked at the partially filled house, then commented, 'Those Republicans are sure sore losers.'

Many of those in attendance – Marge Durante, Angie Dickinson and others interviewed for this book – were vague about the specific acts. They remembered the joke numbers, such as Helen Traubel singing a song dedicated to Jacqueline Kennedy who had given birth to her son immediately after the election:

Everybody knows, Mrs K., the baby is quite a hit
But if you'd had him earlier, it might have helped a bit.

They mostly remembered the glamour of the night, the respect, the sense that showbusiness and politics had blended in a way never before achieved. The Hollywood establishment had come of age, gaining the stature it had lacked ever since the first show people made the trip west to entertain miners in the boom towns of the gold rush era.

The show ended three hours later. John Kennedy went on stage and said,

> I'm proud to be a Democrat because, since the time of Thomas Jefferson, the Democratic party has been identified with the pursuit of excellence, and we saw excellence tonight. The happy relationship between the arts and politics which has characterized our long history I think reached culmination tonight.
>
> I know we're all indebted to a great friend – Frank Sinatra. Long before he could sing, he used to poll a Democratic precinct back in New Jersey. That precinct has grown to cover a country. But long after he has ceased to sing, he is going to be standing up and speaking for the Democratic party, and I thank him on behalf of all of you tonight. You cannot imagine the work he has done to make this show a success. Tonight there are two shows on Broadway that are closed down because the members of the cast are here. And I want him and my sister Pat's husband, Peter Lawford, to know that we're all indebted to them, and we're proud to have them with us.

It had begun. The best of times and the worst of times for Peter.

One of the first problems the new 'first brother-in-law' faced was isolation from his own roots. In 1956 the General, a man he deeply loved, had died, and there was no chance for a relationship with his mother now that he was considered by the public and the press to be a part of the Kennedy family. May had been growing increasingly emotionally disturbed since her husband's death – apparently his influence had been a controlling factor. She also had no money, and had to live on Peter's past generosity.

Shortly before the election, May Lawford amazed Peter and delighted Los Angeles residents when she hired an elephant, had a 'Vote for Nixon' sign painted, then proceeded to ride down Wilshire Boulevard with it. Afterwards her bitterness continued. She became angry after Kennedy's death when she was invited to a film about the President's brief life and career. She declined, for the following reasons (emphasis and asides are as she wrote them):

I am no longer going to ask for insults. Before Peter's wedding I was invited to lunch *alone* with Mr Kennedy and later a dinner alone with Mrs Kennedy – (quite incorrect).

I was not allowed my correct place at the pre-wedding dinner. I was put in the corner alone with a priest.

My escort for the wedding was a strange man, a Police Inspector, not one of the ushers or the family (which is correct).

During the campaign for Mr Kennedy's $100.00 plate, etc. [the Inaugural Gala], Mrs Lawford offered me a ticket. She said, 'If you can find someone to let you sit at their table?'

I invited the children to a small party in the house. Mrs Lawford said: 'Much too far away. Besides they are flying to Florida in a day or so.'

Peter has been in this house – once four years ago. Mrs Lawford and the children never.

I was invited to visit the children one hour about twice a month by the secretary. I asked the children: 'Do you know who I am?' and they said, 'Yes, your name is May.' I said, 'I am your grandmother.' Both the children said, 'Thank you so much, but we already have one.' I have not bothered them since.

Old Mr Kennedy had a stroke. I did the correct thing and telegraphed my condolences. Three months later I received an official reply from his New York office saying, 'Your telegram received.'

Peter was having trouble adjusting to the Kennedy lifestyle. The family was one in which you either took an active part, as people such as Steve Smith (married to Jean Kennedy) and Sargent Shriver (married to Eunice Kennedy) were able to do, or they attempted to run over you. It was also a self-destructive life. Card games went until two or three in the morning, everyone drinking and smoking relatively heavily. Early in the marriage, Joseph Kennedy mentioned this when writing to his daughter Pat. In a letter dated 25 June 1956 he commented: 'In the meantime take very good care of yourself, don't drink too much Scotch, nor smoke too many cigarettes and stay up so late at night. How you do stay so beautiful doing all these things is the eight [sic] wonders of the world.' By the time Kennedy was in office, Peter was a heavy user of sleeping pills and alcohol to enable him to unwind. He also needed stimulants when working, in order to maintain the pace.

Peter's involvement with nightclub entertainers did not help. Nightclub entertainers become accustomed to turning night into day, and their bodies adjust to the pace. Actors like Peter, on the other hand, keep hours that would surprise most of their fans. If a movie is being filmed at eight o'clock in the morning in order to take advantage of the early morning light, make-up and costume preparation might begin two, three or even four hours earlier. Staying up past eight or nine o'clock at night can be exhausting with such a schedule. Peter, trying to live in two worlds, was increasingly punishing his body.

Part of Peter's lifestyle involved poker games at the house. The participants ranged from high-stakes players such as Milton Berle and Ernie Kovacs to casuals such as Pat Newcomb, Marilyn Monroe and Judy Garland. Peter himself was an active, though not very skilled, player.

The closeness of the Kennedy family was uncomfortable for Peter. Joe Kennedy commented that his children were so close to each other, he was surprised that they had ever married. The relationship was not incestuous, yet it did not leave room for an outsider who could not adjust. Peter once said that going up against the Kennedys was like going against a Panzer division. They could be brutal, even in fun. He hated the fact that the best joke the family could think of was tossing a guest into the swimming pool with his or her clothing on. The Kennedys found such slapstick delightful, never realizing that not only might it not be appreciated, but in many instances the owner could not afford to have water-damaged clothing and jewellery, especially watches, repaired or replaced.

What was perhaps Peter's worst moment came during a visit to the family home in Cape Cod. A touch football game was being played, something in which Peter participated reluctantly. Because of the way he had been raised, and because of his infirmity, Peter was not comfortable playing team sports. His body might be lean and muscular, his skills at tennis and surfing might be on the professional level, but those were solo activities. Working as part of a team, being struck ('touch' was a misnomer considering the way that the family, including the women, played the game) by the others and engaging in such sports in general were all foreign to Peter. He did not know what to expect when Steve Smith told the others: 'Get Peter.'

Suddenly the 'touch' part of the game became tackle. Peter was struck several times, the wind was knocked out of him and a couple of ribs were broken. He was upset, feeling that they had brutalized him because he was an only child, raised throughout the world, never knowing a family in the way that they had always done. He felt as though some of them, such as Steve Smith, wanted to put him down, to show him his place. Others, he felt, just considered these actions an exuberant introduction to a 'real' family. Either way, the Kennedy family way of doing things was always something he disliked.

Oddly, Peter felt that in other ways the family seemed to like him and to respect his profession. But Steve Smith, who became powerful by virtue of handling the funds of the family foundation which controls the Kennedy wealth, seems to have acted like a school bully towards him.

One reason for Peter's hostility to Steve Smith was Smith's alleged treatment of his wife. Pat Lawford and Jean Smith used to go out together to buy clothes, and it was during one of these trips that Jean told the story. According to Peter, Jean had met an Italian man with whom she had fallen in love. She told Pat that she had made up her mind to leave Steve because she was tired of his emotional abuse. Steve had been having affairs, a common situation with all the males in the family, and Jean decided that she had had enough. She went to New York, packed and made arrangements to fly to Paris.

According to Peter, Jean left a note on the mantelpiece for Steve. It said that she had had enough. She was not going to be the martyr her mother had been when her father was having his affairs. She wanted to be happy, to have her own life. She said that she was filing for a divorce and that they would work out the arrangements later.

Jean reached Paris, only to find that the man she loved had decided not to get involved with her. She had to return home, knowing that Steve had found the note. Ever since, according to Peter, they had stayed together but Steve had treated her miserably. It was a situation that Peter found tragic.

Eunice Kennedy Shriver always disturbed Peter when they had to eat together because, he said, she would eat off the plates of others. If he was sitting next to her and she liked the look of something on his plate, she would reach over and taste whatever caught her fancy.

There was more to the Kennedy scandals than titillating stories, though. The fact that the Kennedys were users and abusers of others, both within the family and without, reflects a deeper problem than the arrogance of power. All of us who were involved

– and I was to become a desired Kennedy plaything several years later – had a history of abuse which we never tried to overcome.

On a personal level, I was being raised to be the perfect woman for such a family, though I was only five years old when the President was assassinated and Camelot came to an end. I was the accidental child, the child conceived when sex is the only neutral ground for a couple no longer in love and not yet courageous enough to divorce. I was the result of a simple 'fuck' enjoyed only because it meant that they were not battering at each other with their words. I was not a love child. I was not planned. I was no one's joy and both parties' reminder that they had once shared a life, a dream, a hope for the future that proved to be a bitter delusion. Before I was born, my parents were living apart.

I became an appendage, something with which they were saddled whether they wanted me or not. My mother moved to California while my father remained where he was, thousands of miles away. I lived with both of them, eventually making California my main home. Yet no matter where I lived I was an uncomfortable reminder of the past, especially when they moved or to new relationships in which love replaced the former hate.

As my body matured, I became an even more blatant reminder for them. My looks made me a mirror of the past, of both the good days and the bad. I felt that my mother's lovers saw me as a memory of the 'other man', a person to be conquered in whatever way they could. My father's lovers seemed to see me as the 'other woman', since I undoubtedly looked much like my mother had when she first knew my father. And my father, in his sick, perverted mind, developed the need both to love me and to hurt me.

I finally decided that I would leave home, get a job and try to turn my back on the sordid past that had almost destroyed me. I had so little self-esteem that if a man had said to me, 'get on your knees, zip down my pants and perform oral sex on me, bitch!' I would have thought that he loved me. He would have been the first man in my life to tell me what would give him pleasure and not just take what he wanted, hurting me if I could not read his thoughts.

From what I have since learned from Peter, this type of emotional destruction was not unusual among the women who married into the Kennedy family or, in many instances, were involved with the Kennedy men. Some had been physically abused in the past. Others were emotionally battered, though they often did not realize it. Their fathers might have been domineering, alcoholic, emotionally abusive or distant and aloof. But whatever the specific circumstances, we shared a common bond.

Peter, because of his own childhood, slipped nicely into a dual role of abuser and abused during this period. He allowed himself to be subjected to activities that he found demoralizing and humiliating. He accepted the role of an outsider, bearing his pain without letting Pat see the extent of his vulnerability. At the same time he played out the role that Joe Kennedy had performed. He indulged himself sexually, never committing himself fully to the woman for whom he expressed love.

Oddly, Peter's attitude towards his wife probably saved her some of the emotionally shattering sexual requests that Peter was able to make of me. In retrospect I understand things better than I did then. I was younger and desperate to please Peter. Pat Kennedy was a mature woman, experienced, and expected Peter to respect her ways. Also, Peter was older by the time he met me. He had succeeded as a playboy and a sexual 'swordsman'. He didn't want to waste his time with someone who was not going to treat him the way he wanted and I didn't want to lose his affection and attention. Thus I was malleable which Peter sensed right away. Pat Kennedy was far more rigid and imposing at the time they were married. Her Catholic upbringing, her nightly prayers and other acts of devotion were unnerving for him. He could not tell her that he liked to be restrained and abused. He could not show her that intercourse, an act in which a man and woman can become intensely sensitive to one another, both physically and emotionally, did not give him great pleasure. He could not tell her that he wanted to see two women fondling each other, then giving him oral sex which he provided, in turn, for them. They were both the high points of his sexual pleasure and dirty little secrets about which he felt uncomfortable. During the Kennedy years he had to seek such activities outside the home, a fact that destroyed their marriage by the time Kennedy was in his second year in office.

Peter found a kindred spirit in Jack Kennedy, a man who had no respect for a woman's emotions and who delighted in the idea of trying anything sexually. He liked oral sex because it freed him to do other things. He had no foreplay, the woman either being sexually aroused and lubricated before the entered or else suffering a painful experience not a great deal different from rape.

I am bothered by the idea that Peter was, at times, the procurer of women for his brother-in-law, a true statement that people do not wish to face. Kitty Kelley claimed in her book on Sinatra that Peter felt that Frank Sinatra was the pimp for Kennedy and Peter was the procurer for Sinatra. I doubt that he felt this way, and I doubt that such a scenario was true. But Peter admitted to myself and others that he obtained women for Kennedy, a need that someone had to fulfil.

It is too easy to dismiss the claim of Peter's role as being unfounded. Jack Kennedy was handsome, rich and powerful, a combination that many women find the ultimate aphrodisiac. Yet he was President of the United States, a man constantly before the public eye. He was given privacy when he stayed with Peter and Pat, and a man like Peter was in a position to arrange for Kennedy to have private assignations with women.

Peter Lawford in 1938, the year of his Hollywood debut.
(*UPI/NFA Stills*)

By 1946 the star was born. At
twenty-three he'd become a
Hollywood favourite.
(UPI/NFA Stills)

In 1954 he joined the Kennedy clan with
his marriage to Patricia Kennedy.
(Special Collections, Arizona State University).

Buddies.
With brother-in-law, John F.
Kennedy.
(*Peter Lawford Collection*)

The couple seemed close, but in 1966 the marriage was over.
(*Kobal Collection*)

Lawford, Sammy Davis Jnr, Sinatra and Martin. *(Special Collections, Arizona State University Library)*

Frank Sinatra and Peter Lawford. *(Sammy Davis Jnr)*

On location of *The Longest Day*, 1961.
(*Popperfoto*)

Old friends: With Marilyn Monroe.
(*Peter Lawford Collection*)

A final, happy marriage to Patricia Seaton, in 1983. (*Peter Lawford Collection*)

With Patricia, shortly before his
death. (*Peter C. Borsari*)

Peter Lawford in 1938, the year of his Hollywood debut.
(UPI/NFA Stills)

By 1946 the star was born. At twenty-three he'd become a Hollywood favourite.
(*UPI/NFA Stills*)

In 1954 he joined the Kennedy clan with his marriage to Patricia Kennedy.
(*Special Collections, Arizona State University*).

Buddies. With brother-in-law, John F. Kennedy. (*Peter Lawford Collection*)

The couple seemed close, but in 1966 the marriage was over. (*Kobal Collection*)

Lawford, Sammy Davis Jnr, Sinatra
and Martin. *(Special Collections,
Arizona State University Library)*

Frank Sinatra and Peter Lawford.
(Sammy Davis Jnr)

On location of *The Longest Day*, 1961.
(*Popperfoto*)

Old friends: With Marilyn Monroe.
(Peter Lawford Collection)

A final, happy marriage to Patricia
Seaton, in 1983. (*Peter Lawford
Collection*)

With Patricia, shortly before his
death. (*Peter C. Borsari*)

If the woman was in showbusiness, such as Marilyn Monroe, it was easy for Peter to travel with her or be seen with her. Two actors out together implied business, especially if there was no hint of an intimate relationship. Peter could get hold of the woman, help her enter either his own home or some other rendezvous location, then discreetly step aside when Kennedy arrived.

This is not to say that there weren't women in the White House, including aides, longer-term girlfriends such as Judith Campbell, and casual acquaintances. Memoirs by former White House employees and statements made by Secret Service agents assigned to the capital all report numerous women. Usually these affairs occurred when Jackie was away, though that was not always the situation. At least once, Kennedy was caught by his wife quite literally with his pants down. But on the road, especially in the Los Angeles area, Kennedy needed someone to help, and it was Peter who provided the favour.

It is difficult to understand why Peter agreed to do this. One reason that Peter discussed was the fact that he genuinely loved Jack Kennedy as a brother. They were friends in a way Peter never was with any other man except Joe Naar. Even those who were close to him describe Peter as being capable of aloofness. 'I'm sorry I didn't take the time to get to know him better,' was a comment regularly heard when researching this book, even from men who seemed to be close to Peter when he was alive.

A second reason, though Peter never expressed it, was that he might have done it to spite Bobby Kennedy, the moralist who tried to stop the affairs, who played the heavy with women even before Jack had had his 'three different ways' with them. Constantly fulfilling Jack's desire for girls may have been Peter's way of tweaking Bobby's nose.

A third possible reason, also unexpressed, was an emotional one. Peter sold his soul to the Kennedys.

They seemed to break whatever spirit he had when he came to relationships. It was as though, once he decided to gain their favour, he feared losing it. He could not say no to their desires, even long after the intensity of the family hold on him was broken.

The casual attitude in the White House was typified by an incident that occurred almost immediately after Jack took office.

Peter, Jack and several of Jack's friends from his school and Harvard days were in the White House and noticed the Lincoln bedroom, a room that would go relatively unused throughout his term in office except when Jack wished to have a little fun. The men took out some money which Jack would hold and which would be paid to the first among them to have sex in the Lincoln bedroom with a woman other than his wife. Peter was determined to win the bet.

The opportunity arose when Peter was on a cross-country flight. He had business in New York but planned to stop first at the White House. There was an extremely attractive stewardess on the flight to whom Peter was drawn at once. He was flying non-stop, first class, the flight was long and there was plenty of time to talk. By the time they were ready to land the stewardess had agreed to spend the day with Peter at the White House.

A limousine was waiting for Peter at the airport and his bags were taken for him. They drove to the White House where a guard stopped the car, glanced in and said, 'Oh, it's you, Mr Lawford. Go right inside.' The woman was impressed, and it was obvious to Peter.

They arrived in time for breakfast with the President. The stewardess was suddenly in the middle of a world of fame, power and money, a world Peter was certain would serve as an aphrodisiac. After breakfast Kennedy told Peter that he had taken the liberty of having the luggage placed in Peter's 'usual suite', the Lincoln bedroom. The stage was set. Peter could almost count the money.

The couple adjourned to the Lincoln bedroom, where they talked and enjoyed each other's company. An hour passed, then two. Neither had made any sexual advances, yet Peter knew the stewardess was enjoying herself. It was time to become more aggressive.

He kissed her, and she responded – though not with the passion he had hoped. He touched her breasts; her body stiffened slightly, but she did not reject him. Then he moved in. If they did not get their clothes off and climb into bed quickly it would be lunchtime and too late for sex. It was at this moment that the woman pushed him roughly back.

'I'm sorry,' she told Peter. 'I like you and I'm having a wonderful time here, but please don't try to have sex with me. For the past five years I've been involved in a very loving, very meaningful relationship and I simply cannot betray her.'

Thinking fast, Peter managed to calm her and keep her from thinking badly of him. They had genuinely enjoyed each other's company and she agreed to play along at lunch, never indicating what had – and had not – happened between them. She did not know about the bet, but she did realize that, had she liked men, they would have gone to bed together and she might have enjoyed it. Jack Kennedy watched the way Peter treated her, making moves and gestures that seemed to imply that they were a lot closer than they had been at breakfast. Afterwards Jack called Peter to one side. He brought out the money he had been holding, gave it to him and said, 'You son-of-a-bitch! I knew you'd be the one to win the bet.' Peter never told him the truth.

There were numerous other stories of those Kennedy years – good times and odd times, as a family that had achieved the ultimate public power in the United States took full advantage of it in their private lives. And when it came to Jack, Peter was right along beside him in many instances, a trusted intimate.

Fiddle and Faddle were an unlikely pair of Kennedy loyalists who actively campaigned for him during his run for the Presidency. Most people have forgotten their real names and only recall the codenames assigned to them by the Secret Service. They were anxious to meet him, and he had been told so much about them that he felt the same way. They turned out to be extremely attractive women who were quite willing to share sexual favours with the President. When he took office, he brought them in as secretaries.

The incident that remained foremost in Peter's mind concerned some vials of amyl nitrate, otherwise known as 'poppers'. The drug, which smells like ether, is extremely dangerous, yet some people use it in small quantities to increase their sexual awareness. They take the drug just as they are achieving orgasm, in order to heighten the experience. What they don't realize, often until it is too late, is that the drug affects the heart and respiratory system. No one knows just what his or her body can handle until they try the drug, and a single dose can be fatal for some people.

Peter Sellers was a classic example of a man who experimented with amyl nitrate once too often. He took several poppers at once, suffering a near-fatal heart attack. His health was so damaged that the drug was probably a major contributor to his death.

On this occasion Peter had some poppers on him and Jack Kennedy wanted to try one. Peter, shocked, refused. He explained that Jack was the President of the United States and could not risk his health for a sexual experience. Instead, either Fiddle or Faddle – Peter never could remember which – was given the drug. She was naked on the floor at the time, her body turning quite red from the changes in circulation. Kennedy watched in fascination.

Peter enjoyed playing tricks on friends during the Camelot days. For example, there was the time that he, his manager Milt Ebbins and Kennedy were flying on Air Force One. Peter was accustomed to the plane and the service provided, having flown with Kennedy many times. His manager, on the other hand, was new to the experience.

The attitude on board Air Force One was one of great deference and discretion. The first time Peter flew, the plane did not have Peter's favourite Tanqueray gin – only Beefeater. However, they made note of his preference and, from that time, on any time Peter flew his gin was in stock. The Secret Service and the military personnel also understood that the plane was a place for privacy. No matter what might occur, from sex to the use of illegal substances, no one was going to say anything unless the President's life was in danger. But Milt Ebbins did not know this.

After the usual exhaustive security checks of the air-craft Peter and Milt were settled in an area with the Secret Service agents; Kennedy had his own private quarters. Milt mentioned that he was tired because he had spent the night with a number of jazz musicians. One of them knew Peter and had given Milt a present for him – three extremely potent marijuana cigarettes.

Milt was not a boozer or a drug abuser. Although he worked with people who used drugs, their lifestyle was not his and he merely accepted it as being a part of their world. He never thought about the possible implications of giving Peter three joints on the presidential aircraft.

'Not now, Milt,' said Peter, pointing out the Secret Service agents.

Ebbins, startled, accidentally dropped the joints.

Peter, seemingly annoyed, quickly covered them with his foot. Then he waved at the agents as though to tell them that everything was fine and discreetly picked up the joints. Then he looked at Milt and said quietly, 'What the fuck do you think you're doing here? You just dropped grass on Air Force One, you shit.'

Peter said that Milt's hat wilted and there was sweat pouring from his forehead.

'We got a problem,' said Peter, well aware that the Secret Service had seen everything and did not care.

There was no way they were going to arrest the President's brother-in-law on Air Force One. But he delighted in practical jokes, had a love/hate relationship with his manager, and enjoyed watching him sweat. More than that, he was annoyed that Milt, not knowing how casually these things were treated, should have been so unthinking as to bring marijuana on board.

'What are we going to do?' Milt said, frightened.

'You've got three choices,' Peter told him. 'Your first choice is that you can flush them, but they inspect the shit when we get off the plane.' It was completely untrue. 'You can smoke them,' said Peter, offering a different suggestion. Both knew that that was ridiculous under the circumstances, for marijuana has a very distinctive smell. 'Or you can eat them,' Peter concluded.

Forty-five minutes later Peter was watching an extremely high Milt Ebbins, to whom the world had become a wonderful place. When lunch was announced and the two men went back to join Kennedy, Milt was wildly happy. All through the meal he interrupted the President, often spouting nonsense. Kennedy was annoyed with the man's seeming rudeness and strange behaviour.

Later, when both Ebbins and Kennedy knew the full story, the President was delighted with the joke. His manager, though, was hurt and embarrassed and did not speak to Peter for quite some time afterwards.

The relationship with Ebbins was to become an extremely volatile one. When Peter eventually fired him we were living in an apartment with a balcony that overlooked the car parking area. Peter went out onto the balcony and urinated over the side, sprinkling Ebbins' Jaguar. It was crude, but it was typical Peter. At one time he would walk over to the television set and piss on it if the entertainment it offered seemed offensive to him. I always knew that whenever Richard Nixon was on I had better be ready with paper towels and disinfectant.

Peter delighted in Kennedy's humour and lack of pretension. He told me about the first day that Jack was in the White House and the red telephone rang. It was the hotline, and would only be used in dire national emergency such as an attack by Russia. Kennedy had no idea what to do and just stared at the telephone, listened to it ring and said, 'I'm not going to answer it.' He was terrified of what it might mean. The reality was very simple – a wiring problem. The telephone had rung by accident.

Kennedy was also at odds with Air Force General Curtis LeMay, a man who he felt was a warmonger. During Kennedy's first press conference, someone found out about the red phone ringing by mistake and asked Kennedy what he would do if the emergency was real. Peter said that Kennedy paused for a moment, then said that if we had to attack Russia, he was going to make sure that Curtis LeMay was in the lead aircraft.

There was a time when both Peter and Winston Churchill were at the White House with Kennedy. Peter was in awe of Churchill, who had been such a strong influence in keeping the British united during the Battle of Britain.

Churchill stayed on the second floor and had a tendency to be rather lax about his personal habits. He was frequently seen wandering around wearing a towel and nothing else.

One night, about 2.30 a.m., Kennedy knocked on the door of Peter's bedroom and asked him to follow him. Peter and Jack went down the passage like two little boys having an adventure they knew was naughty. Then, before Peter could see what was going to happen, the President went and got a camera. Suddenly Peter saw Churchill just as Kennedy began snapping pictures. The former Prime Minister was stark naked, passed out on the back stairs, cradling a bottle of port.

There were additional games on the West Coast. Jack Kennedy delighted in upsetting the Secret Service because they placed so many restrictions on his life. When he stayed with Peter and Pat, he would frequently find a way to sneak out and go swimming in the ocean before they could find him. They were worried about his going on the beach, both because there was public access and because he could get into difficulties and drown. Yet he felt the precautions were foolish and thought it was funny to see them rushing into the water, fully dressed, to protect him.

Peter and the President, along with the Secret Service guards, would go to a bar that Peter said was little more than a shack. It was called Sip-n-Surf and was the hangout for the surfing crowd. There they would both pick up girls, taking them back to the house for sex when Pat was away for a few hours. While Pat probably did not care about her brother's actions, both because of the way they were raised and because she did not like Jackie, she must have smelled another woman's perfume on Peter or recognized that the bed was not the way she had left it. But this was the period when divorce could not be considered because of the united family image needed for the second term campaign. She might have said something to Peter, or she may have suffered silently. Either way, his unthinkingly cruel actions further destroyed what little was left of their relationship.

Despite the games with Jack, Peter was deeply moved by the White House. He became close friends with Jackie and learned from her the history of the building. She was the first person actively to pursue the much-needed renovation of the building. She raised money, located antiques that had been buried in storage rooms, and obtained long-term loans of items which she considered important for the history of the place.

I didn't realize how much Peter loved the place or how many memories it would come to hold for him until many years later we attended a dinner there. It was a rather odd time in our lives, when Peter had become involved with a group called the National Organization to Reform the Marijuana Laws (NORML). I remember

126

going to meetings in a building in Washington where the room was illuminated by blue lights, Ravi Shankar's sitar music was playing in the background, and everyone sat around smoking marijuana and saying things like, 'We've got to change the laws.' They seemed like a group of meaningless nuts and I always wondered what we were doing there, but the involvement somehow resulted in our being invited to the White House.

During the dinner Peter told me about the building, including stories of Dolly Madison hanging her washing to dry in the East Room in the early years of the nineteenth century. Then, as he looked around and remembered, he suddenly became very quiet. I could tell he was remembering Jack, the parties, the history and the fun. Tears filled his eyes, his face reflecting the depth of emotion I had never known was there. It was a time that brought him great happiness.

10

Sinatra, Monroe and the Death of Camelot

He's so self-centred, when he has sex he shouts out his own name.

Comedian Jackie Gayle

Gravity has a way of making everyone the same.
Marilyn Monroe, speaking about the realities of
being known for a big bust line

Ladies and gentlemen, the 'late' Marilyn Monroe.
Peter Lawford introducing Marilyn Monroe during
a party held for Jack Kennedy at Madison Square
Garden just a few months before her death

The tragedy could not have been predicted. Peter had no idea that before Jack Kennedy could run for a second term of office his own marriage and his relationship with Frank Sinatra would be in ruins, Marilyn Monroe would be dead by her own hand and his brother-in-law would be destroyed by an assassin's bullet. Two of the incidents were out of Peter's control. The divorce was brought about partly by his self-indulgence, but Monroe's death was one that would haunt him for the remainder of his life. Compounding the tragedy was the fact that it occurred just after his relationship with Frank Sinatra was shattered.

The situation that caused his break with Sinatra in March 1962 seems, at first, to have been fairly trivial.

However, you have to consider the fragile egos of showbusiness personalities who have maintained intense rivalries on their way to the top.

The problem began when John Kennedy had to fly to Palm Springs and Sinatra offered to let him use his home. This was not the first time that Sinatra had had Kennedy as a house guest. During the 1960 Presidential campaign Kennedy stayed with Sinatra, an incident so important to the singer that he had a plaque placed on the wall of the room reading: 'John F. Kennedy Slept Here November 6th and 7th, 1960.' (Oddly, the dates listed are incorrect, though the incident did occur.)

For this second visit Sinatra went to great expense to ensure that the house would be right for the President, described by his daughter Nancy in her book *Frank Sinatra: My Father.*

With the President coming, F.S. added a pair of two-bedroom cottages out by the pool. In the main house he built a big dining room with a cathedral ceiling, made the tiny kitchen into a butler's pantry, and added an industrial-type kitchen. He turned the little guest room into a library but left the J.F.K. plaque on the door. He pushed the living room and bar walls out a few feet and brought in giant boulders and cactus plants to shield the pool area from the adjacent golf course. He redecorated everything except his own bedroom, which seemed small now compared to the rest of the house. He painted and papered and carpeted and draped. Some of this, much of this, he would have done anyhow but with the understanding that he would be entertaining J.F.K., he had a cement landing pad for a helicopter constructed.

What Sinatra did not realize was the Bobby Kennedy hated him and wanted the relationship to end. This was a period when many activities were taking place that could be embarrassing to Kennedy if they ever were revealed.

For example, Bobby Kennedy had taken on the Teamsters and he was looking into various underworld figures, including Sinatra's friend Sam Giancana. As early as 1960 Bobby had been concerned with Sinatra's relationship with the alleged Chicago Mafia leader. He had had special agents look into the question of whether Sinatra had Phyllis McGuire cast in the movie *Come Blow Your Horn* because he liked her acting or because she was Giancana's girlfriend. Bobby had also been angry to learn that Judith Campbell, a former girlfriend of Sinatra's, was having sex with both John Kennedy and Giancana.

Later, after she had written a book detailing part of her affair, Peter wrote about Judith Campbell, then locked away the papers. But Peter knew more than she had included in her book and felt a need to record that information on paper, hiding it away because he feared its release while some of the people involved were still alive. It was for the same reason that he never revealed the names of the people who ordered the Kennedy assassination – names he knew well. All he would say was that it was Mafia-orchestrated in conjunction with a wealthy Texas family who felt that their mutual oil investment interests were threatened by Kennedy's stance on certain areas of business. Lyndon Johnson was perceived as either more controllable or more sympathetic, and so was not a threat. Only Kennedy had to die.

Peter explained that the Warren Commission was a whitewash, though he did not say if the members were bribed or if the witnesses and experts were corrupted to some degree. Had Peter lived longer, he might have revealed all that he knew. But at the time of his death all that Peter left behind was these comments concerning Judith Campbell and one aspect of the Kennedy/Mafia connection:

She was, in the words of the first man who married her, a very quiet family type of girl, someone who didn't have any convictions about anything at all. To her lawyer, she was a very warm, charming person, private, self-contained and not a publicity seeker.

True enough, the lady modestly described herself as nothing more than a happily married housewife. To meet her on the street or in a supermarket, you would think her a rather ordinary woman pushing middle age, tan, well kept, in a way that southern California women are always tan and well kept. Not striking, not someone you would look twice at, not different at all, save for one way, a way which would forever make Judith Campbell Exner *that* woman. For Judy was a mob moll and the mistress of my brother-in-law, the President of the United States.

The bare outlines of this story are by now familiar, repeated endlessly with a smirk, a smile, and a leer, how in 1960, Judy, then 23, an aspiring actress, became the consort of Jack Kennedy. What made Judy more than just another presidential girl friend was the other company she kept, notably John 'Don Giovanni' Rosselli and Salvatore Sam 'Momo' Giancana, both members in good standing of organized crime, not to mention the Central Intelligence Agency. This is a lurid tale, and the more one probes it, the more lurid it will become, not merely for sex, for the diminishing of the Kennedy legend, but for its utter sleaziness, the image to be projected of party girls, of swarthy men in shiny suits, now being packaged and auctioned to the highest bidder.

Then, referring to her book, he said that it

merely confirmed what had already appeared in the press or in the Church Committee report, that she had been introduced to Kennedy in Las Vegas in February, 1960, by a mutual friend who turns out to be Frank Sinatra, and they had had a close personal relationship for the next two years during which time they lunched privately in the Oval Office and on other occasions she was acquainted with Rosselli and Giancana. And she had made some 70 phone calls, that all her conversations with the president reflected man–woman bedroom talk.

Peter continued, 'After the last ten years, we should have lost our capacity for shock. Nothing is impossible any more. The sensational has become commonplace.' Then, facetiously, he added, 'Amelia Earhart living in the Bermuda Triangle. Martha Mitchell being poisoned for what she knows. Why not?

'But somehow this is the one story no one ever wanted to hear, the one myth the country wanted left intact.'

Peter was fascinated by the eventual cover-up that was involved with Judith Campbell and the organized crime connections with the Kennedy White House. He noted: 'Out of literally thousands of Washington lawyers, the Church Committee [named after investigator Senator Frank Church] selected a member of Sargent Shriver's law firm to represent Mrs Exner.' Shriver, of course, was Kennedy's brother-in-law. And Peter was constantly aware of such matters, either playing along or remaining silent, always aware that Frank Sinatra remained on the periphery.

Sinatra had long flouted convention in what, for Bobby Kennedy, was an unconventional and disreputable lifestyle. Sinatra was never a part of the Mafia. Known members laugh at the idea because Sinatra lacked most of the characteristics needed to succeed within that closed society. However, he was friends with many of the leaders and happy to spend time with them. For Bobby, who came of age with the McCarthy hearings, even a friendship could damn you.

At the same time Jack Kennedy, undoubtedly with his brother's awareness, had been negotiating behind the scenes with Giancana to have Cuban leader Fidel Castro assassinated. The Mafia had been involved with nightclubs and gambling in Cuba prior to the revolution against President Batista. The United States had admitted the corruption in the country, including the fact that there seemed to be no middle class under Batista. You were either rich, and possibly corrupt, or you were so poor that malnutrition and disease were rife. Castro had promised a better life, been supported by the United States, then moved into the Communist camp so fully that Russia was given permission to have nuclear missiles on the island just ninety miles away from the coast of Florida.

The Kennedys felt that the Mafia would be an ideal resource. They had contacts in Cuba and a vested interest in restoring the lifestyle that had once made Havana far more glamorous than Las Vegas. They were also used to the idea of using assassination as a means of achieving their business ends.

Eventually several possibilities were seriously considered. These included supplying Castro with poisoned cigars, and giving him a wetsuit for skin diving that would be chemically treated to cause cramping and death that would appear accidental.

The New York City Police Department eventually arrested the top members of a drug ring financed by Fidel Castro and run from Cuba by Che Guevara and Raul Castro, Fidel's brother. Its members were dedicated to corrupting an entire generation of American youth in order to destroy the moral fibre of the USA and eventually devastate the country. The year the arrests were made $350 million was involved, a large sum for the 1960s.

The Kennedys were obviously playing both ends against the middle. They were secretly working with organized crime at the same time that they were fighting it. Bobby may or may not have been bothered by the irony of such actions, but the public image he wanted his brother to have did not allow any connection with 'mobbed up' figures such as Sinatra. He decided that the best play would be to declare Sinatra's home a security risk. Technically, Bobby Kennedy's statement was true. Access to the house was fairly open, and anyone determined to kill the President had several approaches from which to make an attack.

A search for another house began. The one that was eventually rented, along with a house on each side to secure the area better, was at the base of a mountain that provided natural protection from attack. There was only one road in and out, again adding to the security. However, there was one serious drawback: the house was owned by a Republican Party stalwart and well-known singer named Bing Crosby.

Jack told Peter the truth. Bobby had convinced him that, as President, he could not go to Sinatra's house and sleep under the same roof as Sam Giancana. The situation would look terrible politically. But Peter was frightened of what Frank would think when Kennedy asked him to call the singer to explain the changes made necessary by security considerations. He and Jack had been joking about Sinatra building the Western White House. They knew about the changes that had been made, including extra telephone lines and essential special communications equipment. There was even going to be a flagpole to fly the Presidential flag when Kennedy was present. Frank had seen one at the Kennedy compound in Hyannis and liked the idea.

No one had ever encouraged Sinatra to make such changes. Neither Jack nor Peter had ever said whether the plans fitted the President's wishes. However, Kennedy was probably looking forward to relaxing with Sinatra, being briefed on the latest showbusiness gossip and introduced to new women.

Peter finally made the call to Sinatra, telling him the situation. Perhaps Sinatra would have understood the political image problem – perhaps something could have been worked out. But the fact that the President was staying in the home of Republican singer Bing Crosby after Sinatra had been a major Democratic Party fund-raiser since the days of Roosevelt was too much.

Sinatra was irrational in his anger towards Peter, completely out of control, blaming him as though Peter had greater influence than he did. That anger extended even beyond Peter. He stopped speaking to Jimmy Van Heusen, the songwriter who lived next door to Crosby and whose house had been rented for the Secret Service's use. However, he made up with Van Heusen a few weeks later.

When Kennedy arrived in Palm Springs on the weekend of 24–26 March, Peter explained how upset Sinatra had been. The President agreed to call, telling Sinatra it was a security decision and asking him to not blame Peter. But Peter told me Frank knew that Bobby Kennedy was behind the 'security' excuse, and that he was aware of the real reason for the snub. Sinatra hated both men for covering up Bobby's vendetta. He never spoke to Peter again, cutting him out of the movies they had been scheduled to make together, including *Robin and the Seven Hoods* and *Four for Texas*.

Peter would later become obsessed with Sinatra's reaction. He came to the conclusion that the singer had blacklisted him in Hollywood. He felt that after Jack Haley, Jr used him in the film history of MGM, *That's Entertainment*, the only reason he wasn't used in the sequel was because Sinatra had refused to appear in it if Lawford filmed a segment. In truth, according to Haley, he never had any intention of using Peter or any other MGM star as a segment narrator for more than one of the films. He wanted the sequel to be unique, with different personalities appearing to talk about the clips.

Conversations with other producers and directors in Hollywood revealed that at no time did Sinatra try to keep Peter from working. One producer, who asked to remain anonymous, laughed when told of Peter's allegations. He said, 'A lot of us hate Sinatra's arrogance. If that son of a bitch ever tried to keep anyone from working, I'd have hired that actor for that reason alone. And I can name a dozen other major producers who feel the same. But seriously, Sinatra's just not that kind of guy. I may hate him, but he's not so mean-spirited and petty as to try to keep anybody from working, except maybe on his own projects, and that's his right.'

The break with Sinatra was shattering for Peter. He had never been all that close to the man, yet he admired his singing, respected his abilities as an entertainer and enjoyed the work they did together. Suddenly he was excluded from that world. There would be no more Clan. There would be no more playing in nightclubs with Sammy, Joey, Frank and Dean.

Peter would still play Las Vegas and other locations, but he would be doing it only with Jimmy Durante, who used him for twelve weeks a year plus hiring him as a guest on his television show. He loved Jimmy like a father, yet the joy of that relationship could not ease the pain of losing the other. He was deeply hurt.

There was no way for Peter to anticipate the realities he was to face almost immediately after his break with Sinatra. Two more important relationships in his life were about to end, the next one being his friendship with Marilyn Monroe.

Monroe understood showbusiness and self-promotion, and liked to dazzle columnists with titillating lines that were never so naughty that they could not be quoted.

'What do you wear to bed?'
'Just some Chanel No. 5.'
'Is that all you have on?'
'Oh, no.'
'What else do you have on?'
'The radio.'

It was great copy, though it was not original. Marilyn used old vaudeville routines to help her maintain a controlled image when being interviewed. She had a quick wit, but she did not leave matters to chance.

Marilyn was married several times and had several lovers. Towards the end of her life she was rumoured to take a new lover every time she was depressed. Since she was frequently depressed, sex became a casual obsession and she had many one-night stands.

Joe Naar talked about the time when he spent the night on the couch in Marilyn's home. They had been out together and he was too tired and had had too much to drink to want to return home. He was fascinated by Marilyn, found her extremely erotic, and shared what seemed to be every male's fantasy in those days of wanting to take her to bed. He also knew that she had given him signals to indicate that, if he made a move, she would happily respond. The night he stayed in her house, 'It was like a fantasy,' Naar later explained. 'I was lying on the couch and Marilyn was in the next room. I knew that if I got up and went in there, I could go to bed with her. But I was so scared, I did nothing. I just lay there, hoping she would come out to me. She didn't and I didn't. I don't think most men would believe me but I just didn't have the nerve.'

Many others did have the nerve, including the great baseball player Joe DiMaggio. He was considered one of the nation's greatest athletes and she was America's reigning sex symbol when they met in the 1950s. She rebuffed his early attempts at getting a date, then called him to ask him out. Their stormy marriage lasted less than a year.

Marilyn's last husband was playwright Arthur Miller, considered one of the great intellectuals of the day. She was impressed with Miller's genius, his gentleness, and the fact that he was totally different from any of the other men she had known. Marilyn was defensive when asked why Arthur Miller never wrote a play for her, yet he explained that he was not that type of writer. However, he did dedicate a collection of plays to her. Monroe commented that the dedication was the best thing that had ever happened to her; then she said, 'No, the best thing was when he married me.'

Marilyn also dated billionaire Howard Hughes, a man whose name was linked with some of America's most beautiful women. Hughes became extremely possessive and even assigned bodyguards to prevent other men from coming into her home. Joe Naar remembered one incident when Marilyn had asked Peter to stop by, yet when he and Peter arrived outside her home the guards refused to let them in. The fact that the call was purely social did not matter. They had their orders, and there was no way that Peter and Joe were going to be admitted. The Hughes affair was very brief – apparently he was only interested in her between more serious relationships.

When John Kennedy decided that he wanted to have an affair with Marilyn Monroe, there was no reason why she should be surprised. She was the most desired woman in the United States. She had been married to the leading athlete and leading intellectual of the day, so why not the leading politician? What she did not realize was that Kennedy did not want to have sex with Marilyn. He wanted to have sex with the greatest movie star of the day. He wanted to fuck her. He wanted to dominate her. He wanted her because of her image, not because she was a woman whom he respected. What she was about to experience would be little better than friendly rape, yet because of her fantasies it would be months before she understood what was taking place. And when she did, the information would destroy her.

Jack Kennedy was emulating his father when he asked Peter about meeting Marilyn Monroe. Joe Kennedy had enjoyed the favours of Gloria Swanson, the greatest star of her day. Jack was simply taking on the reigning woman of the screen for his generation.

I think Peter went along with the request at the time because he saw nothing wrong with it. Jack and Marilyn were adults. Marilyn was his friend, and he saw no reason not to introduce her to the President. If the relationship went anywhere, that would be their business. And if it didn't, again there was no problem.

Yet there may have been more to what took place than Peter understood. I say this because of what happened later between myself and Ted Kennedy.

There was something perverted about the way Peter maintained emotional ties with the Kennedy family. He had been hurt by them and they had been hurt by his divorce with Pat in 1965. His son Christopher and daughters Sydney (after his father), Victoria Frances (after Frances 'Frank' Sinatra) and Robin, were being raised as Kennedys, and the family was estranged. Peter had great love for the kids, but he knew neither how to raise them nor how to show his emotions, a situation that will be described later in this book. The important point is that he had been broken by the family, or so it seemed to me, his spirit crushed, his morality destroyed.

Knowing this about Peter, his actions involving Marilyn Monroe and Jack Kennedy can be placed in a more realistic perspective. She was living with the fantasy that every man in America wanted her and that she could have the most desirable among them. Her life had proven the reality of that fantasy, at least so far as DiMaggio and Miller were concerned.

Peter and Jack were schoolboys, bragging about the number of women they had deflowered. They were cavalier about sex and their relationships. They were also living with the reality that both of them, but especially the President, had always been able to have anyone they wanted. No matter how prominent a woman might be, she would always yield to the advances of Jack Kennedy. His cock had been used like a sword, cutting a wide swath through the beauties of Hollywood. Marilyn's prominence had simply elevated her to No. 1 on the Penis Parade.

It is doubtful that Peter ever believed that Marilyn could be hurt by the relationship with the President. She was relatively promiscuous as well as being a savvy adult, but she was vulnerable in a way Peter was unable to admit despite his own history of childhood abuse. Tragically, based on my experience with Teddy Kennedy and Peter, I suspect that even if he had been sensitive to the possible outcome, Peter would still have gone along with the affair. He would not say no to Jack.

After the affair began, Marilyn was excited by the intrigue necessary for the relationship to continue without interruption. Peter used to dress Marilyn in a brown wig, dowdy clothing and glasses, then hand her a pad and pen. She would be sneaked into the Carlyle Hotel as Peter's personal secretary, and he made her take notes. He said that she used to whisper to him, 'Don't do this to me, prick,' but he would just laugh her off. They both knew that the ruse was critical to avoid discovery. Later a number of reporters who had covered the Kennedy administration either talked of the trick or admitted that they had been fooled. Marilyn would take notes furiously wherever they went, those who recognized her refusing to say anything publicly about what was taking place. The vast majority truly did not realize who she was.

The secretary trick was most effective when Peter took Marilyn on Air Force One or some other plane. The public was fascinated by Peter and focused their attention on him. Marilyn would frequently go unnoticed – no one was interested in a secretary when they could see a movie star or the President.

Marilyn was given Kennedy's private number which rang in the personal quarters of the White House. Frequently she would call the President and Jackie would answer. Marilyn brazenly asked for Jack and was able to talk with him despite the presence of his wife. The mere fact that she had the telephone number and used it reinforced Marilyn's belief that she was something more than a casual sex partner and made her believe that Jack Kennedy was going to divorce his wife. In her mind, she would be married to the President before the end of his first term in office. Then she would be First Lady of the United States during the final four years he was destined to serve.

There was only one public moment in the affair between Jack Kennedy and Marilyn. This came during a birthday celebration for Kennedy that was held in Madison Square Garden on 19 May 1962. Twenty thousand people attended, and the entertainment was to be provided by such notables as Maria Callas, Henry

Fonda, Peggy Lee, Jack Benny and Marilyn, who sang 'Happy Birthday'.

Marilyn was notorious for being late for appointments, even when she was needed on the set of a film. Some stories claim that it was because of her insecurity and talked about her terror of not looking her best. Yet the columnist Earl Wilson once wrote of an incident when his wife went to check on Marilyn after she was more than an hour late for a party. She found Marilyn fully dressed but admiring herself in the mirror.

Whatever the reason for Marilyn's persistent lateness, Peter decided it would be fun to use her reputation as the basis for some humour. Peter went to the microphone and announced, 'Mr President, on this occasion of your birthday, this lovely lady is not only pulchritudinous but punctual. Mr President – Marilyn Monroe!'

The audience, cheering, turned to watch her entrance. She did not appear.

Other acts followed, then Peter said, 'A woman of whom it may truly be said – she needs no introduction.' There was a drum roll, heads turned, and again nothing happened.

Finally, after several more acts, Peter said, 'Mr President, because, in the history of showbusiness, perhaps there has been no one female who has meant so much, who has done more ... Mr President ... the *late* Marilyn Monroe!' And then she was pushed from the wings onto the stage.

Marilyn stood by the microphone, taking time to collect herself, to look at Kennedy and the audience, before softly, almost hesitantly, singing 'Happy Birthday'. Then, after the applause, she began singing with more fervour a song specially written by Richard Adler to the tune of 'Thanks for the memory', Bob Hope's signature tune.

*

> Thanks, Mr President,
> For all the things you've done,
> The battles that you've won,
> The way you deal with US Steel,
> And our problems by the ton,
> We thank you, so much.

The public display of affection was seemingly nothing more than a showbusiness salute to a President who delighted in the entertainment world. However Bobby Kennedy, the family moralist, realized that Marilyn was going too far. She had lost any sense of discretion in the way she was making telephone calls. Soon there would be a chance that information might be revealed publicly. Kennedy's image could be tarnished. The second term might be jeopardized by a woman who was, in reality, just another of Jack's 'fucks'. He was determined to stop her.

Oddly, during this period Marilyn moved into the beach house owned by Peter and Pat. At times Jack would be there having sex with Marilyn, separated from the Lawfords by no more than six feet of space. Yet this was tolerated and, apparently, encouraged.

Peter also acted as the official recorder of these events. There was a beautiful marble and onyx bathroom serving the spare bedroom. Jack liked to get in the tub, then have Marilyn climb on top of him while they had sex in the water. Peter would be asked to take photographs, for the President delighted in having his activities recorded.

Such semi-voyeuristic tendencies on Jack Kennedy's part were an open secret among some members of the family. After the President's death, as many of the photographs as could be found were destroyed. Since no one knew who had taken them all or where they might have gone, there was great fear that some might have survived. Peter, for one, was not asked to destroy his, apparently because no one realized that he had any, and he retained them after his divorce. He did not want to look at them. He did not want to use them for blackmail or titillate others. They were simply not that important, and so they were dumped in a box and forgotten. To this day the Kennedy family is still concerned that one or more of these images might turn up.

Pat grew fond of Marilyn, and was happy to have her stay in the house after Jack returned to Washington. However, Marilyn seemed troubled by the affair and the circumstances of her life at that time. Peter said that many a night he would be awakened by Marilyn coming to the bedroom he shared with Pat. She would open the door, then stand at the entrance in her robe. Peter would feign sleep. He said she would just stand there, watching the couple or staring through their window at the ocean just beyond. She thought that they were the perfect married couple, devoted to each other, completely happy. Marilyn did not know about Peter's affairs or the fact that the marriage was essentially over. It was as though they were a role model for her to study, a picture of happiness she desperately wanted and was uncertain she would ever achieve. One morning, as Peter lay in bed with Pat, Monroe abruptly turned and, before leaving the room, quietly said, 'How come I can't be as happy as you two?' It was a statement that haunted Peter.

What happened later, in August 1962, has been the subject of countless hours of debate and more nonsense than any other issue related to the Kennedy Presidency except his assassination. This is the story of the death of Marilyn Monroe. Even the so-called 'facts' revealed in numerous books have been distorted. In one instance I was contacted by the author of as seemingly definitive volume on Marilyn who told me that he had made mistakes and was planning a follow-up book to correct them.

The most widely circulated story has Bobby Kennedy helping to murder Marilyn to shut her up. The most outrageous of the frequently quoted versions of this story has Bobby and a doctor going to see Marilyn. Suddenly Bobby grabs her while the doctor fills his syringe in preparation for the fatal injection. Then Marilyn is jabbed in the armpit where no mark will be visible to the coroner. From that point on, death is a foregone conclusion.

There are many counters to the story about Marilyn's 'murder', including the lack of physical evidence. However, the critics all say that such a dearth of proof only helps to show the accuracy of the charges. The CIA must have been involved because they can fake anything.

There was also a story that the body was removed after death, rushed to a hospital, then returned to the house when it was obvious that nothing could be done for her. However, a homicide detective familiar with the scene the night Marilyn died said that the body could not have been moved. When someone dies, blood pools in the body based upon the way the corpse is positioned. Any movement of the body causes that pooling to change in an extremely obvious and unfakeable manner, and Marilyn's body showed no such signs. So this story is just another fantasy.

The truth is quite simple and much less dramatic. As to those critics who keep insisting that the murder story is true, and that the death was obviously meant to avoid White House embarrassment, the easiest counter is the dozens of women who are still alive. If Marilyn was murdered, why not the legendary Fiddle and Faddle? Why was Judith Campbell, a woman who was not only Kennedy's lover but someone who could and did link him with singer Frank Sinatra and alleged Mafia leader Sam Giancana, allowed to live?

So what did happen? An unstable woman was pushed beyond her limits by the unfeeling actions of Jack Kennedy, Bobby Kennedy and, in a sense, Peter.

The situation started when Bobby had a conversation with Marilyn concerning her constant calling of the private quarters of the White House. She was told that she was not going to be First Lady. She was not even a serious affair for the President: 'You're just another of Jack's fucks.'

Peter confirmed the harsh reality that Marilyn was facing. It seems that no effort was made to let her down easily. Shock therapy was best for the playboys of Capitol Hill. Tell Marilyn the truth and watch her fall to pieces.

Marilyn went to the Cal-Neva Lodge, a resort in which Frank Sinatra had had an interest at one time and a popular place for entertainment figures to rest and play. There she proceeded to overdose on prescription drugs. Her stomach had to be pumped and she was returned home.

If any of Marilyn's friends made any effort to help her through her suicidal depression, that information has not been uncovered. Certainly Peter took no action. She had been suicidal so many times in the past, always being saved at the last minute, that no one took her seriously. They saw the overdoses as a cry for attention, a chance to be on centre stage without going too far and really dying. No one stopped to think that she was emotionally disturbed and essentially alone despite the loving support of her secretary and housekeeper, and that death was a way to prove her seriousness.

There are conflicting reports of what happened just prior to Marilyn's overdose. Many of these come from people who simply lied. A woman who knew Peter for a few weeks claimed Peter told her everything about that night, then proceeded to relate a story that contradicted everything Peter had said and documented for me during our ten and a half years together. The fact that the woman was paid exceedingly well for the information is further indication of her lack of credibility.

Then there were the private investigators and security experts, the medical professionals and others. If you could get your name in a book, the newspapers or a magazine article, if you could appear on a television show, then you 'knew' what happened the night of the death. The people who truly knew what happened – Peter, for example, Marilyn's secretary Pat Newcomb, and several others – simply avoided the press. They had their own grieving to handle. They also felt that discretion was best because they did not want Marilyn abused in death as much as she had been abused in life.

One story even has Peter telling Marilyn, 'Pull yourself together. But, my God, whatever you do don't leave any notes behind.' Such a statement was so out of Peter's character that no one believes it with the possible exception of the person who originated it. The statement implies that he realized she was going to kill herself and deliberately let it happen, his only precaution being the avoidance of scandal. Peter may have been callous, but he was unthinking about the consequences of his actions. He realized that he had, in part, possibly been responsible for Marilyn's death and that knowledge helped to destroy him. He could never deliberately commit murder, and he would have been in a sense guilty of murder if he had actually made that comment.

Then there is the issue of where Bobby Kennedy was that night of 4 August 1962. Bobby had gone with his family to San Francisco, allegedly travelling briefly to Los Angeles in order to see Marilyn. There are conflicting stories related to this trip and no documentation has been uncovered to confirm or deny such a visit. However, Peter claimed that Bobby did come down briefly in order to talk to Marilyn, returning before that evening. Reports that Bobby stayed the night with Peter are inaccurate, especially since there were numerous witnesses to the activities of Peter and others involved, none of whom remembers Bobby staying in Los Angeles. Regardless of whether he did or did not delay his trip back – and witnesses to the family's activities in San Francisco seem to confirm that he had returned there well before the calls preceding her death began – he was not involved with any murder or cover-up.

Peter had arranged a quiet dinner party with a few friends, including Joe and Dolores Naar, Bullets Durgom and Marilyn. It was to be a typical Lawford party with Chinese takeaway food being eaten out of the cartons. Everything was casual.

Peter knew Marilyn was depressed about having to face the reality of her relationship with the President, and she was despondent when they talked on the telephone around 5 p.m. Peter wanted her to come over for dinner, but she would not. As Peter explained to Naar, Marilyn claimed to be tired and wanted to stay at home.

She made another call around 7.30 p.m. 'Say goodbye to Jack, say goodbye to Pat, and say goodbye to yourself, because you're a nice guy.' This call was upsetting, but not to the degree that might be imagined. Peter allegedly commented to one of the guests, 'It's phone-dangling time again.' He knew that Marilyn was making one of her dramatic suicide gestures, though he had no reason to think she was trying to kill herself for real. He had been through this type of thing with her before, which made him far less concerned than someone else might have been.

Peter realized that he ought to go and see Marilyn, yet he was an extremely weak man. He tried to reach her several times after that, but the line was always engaged. He lived approximately four miles from Marilyn, yet he did not go over. Instead, rather than calling the police, a doctor or even a friend, he called his manager, Milt Ebbins.

This was one of several instances when Peter used his manager as a father figure to avoid personal involvement. He did not particularly like Milt and their relationship was frequently strained, yet he was so weak that he was willing to sublimate his better judgement for whatever advice Milt might give him. And to Peter's relief, that advice seemed to free Peter from responsibility at the moment.

'You can't go over there,' Ebbins told him. 'You're brother-in-law of the President of the United States.

Your wife's away. Let me get in touch with her lawyer or doctor. They should be the ones to go over.'

The advice was brilliant. A woman may be dying, so her lawyer should be called? The situation would be humorous if it was not so tragic.

Peter made other calls, including one to Joe Naar at home. The Naars lived only a short distance from Marilyn. Joe could easily walk over there and check on her, breaking into the house if something was wrong. The Naars had left Peter's house before eleven and were getting undressed when Peter called to ask Joe to check on Marilyn. Then he thought better of it, especially after Milt Ebbins' comments, so he called the Naars again and told Joe not to bother.

No one called the police or any other agency that might have been equipped to handle an emergency such as an overdose. Each person tried to pass responsibility on to someone else, with the exception of Joe Naar who simply thought Peter had things under control. By the time anyone arrived who could truly do something, so much time had elapsed that Marilyn was dead.

Could Marilyn have been saved through earlier action? Peter certainly thought so. He was haunted by her death, maintaining a sense of personal responsibility for her loss for the rest of his life. He spoke of that responsibility to Pat Newcomb and others. He may also have led himself even further along the path of self-destruction as a result of his reactions to that night.

Marilyn was a drug addict, addicted not to heroin or cocaine but to prescription drugs. Not everyone understands their dangers. Suppose your normal prescription is for 5 mg. You take the drug for weeks or months, then develop a tolerance level for that amount so, either on your own or with your doctor's approval, you start taking 10 mg to achieve the same effect. Once that dose no longer seems to work, you try 15 mg. But many drugs have a fatal dosage, and no matter how much of a tolerance you seem to be developing, the moment you take, say, 30 mg you will die. You may never have intended to die. You may have had every reason to live. But unless your doctor or someone else knows that you have been gradually increasing the amount in excess of the approved dosage, your death may be listed as suicide.

The truth is that if anyone 'killed' Marilyn Monroe, it was Peter who failed to act in a constructive manner. The death may have been a suicide. It may have been a plea for attention. And it may have been an accidental overdose caused by Marilyn's not realizing that she had taken too large a quantity of a drug with a lethal dosage level. An addict taking an overdose of a familiar drug routinely dies with no trace of the pills in the stomach, and the coroner who handled Marilyn's autopsy confirmed that this was true in Marilyn's case. Her death was not ordered by the Kennedy family, members of organized crime or anyone else who has been the subject of one of the conspiracy theories. It was a tragic situation made all the more horrible because of the human inactions surrounding it.

Peter was reeling from the emotions of the events happening all around him over which he seemingly had no control. He was seeking regular sex outside his marriage, a fact that greatly troubled Pat Kennedy. She realized that their relationship was coming to an end, though the combination of her Catholic upbringing and the fact that a divorce in the family could destroy John Kennedy's hopes for a second term prevented anything from being made public. However, Peter had a private talk with his brother-in-law at the White House, explaining that the marriage existed in name only.

Yet life continued for Peter. He was getting less and less work, though he was still popular. The money was still coming from royalties from re-shown films, residuals, commercials and voice-overs and other sources, and he was still in the midst of the good life. In addition, he continued to do nightclub work with Jimmy Durante for several weeks a year, an activity that delighted him. In fact, it was while Peter was playing Harrah's Club in Lake Tahoe that the President was shot on 22 November 1963. Peter later discussed the events of that night with a reporter called Jerry Le Blanc:

The second show ends at 4 a.m. so you sleep late. And that's where I was when it happened – in a sound sleep. I remember waking up that morning. Somebody was shaking me and I thought, 'they aren't supposed to be shaking me. Why are they shaking me?'

The first thing my eyes focused on was an SS button – the Secret Service – and I said to myself, 'What the hell is he doing here?' . . .

I didn't recognize the agent. He was from the Reno detail, and he said, 'I think you better get up.' I got up, and of course I immediately knew something was terribly wrong. Then he just said flatly, 'The President's been shot.'

'How bad?' I remembered asking immediately. Actually at that moment Kennedy was already dead, but the Secret Service man didn't officially want to tell me. It wasn't his place to. The country didn't know it yet. If you recall, it was all over in the car.

I got on the phone with Pat and Harrah's lent me their private plane and I flew to meet her. The rest, it was like a terrible dream. Those days, right through the funeral in Washington, which was like an Irish wake. You know, everybody was up – drinking, smiling and trying to make the best of it. There were even bad jokes about what costumes we were wearing. Not being Irish, I tried to get into the swing of it, but I was thoroughly destroyed. Looking back, I realize the way President Kennedy's death was handled was really the best way, even with the bad jokes.

I think John F. would have looked on too much grief as unproductive. I'm sure of that. But my initial feeling was shock and sorrow – the obvious things – and an immediate resentment, yes, against the people who live in Texas. But you can't go on like that. To have taken an attitude that everybody in Texas stinks is stupid. Ridiculous.

Oh, if you want to dig deep, they're a part of it, but so many other people were, too. Texans weren't the force behind an assassination movement. It wasn't Texans in the Ambassador Hotel [in Los Angeles, where Bobby Kennedy would be killed almost five years later]. I think the violence that killed the Kennedys goes back to the Adlai Stevenson thing, where a woman hit him with a picket sign, an incident like that, political emotion gone crazy. There was a terrible political fight going on down in Texas and that's what brought Kennedy there.

Peter added,

John F. rang me in Tahoe two days before the assassination – that was the last I'd heard from him – and he said, 'Guess what? Jackie's finally decided to go.' She hadn't been planning to go [to Dallas]. She was angry about something. He was pleased she changed her mind. 'Isn't that terrific, we're going to go, we're off,' he said. And I remember he asked when I would be going back to Palm Springs – things like that.

Jack Kennedy's assassination had a greater effect than just grief for the man whom Peter loved as a brother. Peter's world fell apart. Marilyn was dead because he had been too weak to do more than call his manager about her warning that she was in trouble from the drugs. Sinatra was no longer speaking to him, a fact that might not have been so bad personally, but it affected his relationship with men whom he liked and admired, such as Sammy Davis and Joey Bishop, and his plans for future films. Then Kennedy was killed and Pat gathered up their children and returned to the East. She was through with Peter, through with the California lifestyle, anxious to return to the familiar surroundings of New York and Hyannis.

Camelot was dead and Peter was fatally wounded. Yet more than ten years would pass before anyone knew it and, even then, those of us who loved him wanted to deny the reality of his unstoppable decline.

11

Life in Limbo

When I was making Son of Lassie, *I had my first run-in with the star system. First of all, the dog had a dressing room, but I didn't. When we were shooting scenes in Canada of Lassie and the rapids, they had the dog all wired and roped so that they wouldn't lose him, and I was floundering around in the water with very little protection. Lassie was insured for a million dollars, and I had the suspicion that if I was insured at all, it was for a substantially smaller amount.*

Peter Lawford

The film industry was rough on stars in the making as they ascended the ladder of success. It was even rougher when you were perceived to be on the way down. Peter's friends felt that he went into a decline following the deaths of Marilyn Monroe and John Kennedy, and the shattering of the business and personal relationship with Frank Sinatra.

Peter was never one to go along with the dictates of fashion. He liked to be comfortable, and that meant going about in his beach attire. Jeans, an old sweat shirt, a surfboard ... That was Peter's style, even near the end when he was barely strong enough for the surfing he loved until his death. The idea that he would become a part of the hippie scene, wearing a Nehru jacket and love beads, was out of character. It was as though the old Peter Lawford had failed at everything that mattered to him. Friends were dead, his career on the decline, his marriage over. Peter

Lawford's way had not worked, so why not join the masses? Become laid back in a room where the decibel level of the music could shatter your eardrums. Smoke a joint, drink some alcohol, look like everyone else and mellow out.

Jack Haley, Jr commented on what seemed to happen professionally from the period when Peter was gradually fading from the MGM star system through the sixties.

'They were letting everyone go out there [MGM]. . . . you know, one by one they dropped them. William Powell they never dropped. He had a lifetime contract. They paid him every week until he died.

'The musicals were winding up. The parts Peter was playing weren't fashionable. You know, all of a sudden you've got Marlon Brando, Monty Clift – intense actors, and he was sort of a lightweight because he wasn't told enough to do what Cary Grant started to do, which was to go into older roles and pull them off.'

'I think he was terrific in comedy. You know, he would tell you his own testimony about singing and dancing. He said, "I was no threat to Astaire or Kelly." He was not terribly believable as an actor. He loved being a host. He got a great kick out of that. He was terrific at it. I always felt he maybe thought acting was a little unmasculine perhaps. It was just an attitude.

'You know, I grew up with actors my whole life. But occasionally he would catch fire in a picture. But just occasionally. I wish I could think of one great, dramatic scene with Peter Lawford. I'm sure there is one, but I just can't think of it. There must be some out there.' (No one else familiar with Peter's work could think of one, either.)

During this same period, May Lawford was becoming increasingly emotionally disturbed. Whether the woman was mentally ill in the past, troubled by the loss of both her husband and the money they had once had, the death of John Kennedy, or some combination thereof, no one knows. All that is certain is that she was developing a conspiracy theory about people somehow out to do her harm. She was estranged from Peter, and upset because she could not gain the respect in the United States that her position in England should have warranted. She began writing notes which she saved but did not send to any one.

Lady Lawford's state of mind can be seen by one note, dated 3 January 1964, and signed 'Lady May Lawford':

On December 1st I developed a chest cold, neglected until December 5th; when I visited Doctor Bethea, my doctor since '45. He gave me a cough mixture, coughed all day and night. Next day he said, 'Double the dose.' Some days after I became so dizzy could hardly walk. Next decided 'he only accepted emergencies for home calls.' I had to shop for groceries and drove so badly all over the road! [The erratic driving probably had little or nothing to do with the supposed illness. Lady Lawford was a terrible driver who crashed every car she ever owned. Peter bought both his parents cars when he first began to make good money at MGM; his mother crashed hers the first day that she drove it. He and his father stopped letting her drive, though after the General's death she was frequently behind the wheel.] Lay down after lunch, slept soundly and woke up naked in bed in St John's Hospital, 6 or 7 nurses. Doctor said, 'Well, you've got your X-rays and you stay there till I tell you to leave in a day or so!' I pleaded for my wool dress and glasses, etc. After all left the room I got up and went into the hall. Three large elevators – automatic. In one 3 men white uniforms – second shut. Third, just shutting. I just got in and went down (no shoes or underclothes, etc.) Elevator opened and I saw my son and his body-guard! Neither would speak to me and walked away quarrelling. I walked in opposite direction and slowly as if a visitor! As I got to hall door I prayed hard, a door opened and a very drunk taxi driver came in. I said, 'Hurry up, this is my taxi,' and I jumped in. The doctor shouted at me – and fortunately we were gone. Got home, locked myself in. Next day a friend took me to Mr Belli's office [her lawyer], who said – 'That act you put on probably saved you.' He gave me instructions what to do not to be caught again. I had leased a flat and later the real estate men said 'the lady owner didn't want me' – the lease signed and retainer paid!! Neither my son or either of the office managers will speak, write, reply to telegrams, etc., so I have no speech with any one in authority. This has gone on since last year when I did get my son's number through District Attorney and Chief of Police in Honolulu. When he told me the small Ford he ordered for me was LOST!! Since then no word from anyone. Several persons told me of the ever-increasing fact of persons being railroaded into asylums! One of these a well-known doctor known to me since '45. I also saw the British Consul who said he would keep tabs on me, and to ring up frequently.

Lady Lawford also became convinced that Peter was trying to poison her. She went for help to a lawyer, who attempted both to calm and to humour her. He sent her a letter that read:

In view of the number of strange and inexplicable things that have happened to you within the last year or so, and because of the possibility of some physical danger to you, it is our suggestion that you conduct your daily activity in more or less the following basis.

1. You remain in your home during the night hours from approximately 6 or 7 p.m. until approximately 8 a.m. of the following day.

2. That you limit or restrict your visits to hospitals, either as a visitor or as a patient. In the event that you should require emergency medical attention, you should obviously use either an emergency hospital or notify the police department.

3. That you remain out of strange neighbourhoods.

4. That you select your place to eat with some degree of care. Although we understand that you are now having your main meal at the Ontra Cafeteria where you

are able to select you own choice of food. This seems to be all right.

5. That you refrain, as much as possible, from any trips by plane, train or boat.

6. That you hold little or no conversations with strangers or people that you do not know well.

7. That you be very careful about eating or drinking at any afternoon parties which you may attend.

Basically we believe that the above are no more than common sense safety rules to be helpful in preventing unusual incidents such as those you have advised us have happened to you heretofor. We hope the suggestions will be helpful to you.

Lady Lawford had become a joke to Los Angeles reporters. She had begun to report Unidentified Flying Objects (UFOs) with such frequency that she was the butt of editorial cartoons and less that respectful news stories.

By the time she died, conspiracy theories were rampant in Lady May's mind. Yet she does not seem to have been of particular importance to anyone. She was a lonely woman, seemingly without intimate friends, who had estranged herself from her son and all others who knew her.

Rather than face the fact that the looks and voice that had made him a star in the 1940s now worked against him, Peter lashed out at those representing him. He was represented by the William Morris Agency in Beverly Hills, the largest talent agency in the world and, at the time, the most respected. In a long letter to Abe Lastfogel there he talked about the work he was getting and the fact that it was coming only through friends, not – as it should – from his agent. He ended:

I feel the desperate need for the help and benefits of an imaginative force to work for me and with me. Therefore, I have made the only decision left open to me (and as you are well aware it has not been a hasty one) to move on to other fields – perhaps a little greener with interest.

' Dear Abe, please know how fond I am of you and there are many moments that I will cherish from my long association but I must, in closing, gently say to you that your Motion Picture Department sorely needs a refresher course in selling!

Peter's guest television appearances included several on *Laugh-In*, which was then a new concept. It was a blend of vaudeville, the old Ziegfeld Follies, curtain-dropper sketches and one-liners. There were regulars, including such talent as Goldie Hawn and Lily Tomlin who would go on to become major stars in their own right, and there were guest stars, including national politicians. The hosts of the show were comedians Dan Rowan and Dick Martin, and it was here that Peter met Dan's daughter Mary, who was a dancer.

Peter and Mary Rowan fell in love. It was 1971 and Peter was almost fifty to Mary's twenty-two. Yet he was not marrying her for her youth. The correspondence that Peter saved indicated that he truly adored her, a fact confirmed by his friends. However, Peter's lifestyle involved odd hours, intense drug use, and companions who liked Peter because he had greater access to co-caine and other stimulants than they did. Three years later he and Mary were divorced, though Peter felt that he hid his problems well during this time. He would later write, 'I remarried in 1971 to a lovely girl many years my junior. We were very happy for about 3 years, and then I'm afraid she got restless, needed her own "space" and had to leave me. So there I was alone again.'

Much of Peter's time was spent with friends around the world. His income was on the decline, but he was still working and his lifestyle had long been such that he was able to retain much of his money until his drug habit became too expensive in his last few years.

Many of the friends were experiencing their own crises. Elizabeth Taylor, one of his closest friends, was fighting drink, pills and weight gain. Her lover and two times husband, Richard Burton, was almost dying from alcohol abuse. Members of rock bands whom Peter 'adopted' to share drugs with him were having difficulty handling their own success. And all of them were behaving in ways that were raucous, riotous and/or tragic.

For example, there was the time Peter went to Gstaad in Switzerland to spend Christmas with Elizabeth and Richard. It was the early 1970s and Elizabeth realized that Richard was drinking too much. His liver was in danger of being destroyed and, since she could not keep him away from drugs, she thought that if he switched to marijuana he might be able to recover his health. She was extremely alcoholic and addicted herself at the time, so the idea made sense. Today, when Elizabeth has fully recovered and is more vibrant than she has been in years, such a thought would not occur to her. But then it made sense, since she did not know how else to handle the problem.

To help Richard, Elizabeth alerted all the bartenders in Gstaad that Richard was not to be given anything alcoholic to drink. He liked lemonade, and that is what he was to be given.

Richard was trying to live up to Elizabeth's desires, but he wanted a drug of some sort and he hated smoking marijuana. Peter too tried to encourage him, but Peter would try anything and Burton knew it. Peter made a very poor role model.

Finally Richard had had enough. He decided to go into town, where he could easily get a drink. Peter would accompany him but Elizabeth would stay at home. Elizabeth took Peter aside and warned him not to let Richard have even one drink. She had a vicious temper and Peter was frightened of crossing her. But he also knew that there was no way he could stop Richard doing anything he wanted to do.

The two men stopped at the Palace Hotel where Peter ordered vodka and Richard, much to Peter's relief, ordered lemonade. They sat and talked. Richard finished one lemonade, then went on to the next. By the time Burton had finished his fourth lemonade Peter had noticed some changes in his behaviour. He was not certain what was happening, but the changes worried him. Then, as Burton downed his eighth glass, Peter realized that his companion was, as Peter put it, 'shit-faced drunk'.

Laughing, Richard looked solemnly at Peter and said, 'I'll let you in on something. I have all the waiters paid off. Elizabeth told them not to serve me, but I pay them to spike my lemonade with vodka.'

Peter was suddenly terrified. He was certain that Elizabeth would blame him when she saw the obviously drunk Burton.

Richard, however, was calm. 'I know how to make that bitch shut up,' he said, rising from the table. He led Peter to the Gstaad branch of Van Cleef & Arpel and purchased a piece of jewellery costing several hundred thousand dollars.

Drunk and happy, the two men strolled back up the hill to the house, falling in the snow, singing and laughing. Then, at the top, they had to face Elizabeth, whose first words were, 'Peter, you cock-sucking son-of-a-bitch, I told you not to let him drink. . . .'

Burton then gave Elizabeth the present, which calmed her a little. However, he also explained that Peter had 'made' him drink, refusing to tell her the truth about the waiters.

There was also a Christmas dinner at which Elizabeth behaved in a manner that Peter thought crude. Her servants could not speak English and did not understand most of the words she used. They knew the names of the dishes that were being served, but they were lost beyond that. As a joke, knowing that they would not understand, she said things like 'Give me the fucking roast beef.'

The staff, knowing only the term 'roast beef', would bring the meat to her. 'Now pass the fucking peas,' she would add. She found it hilarious, but Peter felt it was in poor taste.

Richard was a man who was frequently 'on stage', even during dinner parties. Peter said that Richard frequently declaimed speeches from *King Lear* at the dinner table. The guests were always on the edge of their chairs, so powerful were his abilities. But Elizabeth, who had heard it all to many times before, would coldly say, 'Would you shut the fuck up?'

Elizabeth also became friendly with Peter's son, Christopher, when the boy was about the same age as Peter had been when he went to MGM. They went to Disneyland and other places together, either as friends, as she claimed, or as lovers, as the rumours indicated. As mentioned earlier, her one-time lover Henry Wynberg felt that the rumours could not be true. However, he did not really know her then. Peter introduced Elizabeth to Henry because he was concerned about her relationship with Christopher.

One day during these years there was a bizarre incident concerning another of Peter's old friends. Peter was driving along Benedict Canyon Road in Hollywood when he saw a man in a bath robe and pyjamas walking purposefully down the street. It was late at night in an area that does not get much pedestrian traffic, and certainly no pedestrians in night clothes.

When Peter came closer, he realized it was Jack Lemmon. The actor, seemingly quite drunk, had had a fight with his wife, Felicia, and had walked out of the house, determined to spend the night in the Beverly Hills Hotel. The trip was a mile and a half but he was angry enough not to care. Peter told him to get into the car and he would drive him there. When they arrived, Jack strode into the building in his pyjamas and took a room for the night. The staff did not react in any way – the incident was no more unusual than many they had witnessed.

Peter was in awe of Cary Grant, who was a major success in both film and business. Grant did not have the style in real life that he created on the screen – though he was handsome and brilliant he was, as Peter found out, mean.

Peter told me of the time he visited Cary at home, having been invited for dinner. He did not know exactly what to expect, though he realized that with Grant's wealth the meal would be only the finest. That something might be wrong with Peter's reasoning first occured to him when he toured the house. Grant had huge wardrobes filled with clothing, while his wife had only a few dresses. Then they went into the living room to have dinner. To Peter's amazement, Grant, his then wife and Peter each had a free-standing tray placed in front of a chair. And on each tray, the aluminium foil still in place to keep the food hot, was a TV dinner.

Peter was extremely close to Cass Elliot, the over-weight, drug-abusing singer with the group the Mamas and the Papas. Cass would eventually die from a heroin problem, though the officially released cause of death was that she choked while eating a sandwich in bed.

Mama Cass, as she was called in the group, was a friend to Peter, who felt sorry for her. Despite her financial success as a singer, she was a troubled woman who used obesity as a protective shell against others. However, she thought that there might be more to the relationship than there was. When they were together in Peter's apartment one evening, she suddenly leaped on his body, wanting to have sex with him. Not only did he not want to go to bed with her, he was so thin and she was so heavy that he could barely breathe when she attacked him. He laughed about it later, but at the time he thought he would suffocate.

Peter was enamoured with the Beatles, who were then still together as a group. He hung around with Ringo Starr, but Peter and John Lennon were quite hostile to each other.

Lennon, though truly talented, was also rather immature. One night he, his date, Peter, Tom Smothers of the Smothers Brothers comedy act and a few others went into the Troubadour, a club where Tom and Dick Smothers were having a reunion show. The brothers were frequently breaking up, then getting their act back together, and that night they were having a big show.

John was very drunk and very stoned on drugs that night after Tom left the group to go on stage. He looked at the waitress, who was wearing a uniform that included an odd little paper hat and short skirt, and said, 'What's that you've got on your head, a Tampax?' He made other comments as well, all in a loud voice, while Tom and Dick were trying to perform. His actions were rude and disruptive, which Peter could not tolerate. Peter was a gentleman when it came to other performers, a man whom they considered to be a good audience. He would revel in their success during an act, laugh at their jokes and show them respect even when they were bad. The idea that Lennon would act so rudely appalled him.

Peter was extremely strong when angered. He became so angry with Lennon's disruptions that he grabbed him and threw him bodily into the street. Then, outside, he said 'You're a rude son of a bitch! If you can't sit there and be quiet and courteous, get out.'

Lennon started yelling back, but did not go back inside. The next day Peter received a huge basket of flowers from Lennon, asking to be forgiven.

There were women during those years, of course, but nothing serious other than Mary Rowan. It was more a time of drifting, his work on the decline, his friendships changing, his family situation pained.

Peter's relationship with his children was difficult. He had had two bad role models as parents. He had been cared for by nannies and seen by his parents only when washed, dressed and well behaved. His father was a distant hero to whom Peter could never measure up.

He also never stopped his wife doing things that were emotionally destructive to their son.

May Lawford actively hated her son and caused him deep pain. Yet when Peter had children of his own he had no idea what to do with them that might be better. He wanted the children to call him 'Peter' instead of 'Dad' or 'Father' or some similar term. He kept his distance from them, not knowing what else to do.

The divorce went uncontested by Peter, who respected Pat's abilities as a mother. She was the one who had come from a large family. She was the one who knew what it was like to live with brothers and sisters. He felt quite happy with the idea that she should be the principal person to raise them, and to provide them, through the Kennedys, with an extented family.

The problem was that Pat seemed to need male support. The children would later talk of her frequently mentioning 'Uncle Jack' or Uncle Bobby' and the things that they had done in their lives. She was trying to provide strong male role models, but in hearing about their late uncles the children were constantly reminded that they lacked a permanent father.

The children were unquestioningly accepted into the Kennedy family. Upon learning of Robin Lawford's birth, Jack Kennedy sent her a telegram which read: 'Your entrance is timely, as we need a new left end.' Bobby helped Chris Lawford learn to ski at a time when the boy was afraid of what was then, to him, an unfamiliar sport. And the children were always considered Kennedy cousins, not objects to be discarded because Peter had divorced their mother. Yet there was always something lacking, a fact that undoubtedly contributed to Christopher's turning to drugs during the time I was living with Peter. Sadly, as will be explained later, Peter was never able to show his children the deep love he felt for them. I doubt that any of the children ever understood how much he cared.

Peter was damaging his health during this period. At some point after the various deaths and the divorce from Pat, Peter stopped taking care of his body. He ballooned from 163 pounds, the natural weight he carried on his six-foot-three frame, to over 210 pounds. He was bloated from alcohol and lack of exercise, a pathetic figure compared with what he had once been. In addition, his liver was getting so bad that, even before I knew him, one doctor told him that he could die if he went so far as to eat rum cake. He was dangerously reactive to the destructive aspects of alcohol.

Peter had reached the end of the life he had known. He was at a crossroads, the last period at which he might have had a choice in his future. But he would take none of the warnings seriously, a fact of which I would be unaware when I first came to know him.

12

The Second Patricia

It was Friday night, two days before Peter entered the hospital for the last time. He was drifting in and out of a deep sleep, the precursor to a coma he would soon enter, when he managed to talk on the telephone with Milt Ebbins, his manager. 'Peter, where have you been?' Milt asked, concerned when Peter sounded as though he was passing through conscious awareness. Peter replied, 'I've been to heaven.' Then he drifted back to sleep.

Patricia Seaton Lawford

Peter was a dying man when I met him in 1974. He had had a serious pancreas problem in 1969 from which he could only fully recover if he stopped the drinking and the drugs. The fact that he continued with both pleasures meant that his days were numbered. He could be dying of heart disease, cancer, diabetes and the plague, yet he had the attitude that, if his weight was down and his tan was fresh, he was in perfect health.

Peter looked in perfect health when I first met him in On the Rox, a private club on top of the Roxy Theater, then an extremely popular entertainment night spot on Sunset Boulevard. It was an exclusive hang-out for the stars appearing at the Roxy, who were invited there to unwind by the handful of members who owned it. If you knew the right people in showbusiness you too could become part of that scene, and that was how I happened to be there.

Being in On the Rox was like being in someone's private living room. There was a dance floor so small that if more than two couples tried to use it at the same time, they would constantly be bumping into each other. The tables were intimate and you had a feeling that you were always among friends. No one would ask a star for an autograph. No one would disturb them if they just wanted a quiet drink while they thought over the performance they had given earlier that evening. And no one thought it odd if they wanted to cut loose a little after having been on stage for a couple of hours. The liquor flowed freely and the place stayed open until three, four or five o'clock in the morning, much like an after-hours joint.

The night I was there, a girlfriend of mine and I had gone to see Al Jarreau and George Benson perform. We both loved jazz, and she had the connections to get us into the club when the show was over. We had champagne, and the owner talked to us because he and my girlfriend were interested in each other.

Suddenly the door flew open and up the stairs came Peter, Ringo Starr and the Who drummer Keith Moon, along with Peter and Ringo's dates. Peter and I saw each other reflected in the mirror, and we were both intrigued. I found him extremely attractive, and he saw someone whose figure was, at the time, perfection. It was, however, caused by a rather unusual circumstance.

I was born with a bone problem that affected my jaw. There had been degeneration that required major surgery which had been completed a short time before. In order to allow for the area to heal, my jaw had been wired shut. The doctor involved was sensitive to the lifestyle and self-obsession common among teenagers and had done the wiring in such a manner that it was not apparent when looking at my face casually. This was a blessing for a seventeen-year-old like me. However, there was no way to reduce the physical impact of the wiring. I could not open my mouth wide enough to take in solid food and could only take liquids sipped through a straw. The result was a weight loss that left me looking the most attractive I have ever been in my life.

My girlfriend caught me flirting and asked me what I was doing. 'Who is that good-looking man?' I asked her, but she had no idea.

I only knew those actors who were making a name for themselves right then. I knew who Al Pacino was. I would recognize Robert Redford. But Peter Lawford? I had never heard his name, let alone seen one of his old movies. If my mother watched *The Thin Man* series on television, I would not have remembered, having been only a year old when it was running. All I knew was that the man was handsome and seemed to be attracted to me.

Peter sent a bottle of champagne to our table, then came over to speak with us. 'What are you doing?' he asked.

'We're just sitting here,' I told him.

'Here's a bottle of champagne for you,' he said.

'Thank you,' I replied. 'Have a nice night.'

'Yeah,' he said. 'We're just coming out for the evening.'

And that was it. He went back to the girl at his table, a woman I subsequently learned was Deborah Gould, for an extremely brief time the third Mrs Peter Lawford. My friend and I left the club, still not knowing who he was.

During this period I was seeing Henry Wynberg, who was also dating Elizabeth Taylor. For some reason, Elizabeth and I often had affairs with the same men, though usually at radically different times. I even had a brief relationship with Richard Burton, a fact that led Elizabeth to one day comment, 'You and I seem to have the same men in our lives. The only one you didn't fuck was Mike Todd and that was only because you were still in diapers when he died.'

Elizabeth was filming overseas, so Henry was staying in her home and using her Rolls-Royce. I would frequently stay with him at the house, keeping enough clothing there so I could either spend the night or return to my apartment above Sunset Strip. Still a student, I was also at this time working for Lloyd's of London, the insurance group, underwriting aviation business. I had a private pilot's licence and had learned the business through my father.

Three days after meeting Peter, Henry mentioned that he was planning a dinner party which he wanted me to attend. He said there was someone he wanted me to meet.

The night of the party I arrived early so I could dress in some of the clothing I kept at the house. There was a woman already there, wearing a T-shirt that read 'Photo Patrol'. Henry introduced us, saying, 'You know, Patricia's got great boobs.'

And the woman said, 'Show me your boobs.'

I didn't know how serious either of them was, but it made me extremely uncomfortable. I didn't know if they were having fun with me or if they wanted to get involved with something kinky. Either way, I was a kid who had lived a very straight life despite the abuse, and I was certain I didn't want to be involved with any of this.

Then Henry said, 'Deborah has a great ass.'

I could see where this conversation was heading and I wanted nothing to do with it. I excused myself and went to put on an outfit I frequently wore during that period. It consisted of a black silk top, black slacks, a Cartier watch on my wrist and a solid gold Quaalude – sick jewellery if ever it was sold – around my neck. I thought I looked special in this unusual outfit, and I knew that it showed off my new slim figure.

The party was delightful. Handsome, eligible men and beautiful women wandered through the gardens and enjoyed the view of the city. Everyone was open, friendly, getting high. Music was blaring and the liquor flowed free. I turned to Henry in due course and asked him where was the person he wanted me to meet.

It was three o'clock in the morning when the door opened and in walked a man wearing jeans and a casual shirt, looking tanned and gorgeous. It was the man I had met just the other night.

I was over at the bar. He came over, looked at me and did a double take. We spoke for a minute, then separated and I went to Henry, asking him who the man was.

'His name's Peter Lawford,' Henry told me.

'What's he do?'

'He's an actor,' said Henry, annoyed by my naïvety.

'What movies?' I asked.

Henry started rattling off a list. 'I don't know any of those movies,' I said. 'Where did they make them?'

'Here,' he said, irritably. 'In America.'

'Oh,' I said, and returned to the living room, an 'expert' on Peter Lawford.

Then he made his way over to where I was standing and said, 'You know, there's something about you I like.'

'Thank you,' I replied.

'You can't be all bad. You're dressed in black, you have a gold Quaalude and you have a Cartier tank watch.'

'Is that what counts with you?' I asked.

'Oh, so you're a smartass too? I really like that.'

'So?'

'What are you doing?'

'I don't know, but I'm getting very tired and I'd like to go,' I told him.

'Would you like to go now?'

I said yes and he said, 'Can I take you somewhere?'

'I have a car,' I explained.

'Fuck the car!'

'Sure, I'll go,' I said, taken aback.

Peter went to see Henry for a few minutes and I sat down. The party was beginning to dwindle as people drifted away. The woman I had met earlier, Deborah, was seated near me. She looked at me and said, 'What are you doing?'

'I'm leaving,' I told her. 'I'm just waiting for someone.'

As I said that, Peter walked in from the back room and asked if I was ready to go. As I rose, Deborah stood up and said coldly, 'You're going to leave with my husband?'

I was stunned. I had no idea what to say, so I just said nothing. We left and he said he would drive me to Hefner's Playboy mansion where he spent a lot of time.

Peter leaned over to kiss me along the way. It was only then that he noticed that something was not quite right with my face. He stopped the car and turned on the light, and that was when he discovered he had picked up a woman with her jaw wired shut. 'Oh, this is great. I find a girl and her jaw's wired shut,' he said. 'I pick you up. You're nice. I thought you were kind of British through the clenched teeth with those. . . .' Peter was beside himself.

I had been to the Playboy mansion once before, but not in any way that was meaningful. This time it meant driving through the gates at four o'clock in the morning and being greeted by an employee saying, 'Good morning, Mr Lawford. How are you? What can I get you this morning?' We took a jacuzzi and spent the rest of the night there.

I thought the place was wonderful. The guest house room was mirrored on the ceiling and walls. Everything else was black and the bed had a built-in stereo console. There was a velour robe on the door, a small bathroom, and piped music of any type you might desire. The room was soundproofed to provide privacy, and endless electronic games were just outside the door so you could do anything you wanted. You would never be able to tell day from night. If you telephoned the butler he would bring you anything you wanted. I had to keep ordering milk shakes with a straw because of my jaw problem.

I was overwhelmed by Peter, especially when he suggested we stay together the next few days. I had no idea what I should do. I hated my shared apartment. I could not live with my parents. But I knew it would be wrong to leave the apartment because it would stick the other girl with the entire bill each month. Finally, unable to say no and too immature to face all the issues honestly, I decided to move out that day, while my room-mate was still at work.

For the next three days I led a rather odd lifestyle. I had half my possessions in an apartment belonging to a girlfriend of mine, but I spent each night with Peter. Then, on that third night, he told me to move in with him properly.

I called my mother and stepfather to tell them the news. I had always been a quiet kid, getting good grades and never being noticed. Even when I had all my problems with my family, I simply moved out on my own. I did not create a scene or let my school work slack off. This was the first thing I had ever done that got their attention. My father announced that he was going to kill Peter, while my mother told me that it was a great decision.

For the first time in my life I felt powerful. People were taking notice of me. I was moving in with Peter Lawford, the actor, the movie star, the handsome man I barely knew, whose wife I had left at Henry Wynberg's – though the latter was something of which my parents were not aware.

I had just started living with Peter when a friend called and invited me to a party at the Beverly Hills Hotel. The hotel has a combination of rooms, suites and cottages in the grounds. The party was being held in one of these cottages, and to my surprise one of the guests was Deborah Lawford. She took one look at me, slipped the wedding ring from her finger and threw it at me. 'Here!' she yelled. 'You might be needing this, *cunt!*'

The ring struck me in the side of the face, then fell to the floor. I casually picked it up, studied it for a moment then said, 'I'm sure I can do better.'

It was an odd scene. Deborah, though married to Peter, was living with Henry Wynberg at the time and I knew it. Under the circumstances I was unable to feel badly – I did not feel as though I was stealing her husband.

Later I learned the truth of that third marriage. Peter was stoned when he was dating her, using drugs heavily and apparently convinced that she had access to a better supply than he did. In his mind, such a circumstance was an arrangement made in heaven. He wanted to marry her immediately.

The marriage lasted less than a week. Peter sent her over to Henry Wynberg's to live until arrangements could be made for her to go back to her family. It was an incident that was undoubtedly painful for them both, yet it was not a tragic love affair. I doubt whether there was more than a few days of sensual pleasure together as a unifying factor in their relationship.

One week to the day after I began living with Peter, there was a knock at the door. Peter went into the bedroom, shut the door and told me to answer. It was Milt Ebbins, his manager.

I had met Milt and thought of him as a kindly old man. I never realized that he was the person to whom Peter turned whenever he wanted to run away from an emotionally difficult decision. I did not know at the time about Marilyn Monroe's death and the way she had died – possibly because Peter had failed to have the courage to go and see her or call for real help. I did not know that he had wasted time that night talking to Milt Ebbins because he could not bring himself to do anything constructive for far too long a time.

I told Milt that Peter was in the bedroom but that he would be out in a minute. I did not realize this was a set-up, not even when Milt said he wanted to talk to me. Milt told me that I would have to leave Peter right away.

I stared at him in shock. I had left my apartment. I had hurt my former room-mate. I had told my parents I was moving away. And now my actions would seem even more foolish because everything I had thought was my future was being taken from me.

I went back to the bedroom to get my things, but Peter could not look me in the eye. He got up and left, driving away so he wouldn't have to talk with me.

I gathered my possessions and made the most difficult call of my life. I telephoned my mother to tell her that I needed to come over to her place.

I was ashamed, devastated. I had been hurt, my dreams shattered. I felt that I had been humiliated in front of people whose respect I had gained for the first time in my life. My entire world had been altered in ways I could not understand. Unable to face anyone, to deal with what was happening to me, I went to bed and refused to leave except to go to the bathroom. I didn't want to die, yet I didn't want to live. I wanted to will myself into emotional limbo because reality could no longer be understood.

Eight days after I had taken to my bed, the telephone rang for me. Peter was calling, telling me that everything was okay and asking if I was ready to come back. He sent a limousine for me and I returned to my home.

The next night we went to the Palm Restaurant to celebrate being back together again. There were some other friends with us and they ordered lobster for everyone. I tried to protest that I could not eat it, but no one listened. A pair of telephone cable cutters was brought to the table and they snapped my wires so I could eat. Fortunately I was far enough along in the healing process that no damage was done.

I learned several things from that incident. One, of course, was Peter's weakness. He was in the process of getting his divorce from Deborah. He knew that there was no reason it would not be granted, yet he felt that he might have some problems if she could point to the fact that he was already living with another woman. The fact that she was living with Henry Wynberg would not alter his involvement and might cause financial difficulties for him. Californian judges do not favour, in divorce settlements, parties who have already found a new partner.

The second thing I learned was how much I was willing to degrade myself in order to change my lifestyle. I had been hurt so much that someone who wanted me, even if I was going to be taken for granted at times, meant more than my self-respect. I had felt unwanted and abused for too long. Someone who would pay me the attention that Peter was paying, even though his actions had been rude, unthinking and cowardly, was more important than anything I had ever known.

And I also learned just who Peter Lawford was to America. When we left the Palm there were reporters and photographers everywhere, climbing on our cars, on parked vehicles, on anything they could use to get a better vantage point. This man was a major star. His activities were national news. His divorce was known about and I was the new woman in his life. We made gossip column headlines, our pictures everywhere.

The fourth thing I learned that night was that the press is not always accurate in checking information. When I saw my photograph I was often described in the caption as a twenty-two-year-old, unemployed Beverly Hills secretary. Only the Beverly Hills bit was accurate.

There was one other surprise awaiting me at this time. I expected to settle down into a normal sexual relationship. But it did not happen. Days went by, then weeks, and finally we had been together three months without having intercourse. There had been extensive touching and intimate fondling. There had been oral sex after my wires were completely removed. Yet there was never intercourse.

At first I had blamed the wires. I figured that my jaw being kept shut was a turn-off for him. Then I wondered if I wasn't sexy enough for him – if there was something about me that did not please him. Again I had to reject this idea because there was too much intimacy to assume that he did not want me.

Only later was I to learn the truth about Peter. The drugs and alcohol had taken their toll. He had gone from being a stud who could have several women in a day to a man whose body would no longer respond to his mind's desires. Prolonged oral sex could still bring him pleasure. But Peter's drug habits resulted in his becoming a voyeur of pleasure more than a participant.

Nevertheless there was still so much to experience in our new life together. Suddenly I was living in a world that I never knew existed. It was a world of glamour and excitement, of seemingly unlimited wealth, of power and adoration. It was also a world of fans, of people who knew Peter from television and the movies and thought he was the man they had seen on the screen. Peter still had money, so we were able to travel constantly, wherever the whim might take us. I thought nothing of being with Peter on a chartered jet just because he decided that he wanted to catch a show in Las Vegas. He would pay a cab driver to do our grocery shopping. We would take a limousine for a weekend retreat, the hired driver sleeping in a spare room so that he would be constantly available. The fact that Peter no longer had the type of income or earning power that would continue to make such a lifestyle possible was ignored. I had no idea that we were slowly drifting into financial trouble, and Peter's live-for-today attitude showed that he did not care.

Oddly, there was a moment early in Peter's career after MGM when his entire image might have been different. This was when the James Bond movies were first under consideration. It was felt in Hollywood that a movie starring the Bond character might be popular with American audiences and Peter was asked to play the lead. Peter thought about it and talked to Milt Ebbins. As usual, Peter's judgement left something to be desired and Milt's was no better. They felt certain that the story line would be too lightweight and the film would flop. There seemed no reason to link Peter with something obviously destined either to fail or to be forgotten instantly. Peter turned down the opportunity to play the lead, a part that would have turned him from a romantic comedy performer to the role model for macho sophistication. The part was given to the then little-known actor Sean Connery, who became both successful and wealthy as a result.

Thus Peter was typecast as the boy next door to some, the handsome song-and-dance romantic lead to others, and a good-looking lightweight comedy/suspense actor to still others. And the fans who adored him believed he matched these images.

The most frightening fan was a woman whom I encountered when I was first living with Peter and he was in UCLA Medical Center on one of the numerous occasions that his body failed him. He had had a huge non-malignant pancreatic cyst, which meant he was unable to manufacture a particular enzyme essential for digestion. As a result, for several years he had had to take up to six enzyme tablets whenever he ate anything, until the enzyme condition eventually corrected itself. He also had numerous other problems at this time, most of them related to his drug and alcohol abuse.

Peter was on the celebrity floor of the hospital, where the rooms were large and there was a place for husbands or wives to stay. I came to the hospital one night when the room was dark and Peter was sedated, having undergone some extremely painful procedures. I saw a woman in a white uniform unplugging his tubes. The woman – I assumed she was a nurse – seemed to be fussing with the tubes in a strange sort of way. She did not seem to be acting right, yet who was I, a young girl with no medical background, to judge that?

'Excuse me,' I said finally. 'I'm with Mr Lawford, and I'm just wondering what you're doing.'

I moved towards the woman, who was standing at the head of the bed. As I did so, she said, 'Get out of this room!' It was then that I realized she was ripping IV lines from Peter's body.

I leaped at the red button on the wall to call the nursing staff. They were supposed to come running but it was 11.15 at night, when most visitors were gone and life became more casual. No one responded instantly, so I began screaming for help.

When help arrived and we could sort out what was taking place we discovered that the woman had been a hospital employee. She had worked in records and had become obsessed with Peter, convinced that she was his wife. She had since been a patient in the psychiatric section, but had escaped. Whether she was planning to kill Peter, kidnap him or just make him 'more comfortable' by removing the tubes, I never knew. The staff subdued her and returned her to the psychiatric ward.

I was furious with the hospital and have refused to return there to this day. Peter was in a room reserved for celebrities, which should have meant increased security. Yet this woman had been able to walk into the room and, had I not been there when I was, she would probably have killed him.

Peter returned home eventually and, three weeks after this incident, I awoke one morning to find the woman who had attacked him at the hospital asleep in the bushes at our house. She had been released because her actions had not warranted her being held for very long. Letters began arriving from this woman, who signed herself 'Beverly Lawford'. She named all four of Peter's children and told him that they were doing well, that their grades were good. She refused to acknowledge my existence or that of his previous three wives. She knew the names of the children's schools, and wrote as though they were temporarily separated but would be reunited as a family in the near future.

Time passed and I encountered her again. I left the apartment, only to find her waiting outside. She informed me that she was going to kill me, then left. She made no physical move to hurt me, yet I was scared. I had seen what she had done to Peter, the man she supposedly loved. Her statement had to be taken seriously. I called the police, only to be told that nothing could be done. They could not arrest this woman based on a statement she had made. She would have to threaten me physically or assault me before they could do anything.

This was another frightening reality I have had to learn to handle, both when I was with Peter and since his death. There are crazies like 'Beverly Lawford' who become so obsessed with a man that their fantasies are lived as though they are a reality. There are fans who in their minds assume the identity of the celebrity, then apparently kill the star because only one person can have the name (John Lennon's killer may have fallen into this category). And there are fans who seek out not the star but his or her spouse. They want to meet the spouse, date the spouse, emotionally manipulate the spouse, perhaps having sex with the spouse and/or brutalizing the person. Such people may laughingly be called 'star fuckers' before they act, but when someone is raped, knifed, shot or otherwise hurt the words stop being jokes.

I was bothered by 'star fuckers' at times, and was once told by a member of the Beverly Hills Police Department that there was a good chance a particular man would try to kill me. These people follow you everywhere, telephone you, send you letters and generally harass you. They can threaten you and discuss obscene acts they are planning to perform on your body. But law enforcement officers can only react to crime. Because of that, the detective told me I should plan on killing the man myself because I would probably be killed if he kept pursuing me and they could do nothing until he was violent.

The police recognized our problem with Beverly enough to charge her periodically with vagrancy. She could be held for three days, then had to be released. It wasn't much, but it gave us short periods during which we could feel safe.

The situation continued for weeks, then months, then years. It stopped being frightening and became an embarrassment. The woman was found in the grounds of neighbours. They knew that we had nothing to do with it, yet they also knew that the woman was coming around only because of her obsession with Peter. I should never have made assumptions about Beverly. She became so much a part of our life that I let down my guard, forgetting that she had once nearly cost Peter his life.

One day I went to the supermarket, returning home with several bags of groceries. Suddenly Beverly appeared by the front door and slashed at me with a large knife. I blocked her attack with my arm as groceries flew down the steps. We fought until help came, and Beverly was finally arrested for attacking me. We continued hearing from her for a while – she sent notes from jail. Then, three years before Peter's death, Beverly disappeared from our lives. We never heard from her again.

There was a more humorous fan, yet one who quite troubled us. He was a young New York homosexual who had focused on Peter as his lover. He attended the game shows Peter appeared on in New York and wore shirts that read: 'I love you Peter Lawford'. He also carried signs declaring his 'love'.

I felt sorry for the youth when I saw him in the audience of the shows, so I was willing to talk with him. Then one day he asked if I could get Peter to sign some photographs. I saw nothing wrong with that until he handed me a stack of dozens of photographs.

Eventually the fan realized that, since Peter lived in Los Angeles, he would have to come West. He saved up until he could afford the trip, then began showing up around our home. He was younger than I was, yet he knew every movie Peter had made, every television show he had made or appeared on, every song he had sung. For hours he sat in front of our home with a sign, his shirt and a stack of photographs. He was there from around eleven in the morning until well after midnight. Finally we had to call the police and have him moved. We felt as though we were prisoners in our own homes, yet he was harmless. Fortunately he returned to his home on the East Coast and we only received fan mail from him.

Most of the others were more rational. They were people who said that they wished Peter would work more, make more films. A few would come up to him and say, 'Do you remember me? I slept with you in Indiana [or Ohio or wherever].' Peter didn't remember, but he admitted that it was possible. I also received letters from eighty-five-year-old women who said that he had had an affair with them. Since Peter was fifty when I met him, their stories were doubtful.

The other surprise I had in those early days was the realization of how gentle and kind Peter was. There are people who are suckers for a pitch by a beggar. They will reach in their pockets and hand the beggar their change or, in some instances, paper money. But Peter went a step further. He would bring them home for dinner.

I was shocked one day to discover my bathroom being used by a strange man, probably a wino. His clothing was filthy, his body smelled foul and his social graces were non-existent. Peter had let him shower and clean up in my bathroom because 'It's nicer than mine.' Whenever this kind of thing happened he would expect me to cook a meal for the person, something that always shocked me. I kept wanting to tell him to stop, but Peter would not. He wanted to help.

The same was true with animals. He found a stray dog so near death from old age and starvation that the dog could barely move, even after Peter cleaned him and we began feeding him. There was so little life left in the dog that Peter called him the Rock. He had to carry the Rock everywhere, yet Peter did not mind. That dog was going to be loved until he died.

13

The Downside of Life with Peter

The most important thing in acting is honesty. Once you've learned to fake that, you're in.

Samuel Goldwyn

One area that was a real problem between Peter and me was our sex life. Don Brown, a close friend of both of us, said that he felt that Peter had developed a fantasy sex life since the drug abuse had destroyed the image of the great stud. Whether or not stopping the drugs would have removed the problem is academic, because Peter was unable or unwilling to stop. Yet he still insisted upon having his women, usually in pairs. When he could manage an erection, the effort of sex took hours and was always oral. Most of the time he was part voyeur, part oral participant, a thoroughly unsatisfactory lifestyle for me. But as long as Peter could attract women and persuade them to perform, in his mind he remained one of Hollywood's greatest lovers.

Eventually Peter's addiction made having any sort of sexual feelings extremely difficult for him. He needed to be physically stimulated for hours, something no woman could ever handle. However, he solved this need through buying a product called Acujack at a store that sold everything from titillating magazines to sex toys.

Acujack, a kind of male vibrator, became Peter's best friend and companion. When a man attaches it to his penis and turns it on, it is meant to stimulate him to orgasm. The sound it made was much like that of a kitchen blender, but Peter did not care. He would attach himself to it at night, turn it on, and left it go for hours at a time until he eventually achieved some sort of climax.

This new relationship was almost as disgusting as his women, except that it looked ridiculous. After several months of listening to the motor whirr far into the night, I threw the machine out with the kitchen rubbish, hoping it would be gone before Peter woke up. Unfortunately he discovered its loss before the trash collectors arrived and he was able to retrieve it.

Later there was an accident on the freeway, when a man used an Acujack he had plugged into his cigarette lighter so it could be powered by his car battery. When he reached orgasm the machine short-circuited, electrocuting him and causing the car to go out of control, crashing into a pole. He was killed instantly, and I was able to show Peter that his 'friend' could be deadly. Unfortunately he continued using it for the rest of his life.

I loved Peter during those early years together, loved him more than I ever thought it was possible for me to care about another person. He was my best friend, my father, my lover (to the degree he was capable), and, at times, my child. Yet I ached for normal affection. I wanted to be able to go to bed with a man without having to play out some fantasy or remain intimately untouched for the night. Consciously or unconsciously, I knew that the only way our relationship would succeed would be if I periodically took a lover. I didn't know if it would be for a one-night stand or for a long-term relationship. I had no one in mind, I never stopped loving Peter. I never wanted a divorce, but at the same time I could not continue without periodically experiencing a relationship in which everything was rational and all parts of both participants worked as they were intended.

Although we were several years from having the ceremony, Peter and I considered ourselves married almost from the moment we moved in together. He frequently made notes about me to others, referring to me as his common-law wife. When I eventually cheated on him in order to have normal sex, I felt myself as guilty of adultery as I would have felt if I had been married. Technically it was different. Emotionally it was not.

Peter seemed to understand the necessity for me to have a straight sexual relationship outside this marriage. Perhaps there was hurt, deeper hurt than I knew, that he never showed and never expressed. Or perhaps Peter understood that a woman can use casual sex in much the same way as some of the men he knew. Whatever the case, we never discussed the situation, though I learned to my embarrassment and shame that Peter knew what I was doing.

I had met a man while on location in Hawaii. He lived in New York, a city where my father had business and where I occasionally went on trips related to that business. Since I liked the man and wanted to see him again, I thought that it was the perfect cover for having an affair.

The reality of my existence at that time is hard for me to accept now that I am out or it. I was a young girl from an unhappy background who had been used by men. I was in love with Peter, deeply in love with him, yet rebelling against him at the same time. He was incapable of what I considered normal sex. He was a drug addict so heavily addicted to so many different things that he had come to see money only as a vehicle for more drugs. So long as there was more money than the cost of his addiction, then we would have food, shelter and a housekeeper. But nothing was so important to him as the drugs.

Even worse, there was no one to whom I could go to discuss the drugs. When I interviewed friends or colleagues of Peter's I found that none of them realized how addicted he actually was. He hid it well, even from me.

I had been living with Peter for a while, for example, when I wanted to wash my hair and could not find any shampoo. I began looking in the medicine cabinet, then in the cupboard under the basin. There I found a bag filled with hundreds of hypodermic needles. They were all sterile, all identical to what you would find in a doctor's surgery or a hospital. They were used by Peter to inject an intra-muscular pain killer which he took round the clock.

The injections went into his rear end, which is why I had never noticed any needle marks. He did not let me know he was taking them, and he certainly did not want me to know how often. I had no idea then that he carried a pain killer-filled syringe to parties and anywhere else we might go, using the bathroom when he needed an injection. He never showed signs of using the drug, or perhaps no one had seen him for years without his being on it. Whatever the case, it was a shock.

I had severe menstrual problems during that time; the pain was so intense that I might be doubled over on the floor, unable to move until the cramping stopped. I was in the midst of one such experience when Peter suggested I try the same drug. He gave me a shot, which eased my discomfort so that I could function normally. Then, when I had more pain, he gave me another shot and I enjoyed the peace it brought. Gradually, over time, I came to like the feeling of the drug regardless of my 'need' for it. I had no idea that it was highly addictive. In due course Peter and I both began carrying syringes so that we could share the pleasure wherever we went. And still no one knew.

Some of the drugs we took were illegal substances such as cocaine where the market could vary, though the prices were usually high. Others were prescription items, in themselves sometimes expensive, sometimes cheap, but always needed in such quantities that the bills mounted. At one time we were each using a dozen legal pharmaceuticals each. We had to worry about different prescriptions, different doctors and different pharmacies to avoid discovery. However, even if we had been discovered we could probably have continued to get the drugs, because there are a number of pragmatic doctors and pharmacists in Beverly Hills and the surrounding area of Los Angeles. They like celebrity clients. They enjoy having a 'name' who depends upon them in their waiting room or pharmacy. They look the other way when they write prescriptions or fill them. They accept obvious lies about the 'need' for such medications. Inadvertently they destroy patients in order to feed their own egos.

Peter had been a dug addict more years than I had been alive, so he understood that the first thing an addict must do is maintain a source of supply. When he was working regularly, money was no object. Soon after I met him the cash reserves were dwindling and he did anything to get money. He failed to pay taxes. He ignored bills. He borrowed from friends and he stole from me.

The drugs were a constant problem for us. Peter was a major star in Australia when we first got together and one of his jobs was to promote a brand of scotch whisky in that country. We were flown overseas, travelling first class, all expenses paid. We also made certain that we took a supply of cocaine with us because we had no idea whether or not we would be able to get any when we arrived.

Shortly before landing, Peter began talking about the draconian Australian drug laws from which no one was exempt, not even a star. Finally he decided that the answer was for me to smuggle the drugs. I had better ways to hide them than he did, he said. I realized what he was trying to tell me: he wanted me to slip the tiny packages of drugs up into my vaginal area. He tried to say it was no different from using a tampon, but I was disgusted. At the same time, I was as frightened as he was about the idea of being without drugs. I did not think we would be able to function for a prolonged period without getting high first.

So I went into the lavatory on the plane in order to fit the drugs into my body as best as I could. They were extremely uncomfortable and I was lucky not to cut the tissue.

The whisky company had arranged for everything for us. We had the finest possible treatment from everyone, including customs. They did not bother to search our possessions but waved us on the waiting limousine.

When we got into the car I felt extremely uncomfortable. The drugs were moving deeper into my body as I walked about. I wanted to get them out and figured I could reach inside and remove them while we drove. But just at that moment the representative of the company got in the back.

By the time we got to the hotel, I was furious with Peter. Despite what he had told me, there had been no customs search for a star. It was only ordinary travellers who were subjected to thorough checks. I was in pain, and I felt that Peter had betrayed me.

Suddenly I panicked. The drugs were too firmly lodged for me to reach them with my fingers. No matter what I did, they remained embedded. We had to arrange for a doctor to take them out, an extremely painful and embarrassing procedure.

On a trip through Canada, there was a different drug problem. Peter was convinced that the Canadian police used sniffer dogs of all types. That was when we saw the chihuahua. In his paranoid state, Peter decided that this tiny animal was working for law enforcement. We had to get rid of the dugs quickly, our only comforting thought being that we could replace them more easily in Canada than we could in Australia.

I was frequently stoned on drugs during those early months together, yet I recognized what was happening in our lives. Peter was being used because he was generous with drugs. Major entertainers were constantly in our home – John Lennon, Keith Moon and others.

Yet they were not there for brilliant conversation, impromptu instrumental sessions or any form of socialization. They were there because the drugs were available, the liquor flowed and Peter was the perfect host.

I was just another tool to all of them. I would make the drinks, prepare the drugs, then feel as though I had to spend a couple of hours cleaning the house before the maid came in the next morning. I didn't want her to see the evidence of what had been taking place most of the night. Traces of cocaine were cleaned, glass-stained furniture was scoured and pills were hidden away. I was a wreck.

There was no respect for me from the friends, either. One night we had a party but I decided to go to bed. A well-known entertainer who was there was celebrating his birthday. He was full of himself, impressed by his celebrity status and expecting any woman he desired to want him with equal fervour. He walked into the bedroom and announced that I was going to have sex with him in honour of his turning forty.

I was indignant and said no, yet he had had just enough of Peter's 'private stock' that I don't think he recognized I was serious. The next thing I knew, he was trying to get my clothes off. I began screaming, but what with the music and the people being stoned on drugs, no one seemed to hear at first. Finally my friend Don Brown heard my screams, came in and grabbed him. He hit him and threw him out of the house.

Oddly, though I knew I had been saved from rape, the entertainer had no idea that he was trying to do something I genuinely did not want. He was upset about being manhandled and never spoke to me again. After all, he had been in the Lawford's home where anything you wanted you could have – or so it seemed. I had become just another object and, though I never let myself be used, the attitude seemed to be that I had remained faithful to Peter in the house only because no one had asked me to do anything different.

There was even a time when I briefly left Peter in disgust over the abuses. I want to a nearby hotel, informing Peter that I would not return so long as I had to play the part of constant drudge to freeloaders. When he talked me into returning, he had a special treat for me. The living room furniture had been rearranged so that there were lines of cocaine to snort, champagne and a foam pad on which we could have sex.

Unfortunately Peter never quite knew when to stop. We had a beautiful marble fireplace and he wanted the evening to be as romantic as possible. He had put logs in the fire place, then managed to light them without fixing the damper. Partly burned pieces of paper rose up the chimney and then dropped on the awning outside the window, setting the fabric ablaze. Instead of enjoying drugs, drink and sex, we watched the fire department put out the blaze.

The reality of my existence back then is something I continue to fight to this day. I enjoyed the drugs, the way they numbed my senses and dulled my mind so that I could accept whatever was taking place and do whatever Peter wanted. I liked travelling by limousine, by helicopter and by private jet, even if it was just to go a few miles south of Los Angeles to a resort where we could have a weekend away. I never thought about how much money was going out and how little was coming in. I delighted when friends called us 'The Jetsons', a reference to a children's futuristic cartoon show in which everyone always travels by jet. And most of all, I revelled in the fact that my mother called me to talk.

There had been so much stress between my mother and myself, so much pain she had endured as a result of the split with my father, and so much isolation for me that I desperately wanted her approval. She hardly ever called me after I moved out of the house. If anything, she seemed angry because I was not around to help raise my stepbrother and stepsister, even though I was only a child myself at the time I left home.

But after I moved in with Peter, I was Somebody. My mother called me. My mother took me to lunch. My mother wondered what it was that he saw in this ugly duckling daughter of hers when she herself was more beautiful, more worldly and quite successful. Being with Peter got me her attention and, I suspected, both her envy and approval.

In a way my mother and I are like Peter and his son Christopher were. I don't know if we love each other, hate each other, or feel some combination of the two. I think we are each jealous of the other. I think we each long for the respect of the other, for a sense of mutual approval. Yet it seems impossible for us to express our true feelings. When we go out together, we are both liable to drink too much to ease the fear and the pain. When I am in trouble, I want to run to her for help, for comfort, for advice. Yet I am afraid of rejection, fearful of scorn if she sees weakness in my actions, terrified of any perception that she might have that I 'owe her' for her kindness. At the same time, neither one of us is willing to be vulnerable to the other. We are two strangers who want either to have a friendship or not be together ever again, yet we lack the courage to discover our potential as mother and adult child.

I can express such feelings now, even though I am still wrestling with these overpowering emotions so many years after I left home. At the time I moved in with Peter, I understood none of my subconscious motivation. All I knew was that when I lived with Peter, I also gained attention from my mother. When I was apart from him, I scarcely heard from her. Debasing myself physically and sexually to be with Peter was a seemingly small price to pay to gain what I took as her respect.

I lived with Peter during the most destructive period of his life. Even today I am haunted by dreams of the way he looked at the end, his body emaciated, incontinent, fool-smelling, decaying. Yet when I look past all that, I remember the suave, debonair, loving, brilliant, witty gentleman who was the best friend I had ever had.

I was lucky. Had Peter proven to be less of a man than he was, I might have stayed with him all the same. I might have subjected myself to more abuse just because my presence with Peter gained my mother's attention and, perhaps, a touch of her approval. But I did not have to learn how far I would go in a destructive setting. I was not forced to such limits because Peter was not that type of man.

I still remember the time he bought me a teddy bear, for example. It was a rather adolescent wish, but I was very young for much of the time we spent together. The teddy bear was a large one, a toy meant for adults. It cost an outrageous $350. Peter pointed out how ridiculous such a purchase would be. He hated the bear to begin with, and the price tag made it seem all the more foolish. In addition he was beginning to be strapped for money, something I did not then realize, and he did not like buying me a luxury item that might one day mean fewer drugs for himself. I begged and carried on, acting childish over this bear, yet I was serious about wanting it and would not give in. Reluctantly he purchased it for me, cursing me the entire time.

We were out late the night we bought it and Peter had an early morning call for a show. As was my habit, I slept in after he left. It was then that I saw the bear hanging from the bedpost, a noose made from one of Peter's neckties around its neck. There was a 'suicide note' from the bear saying that it could not handle the stress of our constant bickering, and so it had chosen to end it all.

There was an air of tragedy in Peter's relationships. He was constantly reminded that he was not the man he had once been in terms of work, relationships and other aspects of his life.

One night Don Brown came to our house unexpectedly, thrilled because he had closed a very lucrative business deal. To celebrate he announced that we were all going to fly by private jet to Las Vegas, where we could catch Frank Sinatra's act at the Sands. Don and

I knew of Peter's falling out with Sinatra over the Kennedy issue, yet that didn't matter. Sinatra has always been one of my favourite singers. He is a stylist who was without equal for most of his career, and Peter and I had many of his albums. The evening would be delightful.

We flew over, went into the room where Sinatra would be appearing and waited eagerly for the show to begin. Naturally Peter was recognized when we entered and word must have got back to Frank. All I know is that the show did not start as scheduled. Instead, two very large men came up to the table and explained that Mr Sinatra would not perform so long as Peter was in the room. Either we left or there would be no show for anyone. Peter was deeply hurt. We left, did some gambling and returned home. It was an incident he did not wish to discuss any further, yet it was another blow to his ego.

Then there were the jobs that Milt Ebbins discussed that never came to be. Whether Peter was ever seriously being considered, I do not know. It may be that Milt just wanted to give Peter a little hope when he knew he was despondent. Yet the thought that he might have work, coupled with the reality of finding that he was not being hired, proved devastating for Peter. Perhaps if he had been able to hang on emotionally until soap operas became prime-time programmes and handsome, older men with a British accent were in demand, everything would have worked for him. Yet it did not happen. The drugs were taking their toll. His body was deteriorating. His mind was affected by the chemicals he poured into his system.

I began to think that there were as many different Peter Lawfords as there were different types of pills in our medicine chest and hidden around the house. He could be charming, gentle, sensitive and kind. He could be a lover of animals who saw joy in all the creatures God created. He could be the sex-mad director, a sort of Otto Preminger of the bedroom who would arrange two naked women with special lighting and props, touching them, moving them about and generally putting on a production whose climax was never satisfactory. And he could be the crazed madman who seemed destined one day to kill either himself or someone else.

We had an argument one day and I decided to walk out and go to a nearby hotel to meet a friend for a drink. It was a way to calm myself with someone whose companionship I enjoyed. I was not gone for long, but it was long enough for Peter to take one of his 'madman' pills (I never knew what drugs would cause an adverse reaction and neither did he. In general, he could flip out one way on Monday and a different way on Tuesday, both times with the same drugs.) I returned home, reached into the refrigerator and took out a bottle of my favourite grape juice.

Before I could close the door I felt something cold against my head. Peter was holding a loaded revolver against me threatening to blow my brains out for leaving him. He had decided that I must have had a rendezvous with some lover. Fortunately he did not feel as though he had to act out his madness, and eventually he put away the gun.

Peter was losing control over the drugs. He had hidden his addictions for many years. He bragged about drinking vodka in great quantity because vodka didn't 'stink' like liquor. He resented it when I told him that it all stank because his self-image of being a fastidious gentleman, even while on drugs, was in reality a lie. He took whatever he wanted, and the results caused him to collapse at times. It was not unusual for me to find Peter's body on the floor of our apartment, his respiration so shallow that I had to give him mouth-to-mouth resuscitation.

I was desperate to get Peter help. We had been warned that his liver was deteriorating, that he was in danger of dying if he did not stop drinking. Peter's daily routine was becoming one of drinking, whatever drugs he could afford, and watching television game shows and soap operas all day. He was existing, not living. Our money was almost non-existent and he was reduced to beg, borrow or steal.

I first discovered about Peter's stealing from me to buy drugs after I had received a gift of $30,000 from my father. The cheque was placed in a bank account to which Peter had access. When I went to the bank one day to get out some money, I was told that my balance was only $34. Peter had withdrawn the money in order to buy drugs.

I was furious. The closest thing to affection my father had shown was when he gave me that money. He was not trying to buy sexual favours. He was not trying to shut me up to cover the abuse. He actually wanted me to have an inheritance while he was still alive, and he had given me the money in the way a normal father might want his daughter to benefit when the relationship was healthy. While Peter had every right to share that money, he had no right to steal it.

I returned home enraged. Peter was in bed watching a game show on television. 'What happened to my money?' I demanded of Peter.

'What money?' he said blithely.

'My money. My dad's money. The money that he gave me.'

'Don't be so common,' said Peter, acting as though I was an interruption in his day's pleasure.

'There's thirty-odd dollars in that account. The "three" had a few extra zeroes on it before, if you will recall,' I said.

'I don't want to talk about it now,' he said. 'If you're going to bitch, leave this house.'

That was it. I informed him that unless he came up with the money that night, I would indeed leave the house.

Peter ignored me and went back to watching television, pulling the covers up over his head like a little boy using false bravado to save himself from embarrassment. I went out, withdrew $1,500 from another account and returned home. The next day I decided to go to New York to be with the man with whom I had been having an affair.

I don't know what I felt at that point beyond rage. In a perverted way I still considered Peter my lover. I always wanted to please him, doing things I found repugnant even then, though often I would 'anaesthetize' myself with drugs so I could tolerate his requests. Today, my health so damaged from past drug use that something like cocaine would be potentially fatal, I could not repeat those actions. However, then we were still best friends, trusting each other totally except where the drug abuse interfered. He was also my father figure, guiding me into adulthood in ways that were constructive for the most part. We had mutual respect, something I had never known before.

At the same time, I was betrayed. I was angry, hurt, in an adolescent rage. I wanted someone to hold me, to comfort me. So I would go to New York and move in with the man I had been seeing even though, if I analysed things objectively, his attraction was not so powerful as to make me want ever to leave Peter.

The next morning Peter had to leave early for the recording studio. It was my chance to get away.

I took a steamer trunk from the closet and stole everything in the house that I knew had meaning for Peter. Cigarette boxes with John Kennedy's name on them went into the trunk. Items from Peter's marriage to Pat Kennedy were taken. Meanwhile our housekeeper had arrived and could only stare at what I was doing. 'What am I going to tell Mr Lawford?' she asked.

'You're going to tell him to go fuck himself,' I replied, coldly.

'I couldn't tell him that,' she said.

'You're not on the plantation any more,' I told her. 'Tell him to go fuck himself.'

She was shocked, finally lapsing into silence as she watched me strip the house.

I took a cab to the airport and checked in most of the baggage at Air France, taking care to tip the porter who arranged for storage. Then I made my way to American Airlines and flew to New York, paying cash to avoid leaving a paper trail. I was clever. I knew how to cover my tracks. Peter might locate me, but all he would know was that I had gone overseas, probably using a false name. It would be days, weeks or even months before he found me.

New York was a relief. I was welcomed by my lover and taken to his apartment. I could relax and ease my anger.

The first day I was constantly waiting for the telephone to ring, knowing that Peter might magically find me. The second day, still not having heard from Peter, I became cocky. He must be suffering, I told myself. He has no idea where I am. If anything, he thinks I'm wandering around Europe. He must be eating his heart out with misery.

It was midnight when I took pity on Peter. I called him in California, waiting for the anguished voice of the spurned lover barely to croak his greeting. 'Hello?' he said, a lilt in his voice as though he had just won a lottery and the first prize was a lifetime's supply of his favourite drugs. I hung up.

At 6 a.m. I tried again, knowing that it would be three in the morning in Los Angeles. 'Hello?' The same damned voice. Happy. Carefree. Not suffering in the least.

It was my fourth day in New York and I still had not spoken to Peter. He had spent my money and all I had from the relationship were the stupid cigarette boxes, ashtrays and other things that meant nothing to me. I was lonely, miserable, and angry that he was not suffering. The housekeeper hated me. Nothing was as it should have been. Even worse, California had been warm when I left, while New York was suffering heavy snow and ice.

While I was brooding, there was a knock at the door. It was a delivery man, obviously exhausted, surrounded by several boxes. When I took a closer look, I realized that the private lift to the apartment was filled, floor to ceiling, with boxes. The hall was filled with boxes. The area surrounding the door was filled with boxes. There was a narrow little passage along which the delivery man had got through to the apartment door, yet there was so little space that he had to slip the receipt form over the top of the boxes.

'What *is* this?' I asked.

'Lady, I just got a job to do. Will you sign the paper?'

I signed, then stared at the boxes more closely. Each was marked 'Aqua Chem', a name with which I was familiar. It's a brand of safe swimming pool water which we used in California, as did many of our neighbours.

Then the delivery man paused and said, 'By the way, lady, I got something else for you.' He managed to throw a letter over the top.

I recognized the envelope immediately. It was the grey stationery that Peter and I both used. The note, and the boxes, were from him.

I was shocked. I had so carefully covered my tracks. I had used Air France. I had paid cash. I opened the envelope and read the letter. It said, 'Darling Patricia, you forgot the fucking pool, cunt!'

Now I knew why Peter had sounded so happy when he answered the telephone. He wasn't enraged that I had left him. He understood or at last tolerated my lover, since he knew that my commitment would be only physical, not emotional. He had played the ultimate joke on me.

At that moment I knew that I would never leave Peter. His sense of humour touched something in me that kept me with him until his death. There were periods of abuse, and the lack of true intimacy never changed. There would also be one more nightmare period in 1982, a situation that would radically change both of us, but that was a long way off.

14

Family Affairs

[Movies are] without a redeeming feature to warrant their existence ... ministering to the lowest passions of childhood ... proper to suppress them at once.

1907 quote from the *Chicago Tribune* when
the city established the first censorship board
for 'those classes whose age, education and
situation entitle them to protection against
the evil influence of obscene and immoral
representations.'

Peter's greatest pain during those early years seemed to be caused by his trying to come to grips with his children. Peter not only did not know how to love his children, he was afraid of the feelings that, at times, seemed to overwhelm him. It was as though he had difficulty being vulnerable to the emotions the children created for him.

I never knew why the children were a problem for him, though there are a number of possibilities. He was, of course, raised without parental love. Nannies as surrogate mothers did not fulfil the same role as a real, caring mother would have done. And nannies had provided his introduction to sex. Then there were his own insecurities. Peter had difficulty accepting himself as being worthy of love. He had trouble with personal relationships, especially with women and children. He seemed scared of being emotionally vulnerable and tried to build a wall around himself. Sometimes he made this wall through avoidance of people. At other times he created it by leaving himself in a drug-and alcohol-induced haze. You have to be able to accept yourself in order to love another, and Peter seemed to fear that he might be found wanting.

Peter tried to be a pal to his children since he could not bring himself to be a father. Asking them to call him 'Peter' was part of this act. He like to take the children and me to restaurants such as Trader Vic's in New York when we were there, and they frequently stayed with us when they came out to California, sometimes bringing other members of the Kennedy family. In fact, it was not unusual to come home and discover one of Peter's children and several Kennedy cousins sprawled in the living room and around the house. We only had two bedrooms, so the overflow of Kennedys often fanned out about the Los Angeles area to sleep with friends. I jokingly said that the Kennedys never travel alone – they travel in packs.

It was through the children that I first met Pat Kennedy Lawford, a rather embarrassing experience. Peter and I had been living together for only a few months, though the kids had been staying with us from time to time. She would call them at the house and they would call her. Frequently I would be the one who answered the telephone, so I had at least spoken to her.

I was always respectful when I talked to her, addressing her as 'Mrs Lawford' and treating her with deference. She was larger than life to me, both because of the Kennedy name and because she was the late President's sister. She was also Peter's wife of eleven years, the mother of his four children, and seemed to be extremely tough.

Peter and I were temporarily living in New York in an apartment owned by a friend of mine who was out of town. Peter was appearing on a game show that was deservedly short-lived. Peter loved quiz shows. He would pick up around $5,000 for each one, get a trip

200

to New York and be able to see his kids. He was also usually quite good on the shows and behaved just as a celebrity guest was meant to.

Peter and I arrived in New York the evening before his appearance, then went out to clubs. He had an early call, but could cope with the lack of sleep.

After he left I had stayed in bed, drifting back to sleep, when the door buzzer rang. I thought that Peter had forgotten something, so I put on an old, rather tattered robe, did not bother running a comb through my hair and went to the door. I looked a wreck, with smudged black mascara under my eyes because I had been too tired to clean it off the night before. And there standing in the hall was Pat Kennedy Lawford and the three girls.

'What's all this fuss about this young one?' said Pat Kennedy. 'You don't look so red-hot in the morning.'

I realized who she was and said, 'Oh, Mrs Lawford, I'm so sorry. Let me get you some coffee.' I began blithering about, taking them inside, trying to work the coffee maker.

'Get dressed. We're going over to the studio,' she commanded.

I didn't know what to say or do. I was in shock and realized what Peter would feel like when all of us showed at the studio. But there was no arguing with this forceful woman who I knew stayed up late, got up early and had a way of dominating everything. Thoroughly intimidated, I showered and dressed in a record twenty minutes.

The five of us took a cab to the studio. Pat was extremely nice to me – I knew that Peter had warned her to leave me alone and had told her that I was a nice girl. But he certainly never expected us to get together.

As we entered the studio Peter spotted me from the stage. He smiled and mouthed, 'Hi, babe,' then caught a glimpse of his ex-wife and three daughters. 'How the fuck did that happen?' he mouthed.

Our arrival did not affect his performance. He was winning regularly, his partner being a woman from New Jersey who was excited to be on the show, especially with Peter. Finally Peter and his partner reached the big question where they would win the top money and prizes. Like all non-celebrity contestants, the woman would go home only with what she had won, and it looked as if she would get everything they had that day. All they had to do was answer a simple question.

The host took out the question which was: 'Famous singer named John. City in Colorado.'

Peter smiled in recognition, slammed his fist on the buzzer, and said, 'Boulder! John Boulder!'

The woman was horrified, her expression one of pure hatred towards Peter. Pat leaned over to me and said, 'Let's get out of here. We're going to lunch and we're going to have a few drinks.'

Peter had no idea that he had done anything wrong. His interest in music was such that he had never heard of John Denver. When he learned the truth, he was highly amused. From then on, whenever he saw John Denver on television he'd say, 'There's that Boulder chap again.'

The relationship between Peter and his children might have continued longer than it did had it not been for the drugs. Christopher began using drugs with enough frequency eventually to become addicted.

When Christopher turned twenty-one, a party was held in New York which Peter flew out to attend. Pat Kennedy Lawford decided to have some fun with Peter. He had a new pair of jeans, and since Pat was slim-hipped it did not surprise him when she asked to try them on. However, the moment she put them on she went back to the party, leaving Peter in a bedroom with no jeans and no change of clothing. He finally wrapped a towel around his waist and ventured down to the party to locate another glass of vodka and his ex-wife. She did not return his jeans until the end of the evening and he was forced to send someone out to buy him a new pair.

This light-hearted joking hid a more serious problem at Christopher's birthday. Peter's gift to his son, a gift he thought was a proper present, was some cocaine. Later Peter received a thank you note from his son which read:

> Dear Pedro,
> Thanks for making it cross country for my birthday. You were a surprise and the most honored guest of the evening. You made the party and I thank you. Oh, thanks for the gift. Unfortunately it was not one I could hold on to for very long.

It was obvious that each was reaching out to the other as best they could, yet nothing seemed to work.

We were in New York one evening, both Peter and I carrying cocaine for our own use later, when Christopher asked Peter where he could score some coke. Peter had a connection whose name and address he gave to Christopher. Then Peter spent part of the night snorting cocaine with his son. The situation greatly upset me. Peter was thirty-five years older than me, his son three years older than me. In a sense, Peter was the most positive father figure I had ever had and I know that that was a part of my attraction to him. Yet Peter was not my father. He was my lover, my friend, and in no way biologically connected with my existence. The same could not be said for his son. I felt that his snorting cocaine with Christopher was in the worst possible taste, and I told him so the next day when Christopher was not around.

Peter was upset, constantly complaining about my Catholic morality. I had been educated in Catholic schools, and his children had been raised in the Catholic Church. Peter disliked my sense of morality because, as loose as it may have seemed at times, there were limits I could not cross without feeling great guilt.

Yet my anger at his using drugs with his son did seem to affect Peter. I think he realized that it was wrong, yet he could not bring himself to work out what being a father might truly mean. He did not know how to love a child. He did not even realize that it was all right to love his children. He had had no role models except the one that seemed to say that to be affectionate was wrong. Peter became cold, distant, desperately wanting to reach out to his kids and always holding himself back. It was an action that caused his children great pain and the feeling that he did not care for them. The truth was that he cared beyond his ability to cope with such feelings.

The result of all his turmoil was rather brutal. The children were always welcome to visit us and continued to do so. He seemed to like seeing them. But he deliberately cut himself off from them in other ways. For example, Peter and I took a two-week trip to New York in July 1978 and made no effort to see the children. Then Peter sent each child what amounted to a form letter telling them that he was in good health, that he was happy with me and that he loved them, but wasn't going to see them there. I felt it was a very cold action.

The situation was not a unique one in Peter's personal relationships. He had done something just as cold to me when he asked Milt Ebbins to throw me out of the house when he was divorcing Deborah Gould. There had been no mention of what was taking place or any of the underlying reasons. What he did to the children was much the same, the form letter serving to avoid the feelings that seemed to be overwhelming him.

Victoria, the most articulate, sent him a letter that expressed her feelings in an eloquent manner.

Dear Daddy,

I really don't know how to tell you this or how many times I've said this and meant it, but I love you. I don't know if you believe this but I hope to God you do.

I've never really had a chance to sit down and talk to you as father to daughter, but I guess I feel just as close to you as if I had. I guess the circumstances leave it difficult to get to know one another, but I hope this changes in time, Daddy.

I have to tell you I am very upset this year because last year I felt we got really close and then this year that all just fell apart. The reason I call so often is just to say hello and hear you because I do miss you.

When I heard you were ill from Patty, I wanted to go see you so badly and yet couldn't tell you over the telephone. I wanted to see you when you were here simply because I've waited all year. I know you're busy and I understand. I guess I just ask for things too far in advance; things I know I'll never get, but maybe that just takes time too.

I didn't understand what's going on this year when you sent us all a typed letter trying to explain that you were happy, busy, and in good health. All of that makes me happy, but I still don't understand it.

I love you, Daddy, and I never want you to forget it.

Your daughter, always. Victoria.

The letter was deeply moving. It also sat unopened until I removed it from the envelope. Peter did not have the courage to look at letters from his children. Perhaps he feared their rejecting him. Perhaps he was frightened that they could touch his heart in ways he did not want to deal with.

I also think that Peter was shocked that he was living with a woman who was younger than his oldest child. He had to face aspects of his life that he had never considered before.

There were occasional discipline problems with the children that Peter also did not know how to face. The Kennedy money, like many great family fortunes, became diluted by the tremendous number of Joe Kennedy's grandchildren. The money from the trust funds allows them an above-average income compared with most Americans, but it also requires them to hold jobs if they are going to be able to play in the manner to which they were raised. Yet the children were spoiled, and too many of their wishes were met.

I remember one time when Peter and I were away and Christopher stayed at our house. During this period we were both abusing prescription drugs – we had a running charge account at a pharmacy that was delighted to have our large volume of business. Christopher knew about the account and took advantage of it while we were gone. When we returned we discovered that we owed $1,300 primarily for prescription drugs. In addition, Christopher forged a prescription for Darvon, a powerfully painkilling compound, and got arrested for it. Then, a week later, Christopher was in Aspen, Colorado and was again arrested for forging a prescription.

Peter was less concerned that his son might be an addict or heading into a life of crime than he was at the thought that Christopher's actions might damage our credit. We had the perfect set-up for drug abuse and needed the pharmacist's trust as well as the credit line. Again, Peter could not face the reality of the family's situation.

The first time Peter had to face the seriousness of his son's problem was when we returned from a trip and found a large number of emergency vehicles parked just outside our home. Lights were flashing and men were gathered just outside the apartment.

We looked up and saw Christopher on a ledge, preparing to jump. He had overdosed on heroin and he was no longer rational. He had no intention of trying to commit suicide, but his brain was so confused that it seemed perfectly natural for him to walk off the side of the building. Then we saw another figure on a different ledge. He was a friend of Christopher's who had taken PCP (called 'angel dust'). He too was unable to reason logically and had decided to join Christopher in his trip over the side.

We had arrived in a limousine, got out long enough to see that the place was completely surrounded and that trained people were trying to talk the two youths back to safety, and then got back in the car. Peter was terrified not only of what seemed about to happen but also of having to deal with it. He had been running from life for so long that he wanted to tell the driver to go on, that he could not handle being there with the crisis taking place.

We sat in the car, watching what was taking place. Our apartment had been entered and searched and officers were coming out with bags marked 'Evidence'. The law has since been changed, but at that time, every emotion we could have was taking place. We were frightened for what might happen to Christopher, who easily could have gone over the edge. We were concerned about whether or not we could be linked to the drugs that were being confiscated. And we were angry that our main supply had been compromised because, when the crisis was over, that would be the way we'd want to relax.

They even discovered the marijuana plants we were growing in much the same manner as people raise orchids or African violets. About the same time that the agents were able to talk Christopher and his friend back far enough so that they could be grabbed and safely subdued, we watched our largest plant being carried out. This was at a time when possession of marijuana was a criminal offence, even if the amount was so small that it was obviously being used personally, not kept for resale. Peter said, sadly, 'Oh, no, not that plant.' It was one we had carefully nurtured, and it had thrived more than any of the others. We never recognized the tragedy that caused him to express more regret over the loss of the plant than over the chemical turmoil that had caused Christopher to become so irrational for those few moments.

Somehow Peter found both the courage and the maturity to get into the ambulance with his son instead of trying to run away from the responsibility. I stayed behind to deal with the police, pleased that Peter was showing some maturity.

It was very late when Peter returned, his face ashen, his body looking prematurely aged. Christopher had come near to death. The drugs he had taken were depressants. His respiratory system had slowed down to the point where, without treatment, he would have died. The doctors had had to inject Christopher with stimulants to counteract the effects of the depressants. Then he had regained awareness of his surroundings, seen his father, and said, 'Dad, how come you never yell at me? How come you never yelled at me?'

Peter said, 'What do you want me to tell you? Not to do this? Don't do this? Don't do that? If you wanted a father who was going to go after you, you came to the wrong window. I'm not going to do it. I'll talk with you quietly but I'm not going to yell at you.'

I had the feeling that Christopher was longing for his father to show some authority, to set limits, to show that he cared. I don't know if Christopher started with drugs in order to get Peter's attention, to force Peter to react. He may have been like Peter, hurt, running away. Or he may have started with innocent experimentation, then discovered that using the drugs could mask the pain he was feeling. But as the problem progressed he wanted Peter to stop him, to act as he felt a father should.

There would be other times when Peter would be with his son when Christopher was in trouble. Peter had been vomited on, cradling the unconscious youth when he was faced with the possibility of death. His love was intense, obvious to all who saw them during one of Christopher's crisis periods before Christopher sought help and began to gain control of his life.

Yet when the crises were over, when Peter and his son were together, he was unable to express his feelings. Peter could not tell Christopher he was loved. He had no idea how to relate to his son, holding in his feelings, going through life in a way that hurt the person he did not wish to hurt.

In the end, Christopher never realized that his father loved him. He had been unable to reach out to his father other than in anger and in acting out with drugs. The great tragedy was the relationship that might have been had either of them been able to break through the walls they both erected.

15

Till Death Us Do Part

For 35 years I couldn't go to sleep without at least two sleeping pills. And I'd always taken a lot of medication for pain. I'd had 19 major operations, and drugs had become a crutch. I wouldn't take them only when I was in pain. I was taking a lot of Percodan. I'd take Percodan and a couple of drinks before I went out. I just felt I had to get stoned to get over my shyness. Not being a drunk is the only way I'm going to stay alive. Drunk *is a hard word, but I've had to face it. Somebody who drinks too much is a drunk. Somebody who takes too many pills is a junkie. There's no polite way to say it.*

Elizabeth Taylor

I became desperate to find a treatment centre where Peter could get help for his drink problem. I felt certain that there had to be a place where someone would be able to touch a nerve, to say something that would convince Peter to stop his self-abuse. I sensed that he hated himself, but I thought he could learn to see himself as others saw him, to gain respect, love and understanding for the man whom I knew had so much potential left within him.

Eventually I thought of the Betty Ford Center in Rancho Mirage, California. Mrs Ford had been a substance abuser even during the White House years. Yet she had the courage eventually to face her addiction, go in for treatment, then tell the public what had happened to her. She had dedicated herself to helping others with the same problem, and the Center was the ultimate tribute to her caring attitude.

I had been told that the Center might work for Peter, but I was also told something else that I did not wish to hear. A former alcoholic who now worked with alcoholics told me that Peter might be one of those people who had to die.

There is a saying among addicts that you have to hit bottom before you can recover. 'Hitting bottom' means many things to many different addicts. Sometimes it is the threat of losing a job or a loved one that makes the person decide to get help. Sometimes the person simply has a minor traffic accident when he or she thought no one would notice what they had drunk at lunch. No one is hurt in the accident, but it is enough of a shock for the person to admit that there is a problem. And sometimes hitting bottom means actually losing one's job, family, home and self-respect, sleeping in a gutter until forced into a treatment centre.

But there is yet another type of hitting bottom, which occurs when nothing seems to reach the individual involved. Their career ends, their relationships fail, they may use all of their money or they may have enough resources to live on. But the person refuses to quit even as his or her body organs are damaged, then cease to function, as loved ones beg for change, as counsellors give advice, and everything that can be tried *is* tried. Nothing stops the drinking except the person's death. It is the ultimate form of hitting bottom, and my counsellor believed that that would be the reality for Peter.

The idea that Peter might have to die was not something I could contemplate. Peter was going to live and I was going to ensure that he made it. He *had* hit bottom. He was not going any lower. I had given him mouth-to-mouth resuscitation in the past – literally the breath of life. Doctors had written him off as a dead man before and he had proven them wrong. I was going to get that man well, no matter what it took.

The Betty Ford Center did not share my enthusiasm.

They were not happy to accept Peter. They were a serious treatment facility, they wanted me to understand, not a three-ring circus for showbusiness people. The flak continued, yet it did not sound right. This was not the programme I had heard about – there were too many negatives. I was confused and angry, and then I learned the truth. The person with whom I was dealing was politically oriented. Gerald Ford was a Republican. John Kennedy had been a Democrat. And Peter Lawford was the former President's brother-in-law. Fortunately Elizabeth Taylor, a friend of Betty Ford's, was going in for treatment herself and she made certain that they would accept Peter.

The trip to Rancho Mirage would have been a comedy had Peter's life not been at stake. First we flew to Palm Springs, California, the nearest airport. Peter happily consumed little bottles of vodka throughout the flight, becoming quite drunk by the time we landed.

Then we got in a car, which Peter did not quite understand. 'Where are we going?' he asked.

'To Betty Ford's,' I told him.

'That's wonderful,' he said. 'I've always liked Betty Ford.'

Peter was happy and prattled on. We were obviously going over to Betty Ford's house for dinner. It came as quite a surprise when we arrived at the clinic.

I stayed with Peter during the period of detoxification. It was rough for him, since his body had become chemically dependent upon what amounts to a poison. Withdrawal caused extreme discomfort, yet was necessary for his survival. Fortunately he seemed well, and I felt able to return to Los Angeles. However, when I got back to the clinic I found that he had made an attempt to escape into the desert, looking for a liquor store.

Part of the Betty Ford Center programme uses Alcoholics Anonymous booklets, several of which contain self-analysis questions. The notes Peter made are interesting, sometimes painful and sometimes quite revealing. For example, when discussing the topic of selfishness he admitted: 'There is no question, I want what I want now!' Then he added something which showed how insensitive he was letting himself be towards both me and the friends who tried to help him along the way. He said: 'I only hurt myself, not others that I am aware of.' More revealing was Peter's comment about resentment: 'I resent where I'm living right [now]. I had to move from my old place because of lack of funds. It makes one rather frustrated watching one's life going down instead of up – especially at my age. . . .'

Peter was not at first the most cooperative patient, and rebelled against the authority of the Center. However, later Peter went from being belligerent to being extremely cooperative. The staff and I thought that a breakthrough had finally occurred, but the reality was quite different.

I was taking an increasing interest in our finances at this point. The man who worked with Peter on financial matters was concerned at my lavish lifestyle. When we both realized that I knew nothing of our financial situation, I began to check carefully what was happening to our money. That was why I noticed what seemed to be an odd charge on our American Express bill. It was for plane and helicopter charters during the time when Peter was in the Betty Ford Center and I was at home. There was no way Peter could have flown, and I certainly had not used the card for such things. I assumed that a mistake had been made.

There was no error. Peter had had enough of life in the slow lane. Sobriety was fine with him so long as someone else practised it. He had managed to contact a drug dealer who regularly supplied him with whatever he needed. He had the dealer fly cocaine to the Betty Ford Center using a chartered helicopter. The pilot landed in the desert behind the clinic, where no one would normally think to check. Out there a patient will find nothing to drink except cactus juice. It is so isolated that Peter's wandering off back there caused no concern. They did not realize that he met his dealer, did a few lines of cocaine and felt wonderful about everything and everyone. He was much more willing to follow the detoxification programme once he found he could do it without abandoning all his old ways.

Peter emerged from the Betty Ford Center looking wonderful. His body chemistry had stabilized and he had been off alcohol the entire time he was there. I thought that I had found the miracle cure for Peter, only to get a call from a bartender three days later. Peter was so drunk that he had to be brought home.

I am not bragging when I say that Peter and I were probably closer than he had ever been with any other woman in his life. I was with him during a quieter time, when he was able to settle into a relationship more than at any period in the past. He loved me deeply, committing himself to me more than he had done with anyone, despite his sexual hang-ups. And this belief was shared by those interviewed who had known him over the years as he went from wife to wife and girlfriend to girlfriend. Many agreed that his age and health may have had a lot to do with the changes in him, but whatever the case, our feelings were intense. Yet such a relationship was not enough to overcome the drug-induced stupor that prevented him from helping me when I was raped.

It was 1982 when the incident occurred, less than three years before Peter's death. Despite the apparent wildness of my life, I was basically a rather sheltered girl who had been educated by nuns in a strict Catholic environment, and I was extremely naïve when it came to understanding my body and what I should expect from the medical profession. I had seen one gynaecologist but had had very little contact with him when I needed to go to a different doctor. This man had an excellent reputation and a large number a patients in Beverly Hills. He was extremely conservative in appearance and demeanour, so I thought nothing about him.

214

The first problem, though I did not realize it at the time, was that he saw me alone. There is nothing illegal or unethical about a male being alone with a female patient. However, considering the woman's vulnerability and the intimate nature of the various tests that have to be performed, it is normal in the United States for a nurse to be present. I knew nothing of this.

The doctor asked me some questions, including, 'Do you masturbate?'

I was embarrassed and a little shocked, though I assumed that it was a routine question.

'It's a good idea to masturbate before this procedure because it helps you relax,' he continued.

I explained that I was fine, that I was certain it would be unnecessary. I thought how naïve I was to not have known about this. After all, in a way what he was saying made sense.

'I could do it for you, if you like,' he said. Still his expression and tone of voice did not change. He was offering me nothing more than a mild tranquillizer in a completely safe form – or so his voice indicated. His words, on the other hand, were making me nervous.

The procedure was handled without masturbation by either of us. There were no complications and I thought nothing of what happened.

I stayed with the doctor when he moved to a new address.

Subsequently I had some problems with severe cramping that made me realize something was not quite right. I called to ask if I could see him, and he told me to come to his home where he had a surgery. When I went to see him the set-up seemed perfectly normal.

As time passed I learned to trust the gynaecologist. I felt quite unembarrassed telling him of intimate problems that might affect my body, including the fact that Peter and I had never had intercourse. That was why, when I had to go to New York and was quite late with my period, he told me to call at his home surgery. He said that I simply had a recurrence of a hormone

215

imbalance that had troubled me in that past. He would give me a hormone shot that would induce a period and I would be fine. But I still did not have my period, even though there was no way I could have been pregnant. So I called to make another appointment to see him on my return from New York.

I arrived there at the end of his day, the nurse and all other patients having long gone.

'Get up on the table so I can examine you,' he said.

'Okay,' I replied, lying on my back and positioning my feet in the stirrups. It was the standard examining position for all women to take and I could not easily get down. I was relatively helpless, but it caused me no concern whatever. This was my doctor and I trusted him.

The doctor kept his examining instrument in a warmer so that there would be no discomfort when it was inserted in the vagina. He removed it from the warmer and then shoved it inside me.

The pain was intense. He began jabbing at me, my natural instinct being to jam my legs together. I could not rise, could not strike at him, and each time I jerked my legs I only fixed them more firmly in the stirrups. I could feel myself bleeding. He was hurting me, saying nothing as I screamed.

I never felt the doctor enter me. I was already in too much pain from the injuries. I just knew that everything was wrong as he became verbally abusive, saying, 'This is what you've wanted, bitch. You needed a fuck.' He zipped up his trousers, moved to the side of the examining table and struck me. This man was no longer a doctor, a caring healer. He was a rapist, angry with me, violent, barely in control. I had the feeling that he might kill me.

The doctor left the room for a minute and I managed to remove my feet from the stirrups and get down from the table. I could not think about the rape. I could not think about the violence. The only thought in my mind was blood. Somehow Peter had managed to find enough money to make the down payment on a beautiful white lynx coat for me. I was also wearing white slacks and a white sweater, and the upholstery of my car was white. The blood would stain it all. Desperately I tried to find some towels to stop whatever bleeding I could, then absorb the rest. Pieces of flesh were coming out and I knew I was in trouble.

The doctor had set the perimeter alarm so he would know if I tried to get out. However, he was not close enough to stop my escape. I got in the car, started the engine and drove to the emergency room of St John's Hospital.

The staff were wonderful. I wanted to tell them the truth. I wanted to tell them about the doctor who had raped me. I wanted them to know that there was a madman with a licence to practise medicine. But at the same time I realized that if I told the truth, there would be newspaper headlines: 'Wife of Peter Lawford Raped by Gynaecologist!' 'Doctor Said She Had No Sex at Home So He Helped.' The whole idea was a nightmare.

The entertainment industry is rather strange in that there are good crimes and bad crimes with which you can be involved. If you're going to be a victim, do it in a way to which everyone can relate. Be stabbed, mugged, beaten, or thrown off the top of the Arco Plaza Building. Get repeatedly run over by a Bentley in Beverly Hills. But do not get raped by your gynaecologist and expect sympathy or understanding. Peter would have had an even harder time getting work and we would both be the butt of jokes.

'My boyfriend did this to me,' I lied. I let them treat me for the battering without telling them my name. I had locked all my identification in the boot of the car before arriving, so there was no way they could learn who I was while I was being treated. I also informed them that I was walking out the moment they said they were calling the police.

I made a telephone call to Peter to get him pick me up. 'I need you,' I told him. 'Something has happened that is so terrible, I need to see you right away.'

'What is it?' he said, angrily.

'Peter, I'm in the hospital,' I said.

'I don't understand you.'

'Peter, are you loaded?' I asked, realizing that he sounded stoned on drugs.

'Fuck you!' he shouted, slamming down the receiver.

I called a girlfriend, Laurie, and she said she'd be there in ten minutes. She took me home, even though the hospital wanted to keep me for the night. I told Laurie everything and she was furious, going into the house and telling Peter that he had better talk to me.

'What are you doing here?' he asked her, unable to see or think clearly. He was so drugged that Laurie spent the night with me, caring for me while he slept.

I had still been unable to talk to Peter when Laurie brought a local newspaper to show me. It contained a story about my doctor, who had been arrested on eight counts of molestation. He had been caught by an undercover police officer posing as a patient. The story also gave the name of a police officer who was coordinating the investigation and looking for other women who might not have reported their assaults. None of the charges made so far was as serious as mine. Apparently he was becoming more violent, and I had to keep silent because of Peter.

Then I went to another doctor because I still had not had my period. This time there was no hormonal problem. The rape had impregnated me. I was carrying the doctor's child. Had I told the hospital that I had been raped, not just battered by my 'boyfriend', they would have given me a 'morning after' pill. Now I had to have an abortion.

All this was too much for me. Two weeks after the rape I called the police officer whose name had been mentioned in the paper. The officer, a woman, was kind, attractive and very professional. However, Peter still had no idea what had happened, having remained almost constantly on drugs since the day of the rape. All he knew was that a female police officer was at the door. She could handcuff him and hit him with her stick. It would be the ultimate sado-masochistic experience, and it aroused all the sexual fantasies of which he was still capable. I could tell he hoped that she was a present for him. He had occasionally mentioned that he thought a threesome with a policewoman would be wonderful, and he no doubt felt I had finally decided to let him have his fun.

The officer interviewed me privately. I told her everything but stressed that I would not go into court. I was still worried about Peter's career, not realizing that it was over. He was in the process of dying and would never be able to work again. The trouble was that I had seen him haul himself back from serious problems for so long that I still believed he would perform successfully again.

'Do you know what happened here, Mr Lawford?' she said to Peter. Her manner was cold and hard. I had explained that Peter was a drug addict, and as a result she tore into him for his insensitivity, lack of awareness and lack of caring.

I thought I was all right. I thought I was handling things well. Then I discovered that the doctor had sent me a bill to pay for his time when he was raping me. And Peter, his mind fogged with drugs, wondered if I had encouraged the man.

'Peter, I have to get away. I'll be gone five or six days. Goodbye,' I told him, taking a suitcase and leaving our home. It was May and I did not in fact return until October.

I wanted a complete break from Peter. Using what little cash I could get, I changed my name, got a job and lived in Hawaii. I wanted to be on my own, cope with my own life, and not have to experience the destructive ego of Peter Lawford. I also made some trips back to the mainland, including one to Las Vegas where I made contact with Frank Sinatra, the man Peter still considered an enemy.

Oddly it was Frank Sinatra who got me to call Peter after all that time. He told me that he had heard from mutual friends that Peter was in an extremely bad way. He was not coping well without me. Frank encouraged me to telephone.

Peter sounded shattered on the telephone. I loved him and he loved me, that was our reality. He was an alcoholic, a drug addict, a sex addict who could no longer achieve an erection, a weak man in many ways. But Peter was my friend, the one true friend I had ever known. He was my father figure and, in the past, in his own perverted way, my lover. No matter how upset I had been, no matter how positive a move my leaving had been for me, his needs came first. We could not stay apart.

I rushed back, only to find that the situation had got worse than anything I had ever know before. Peter had not cut his hair or his nails the entire time I was gone. He was incontinent, yet had not bothered to change the sheets. If he wet or defecated in bed, he would remain in his own filth. The floors were disgusting. The entire apartment looked like wild animals had been penned up inside.

I was nauseated, disgusted, wanting to vomit and weep at the same time. I mourned the loss of the only source of goodness and strength I had known in recent years. I was angry at the little boy who was unable or unwilling to handle the rudimentary aspects of personal hygiene and survival. And I was terrified of this living dead man who was so sick, so strange, so unlike anyone or anything I had ever known.

I helped Peter clean up. I began ridding the house of his vodka and pills. I fed him healthful meals. And I began attending meetings of Alanon, the Alcoholics Anonymous programme for individuals who are living with alcoholics. There I learned about tough love, that the greatest love of all comes from not pampering someone who has become a dependent personality.

Peter seemed to make an effort. He tried to stop the use of the drugs and alcohol. His mind cleared and he was his old, delightful self. He was on the rebound and doing much better. Yet still there was no work, except for one last movie. Some of his former friends he could not face. Some of them had never been friends but drug using hangers-on who wanted nothing of a sober man. And some were too busy with their own careers to think much about Peter. They also had no idea what shape he was in.

That last movie was a rather pathetic gathering of brilliant 'losers' – men who were major stars yet who had not had a meaningful role in several years. There was Peter, Orson Welles and Tony Curtis, and the film, which mercifully opened and closed within four days, was called *Where Is Parsifal?* It was filmed in England in a decrepit old mansion. The toilet seats were made of wood that was not properly sanded. You had to position yourself with caution because of the splinters. The bedrooms were no more appealing. Ours had a single light bulb in the ceiling, a wardrobe rack and a single bed, and the bathroom was some way away. We stole an eiderdown from another room, yet we were still cold at night because the walls were poorly insulated.

The house was magnificent despite the problems, though. The dining room appeared to be capable of seating a couple of hundred people. I imagined a group of medieval diners throwing food around and wiping their hands on passing dogs during the orgies.

I wanted to be useful on the set and kept trying to find some job to do. What I did not expect was that I would be hired to feed Orson Welles, a request that seemed a little odd. Peter laughed at me, but because he sat with the crew, not the actors, he never realized what was to be involved. The catering for the cast and crew was done by a company that cooked rather heavy food. There was shepherd's pie, steak and kidney pie, mashed potatoes and numerous other filling dishes. After we ate we felt as though we needed a three hour nap. The one exception was Orson Welles.

Welles was one of the greatest actors of his time, with a voice trained to such a degree that listening to him say even the most mundane things could be riveting. He had achieved great fame for projects such as his radio presentation of *The War of the Worlds*, yet he never reached the heights predicted for him. He was a genius who went unappreciated, working on too few films over his career. He was also a rather troubled man who seemed to turn to gluttony for solace in his later years, ballooning to grotesque size.

Orson was late in arriving in England, having taken the wrong directions and somehow ending up in France. A special plane had to be dispatched to Paris because his several hundred pounds of weight would not fit in a normal first-class seat. Then he had to be conveyed by a London cab to the movie location because he was too large to get into a limousine.

Orson played Klingsor, a magician, who was supposed to arrive at the scene in a Daimler. Not surprisingly, they also had to use the London cab for shooting this scene, even though the house was some eighty miles from the city and in an area that looked quite odd for such a vehicle. The back of the cab, that normally seats four quite comfortably, was filled by Orson.

Orson was kept in the basement of the house because the steps to the upper floors, where everyone else was eating, would not hold his bulk of at least 400 pounds. The first mealtime I took a plate and, figuring that he had a healthy appetite, gave him a little of everything – roast beef, Yorkshire pudding and enough other food to create a well-heaped plateful.

Just then the director came over and called me a 'stupid twit' and, worse, berating me for not doing my job.

'There's no reason to be abusive,' I explained. 'I'm just doing what you asked.'

As it turned out, my idea of feeding Orson Welles did not match the man's appetite. I was handed the kind of platter that holds an entire turkey. 'Fill it, and repeat same in fifteen minutes.'

I stared at him, then realized that he was serious. I heaped it with food, then took it down to the basement – having to turn sideways to get down because it was so loaded. The director had told me to knock lightly on the door, say, 'Mr Welles, your dinner is here,' and leave it for him. Then I had to come back upstairs because by that time he'd be ready for the same again.

I did as he said, and after walking up six stairs glanced back. Suddenly the door opened, a hand shot out and the plate was jerked inside so rapidly that it made a whooshing noise going through the air. By the time I had reached the top of the stairs the platter was out, piled with bones. I repeated the process, a pattern I was to follow the entire time we were there.

Orson Welles knew Peter from the time Peter had done *Othello* in London with Orson, and the two of them had gone round together. They also had another connection, since Peter had had an affair with Rita Hayworth whom Orson eventually married. Peter said that having sex with Rita showed him why she and Orson got along so well together. He said that after going to bed Rita got up, went to the refrigerator, sat on the floor and ate everything she could find. The sex act was foreplay for her gluttony, though she still managed to keep her weight down and remain beautiful.

I was shocked, but Peter assured me it was true. 'She was the worst lay in the world,' he said. 'She was always drunk and she was always eating.' In the end I accepted his story, envying Rita her metabolism because, unlike the grotesquely obese though brilliant Orson Welles, she kept her figure.

Orson Welles did not know that Peter and I had been living together when he saw the two of us together on the set. He looked at Peter and said, 'So there you are, Lawford, a man who knows no shame.' His voice was deep and rich, like melodically rolling thunder, the timpani section of some celestial orchestra. 'What are you going with this young one?'

'I've been with her now for about nine years,' Peter said.

'Oh, dear God, help us!' commented Orson.

'I'm the one who's been shoving those barrels of food in front of your door, Mr Welles,' I told him, though I don't know where I got the nerve. Everyone on the set was afraid of him except Peter. He was brilliant, imposing and a little odd from the very slight brain damage caused by the stress that his obesity had placed on his heart.

Welles lived in Hollywood and did not live very long after the movie was made. What touched me, since both Peter and I loved animals, was that he willed his beloved French poodle, Fifi, to his neighbour. It was his first bequest and, I'm certain, in his mind the most important. Except in England, where the quarantine laws were too strict, Orson carried Fifi everywhere.

After that movie, Peter announced that he was bored with life the way we were living it. He said that we should go to Barbados and get formally married. It was a ridiculous idea on the one hand and a wonderful one on the other. I said yes.

We started out for the airport, getting as far as UCLA Medical Center where he had to be admitted as an emergency case. He was suddenly experiencing severe pain and had a distended stomach. There was no way we could go any further. Peter was diagnosed as having a bleeding ulcer that required emergency surgery. I was told that he might not survive.

Peter did live, and the next afternoon we were married in his room. I wore white. Peter wore a hospital gown. And the patient in the next bed (we no longer could afford a private room) vomited through the entire ceremony. When it was over, Peter pointed to the patient, a man who was dying, and said, 'This is a sign of things to come.'

I laughed at Peter's joke. I didn't know it was a prophecy.

Our 'wedding night' was spent together until I finally left at 5 a.m., wondering how much longer he would live. I let his children know that their father was in trouble, but they had heard it all before. Peter hit life-threatening crises the way Marilyn Monroe committed suicide. No matter what happened, Peter recovered. Coldly, their attitude was that they were tired of his slow destruction. If he was going to die, he was going to die. Yet three of the children did visit him. Christopher asked for some of his father's possessions. I pointed out that he was a bit premature since his father was still alive and, with luck, would continue to be.

By the time Peter was able to return home his body was shattered. Over a third of his stomach had been removed: I learned to flush out his stomach, feeding him through a tube with specially prepared liquids. For the first two weeks that meant every ninety minutes around the clock. I had to carry him to the lavatory – fortunately his weight had dropped more than 45 pounds to 120. Yet slowly he was improving.

The doctors were pleased until the gastric tube had to be removed. Suddenly Peter started to bleed uncontrollably. All the liver damage meant that he was no longer able to process the enzyme that allowed blood to clot. He had developed coagulaopathy, a life-threatening condition. Yet again he survived.

The next morning, at home, Peter fell from bed, creating a swelling that suddenly erupted like a geyser, spraying out blood. This time we went to Cedars Sinai Hospital, where I was warned that a blow to the head could kill him. As it was, Peter had to spend three weeks there, recovering. He was also told that if he drank again he would be dead.

By Thanksgiving of 1984 Peter, though on a restricted diet and taking large quantities of medicines, was mobile enough to go to dinner at Elizabeth Taylor's home. At the same time his liver was so damaged that each dose of medicine threatened to destroy the liver and kill him.

I was sleeping less and less each day, becoming severely depressed. We could not afford help, though I discussed with his children the idea of placing him in a nursing home where he could receive round-the-clock attention. The children saw no reason for that.

I was becoming increasingly angry with them. They had access to all the money they needed and could easily have helped their father. But at the same time I was aware that they had been emotionally abused by being raised in that highly disturbed environment. The very fact that Peter could give his son cocaine as a twenty-first birthday present tells much about their relationships.

Yet this was still their father. This was the man who had been with them during the earliest years of their lives, a man who loved them despite his inability to express that love. He was sick, disturbed, dying, and they were too shallow, too hard, or both to care. I was his wife. I was the one who cleaned up his shit, his vomit and his urine. I changed his dressings. I fed him, gave him his medicine and never slept longer than an hour or two at a time as I worked round the clock to keep him alive.

Oddly, Peter maintained his tan, though the colouring was mixed with the yellow of jaundice. He certainly looked and sounded good enough for Elizabeth to think it would do Peter good to have a job. She was going to star in a television movie called *Malice in Wonderland*, the story of two infamous Hollywood gossip columnists, Hedda Hopper and Louella Parsons, and there would be a bit part for him to play. Quietly, behind the scenes, she arranged with the producer, Jay Benson, to meet Peter and hire him.

I tried to explain to Elizabeth that Peter could not handle the task. He was too far gone to be able to perform. Unfortunately Peter hid his problems well and she did not believe me. Jay Benson went along with the idea of giving him the part as a favour to Elizabeth. Peter was terrified of going before the cameras again, but he did not have the nerve to admit it.

Elizabeth did warn Peter that he had better not screw up this chance. She was going out on a limb for him, and did not want his addictions to get in the way. But Peter only laughed. He found Elizabeth's sobriety extremely funny. She had conquered her addiction and was determined to straighten out her life – she had tapped an inner strength that she was not going to lose for anyone. I was extremely impressed at her courage, but aall he could do was tease her. He would refer to the time when she was a drunk and tell her, 'You used to have a personality. You used to be interesting.'

To give him Dutch courage Peter began to drink heavily, then telephoned his old connections in order to buy marijuana and cocaine. He was not going to disappoint Elizabeth. He was going to do the role. I talked to one of Peter's doctors and told him what was going on. The doctor spoke sternly to Peter, yet it all seemed to be a drama staged for my benefit. It was obvious to me that the doctor was willing to go along with whatever Peter wanted. He did not like Peter's self-destructive behaviour, yet he also did not want to alienate Peter Lawford, the movie star, the brother-in-law of the late Jack Kennedy. I was witnessing what I called the Hollywood 'starfucker' phenomenon, and Peter was going to die because of it.

Peter collapsed from all this renewed self-abuse and had to be taken to Cedars Sinai, where they used vitamins and other treatments to try to lower the toxicity in his body. His liver, of course, was not functioning properly and he was now in serious trouble. However, he was mobile by the time he had to go on the set.

I arrived early in the morning to fetch Peter, knowing that I would have to spend the day on the set with him. To my surprise he was not downstairs waiting for me, though he had been checked out of the hospital. Then I spotted him walking down the street, happy as could be. He told me he had gone for a walk, nothing more. It was only after we had got onto the set that I discovered his walk had been to a nearby drugstore where he was able to buy some small bottles of vodka.

For the first time everyone connected with the show understood what was happening. Peter Lawford was not on that set. In his place was a pathetic shell of a man, someone who could not remember his lines, his cues or why he was there. He was yellow from jaundice, his movements were painfully slow. Gone was the quick study. Gone was the natural movement that convinced people he was a trained dancer. Gone was the consummate professional who could be brilliant in a single take or brilliant twenty times over if he took that many times to get a scene to be perfect.

Elizabeth, extremely upset, came over and whispered that she should have listened to me. Peter could not even say, 'Hello, my name is Tony.' The crew kept glaring at me, as though it was my fault that this shambling creature was on the set. Finally I hid, returning only when his dressings needed changing. Aching for Peter's loss, I took him home at the end of the day, only to watch him fall asleep without dinner.

Peter awakened on Saturday long enough to ask for fresh orange juice. He slept for the rest of the day and seemed about to sleep through Sunday when I risked taking thirty minutes to go to the shops. By the time I returned, Peter was incoherent and there was blood all over the apartment. The telephone was also ringing, though I did not answer it and Peter was incapable of knowing it was even there.

Later I learned that the caller was Jay Benson. He was firing Peter from the show.

I dialled the emergency service, but they had to ask questions before they could sent the paramedics and I didn't think we had that much time. So I got Peter into the car and drove him to Cedars Sinai where they admitted him immediately.

Tests were run on him, and I was told it was safe to go home. The moment I arrived the telephone rang. It was the producer of *Malice in Wonderland.*

'I know what you're going to tell me,' I said, too tired to want to deal with any of this, yet knowing that I had to.

He said, 'Do you want me to say it?'

'No,' I replied. 'Let me tell you something. I'm glad you didn't have to tell him. He's collapsed right now.' It was the first acting job from which Peter had ever been fired.

Then I received a telephone call from the hospital, asking me to return. There was possible internal bleeding. He was heading into a coma and might not make of it.

I was determined to keep Peter alive. I returned to the hospital and talked to him. I wanted him thinking, fighting to stay conscious. I was going to will that man to rally and live, just as he had so many times before.

Our friend Jackie Gayle visited him and I insisted he tell Peter jokes. Peter always loved Jackie's humour. He could be outrageous, vulgar or sophisticated, and Peter would normally roar with laughter. He was a great audience and I knew that Jackie would keep him out of his coma. Peter's subconscious mind would hear the jokes and he would respond as he always did.

Laugh, Peter. God damn it, laugh! I was angry. Peter wasn't laughing. Jackie wasn't doing his job. They were a pair of assholes. Peter was going into a coma. Jackie was doing shtick. And neither was responding to the other. If you're so fucking funny, Jackie Gayle, then why aren't you keeping my husband alive? You play the world and you can't keep one man from going into a coma? What the hell good are you?

Peter was dying. My best friend was dying. The children were alerted. Elizabeth came to see us. A few other friends called in. Faces. Nurses. Doctors. Security

229

personnel. Some were familiar. Others I had never seen before in my life. And a few, whom I was certain I did not know, were people with whom I had been close in the past.

My mind was dulled with emotion and lack of sleep. I would eventually experience sleep psychosis, at which point the exhaustion becomes so great that your body can no longer function normally. The more tired you become, the harder it is to rest, until somehow you break the pattern, collapse or die.

It was almost Christmas and there were cards and decorations hanging in the hospital offices. Every effort was being made to make the stay of those who could not go home as pleasant as possible. Yet I saw none of it.

Peter looked at me, said, 'I'm sorry,' then slipped into a coma. He never spoke again.

The children left to go to Jamaica for the holidays. Many of the friends stopped coming. Reporters and photographers were camping out by the hospitals, trying to get interviews. And hovering everywhere was Ron Wise, the public relations director who was trying to help me through my ordeal. He handled the countless telephone calls that came in, he worked with the press and was available to me twenty-four hours a day. He also encouraged me to look my best in the midst of others, knowing that that is how I really wanted to appear at those times.

Sleep was gained in fits and snatches. I read to Peter. I sat by his bed. I slept in the chair. I wandered the floor and read to him again. He was on a life support machine, yet somehow I was determined that he would make it. His body had been abused so much for so many years, surely if he had not died before he could not die now?

And then, at 8.50 a.m. on Christmas Eve, there was movement. Peter's body rose and suddenly blood rushed from every opening. His heart stopped. His lungs stopped. His cell walls, damaged by the drugs, the alcohol and the periodic malnutrition, could no longer hold the life-sustaining fluid. Peter Lawford was dead.

I held the battered, bloody shell of a man and talked to him for the next two hours. I reviewed our life together, laughing, crying, sharing precious memories with someone who could no longer hear. Finally it was time for the body to be removed to the mortuary, yet it seemed as though he had only been dead for five minutes.

Suddenly there was a whirlwind of activity. The children, informed before they reached Jamaica, had landed at Kennedy and were planning a trip back to Los Angeles immediately. The press was notified and arrangements were made to sneak me out of a door so that I would not have to face anyone.

When I got home there was note on the door which read: 'I love you. Call me if you need me. Mommy.' She had not come to our apartment for eight years. Then there was a telephone call for Jackie Onassis. She was gentle, kind, understanding of the horror that I had witnessed. She had undoubtedly arranged for the hospital to call her the moment of Peter's death, for she apparently knew about the nightmare of blood passing from his body. She mentioned the fact that when her husband was assassinated she had held bits of his brain in her hand. And for a moment we were two women, united in grief, who had shared the experience of the disintegration of human flesh, one by a bullet the other by self-abuse, which most people never know in their lifetime.

There was no rest that night, and on Christmas morning I was to witness Peter's cremation. In the meantime telegrams, letters and cards began coming in from every corner of the world. There were messages of condolence from the Reagans at the White House and from mainland China where Peter's father had been long ago. Heads of state checked in. Fans sent letters. It was as though the world had lost a beloved resource who was not forgotten even though his time as a star had long since passed.

Peter had no clothing for the cremation. I went to Carroll & Company, the only clothing store that was open where I could charge clothing for Peter. He had been raised a gentleman and he was going to go out a gentleman, even if he would only wear the clothes a short time before they were burnt in the flames. Christopher, who was the same size as his father, was impressed with the outfit. He asked if he could have it, but I refused.

I rode to the crematorium in the hearse with Peter's body. He was inside a cardboard box and I climbed in the back to look at him once more. I opened the box, touched him, and felt nothing but a cold, stiff shell. Peter was with me and Peter was gone.

The crematorium horrified me. A man came and took the box, loading it on a gurney and rolling him up a ramp. A fireproof number was placed in the box so that, when he was burned at the same time as other bodies, there would be no chance of misidentifying his ashes. The system actually becomes rather painful when you start thinking about it. We walked up a ramp where I was faced with six giant ovens most of them working. At first I panicked, certain I could not burn his corpse. Then I remembered that it was what Peter wanted, so I gave the go-ahead. Four hours later, Peter's ashes were placed in an urn, the numbered tag assuring me I had the proper remains.

On 26 December a memorial service was held for Peter. Kennedys were there, friends from MGM days an others. A friend of mine put something together for me to wear, and then I found myself on Rodeo Drive where some Italian man draped veiling around my hat. I had no idea who was doing what to me and I certainly did not want to go to the service. Peter would have understood. He hated funerals.

The funeral director explained that I would have to carry the urn to the vault in which the ashes would be placed. Peter would be near Marilyn's remains, which would have amused him. Then the director suggested I take a practice walk with a dummy urn apparently used for such a purpose. Suddenly I felt as though I was participating in a perverted wedding ceremony. I was being led down the aisle in preparation for the actual 'show' scheduled for that evening. It was as though there was going to be a casket filled with the remains of the best man, and perhaps a smaller casket containing a dead bridesmaid. It suddenly seemed perverted, a show for ghouls even though there was nothing abnormal about it.

The actual ceremony took forty-five minutes, in pouring rain. The Lawford children followed until I kissed the urn, then placed it in the crypt. I returned to the limousine, relieved that it was over.

Stan Kamen of the William Morris Agency, which had represented Peter, held a party in a private room at La Scala Restaurant. There were many people from Peter's past and it could have been a beautiful tribute to a man who had once been a major star and a source of income for the agency. The problem was that these were primarily not people who had cared about Peter. They just wanted to be a part of the Kennedy mystique. They had abandoned Peter years earlier, leaving him to wallow in despair except when he could be used to make contact with a member of that family.

I was offered the condolences of people who had refused to return Peter's telephone calls. I was told of his greatness by people who looked upon him as being lower than dogshit when he was no longer a major star. Peter had been self-destructive all his life, yet, with the sole exception of the final small role that Elizabeth Taylor had got for him, he had managed to maintain his professionalism, to perform with competence, so long as anyone wanted him.

Finally I returned home and the Lawford children were able to continue on their Jamaican holiday. The mortuary bill came to $10,000, money I no longer had.

There was no life insurance. Those bank accounts that Peter had failed to strip for drug money had been frozen by creditors.

I was not prepared for life without Peter. I was not prepared for life with Peter, for that matter. I was a scared, vulnerable adolescent when we met. I had travelled. I had worked at jobs requiring me to be far more responsible than my years. I had escaped from physical and emotional abuse, developing a veneer of sophisticated toughness. I had a quick mind, a faster tongue and the ability to curse in two languages. Yet the reality was that I had my own future. I am no longer reacting to a drug-induced crisis. I have not abused my body with endless pills and alcohol as I did in the past. I am looking for a job, for a respite for my countless creditors with whom I am trying to make financial arrangements to meet Peter's obligations. I am beginning to mature, to try to like myself and respect my abilities.

Yet I will never forget Peter Lawford, nor will I ever stop loving him. We were symbiotic in our relationship, dissimilar beings who fed off each other, surviving together, thriving where we could, each keeping the other from hitting bottom for more years than Peter's health should have allowed.

The world lost Peter Lawford, the actor. The Kennedy family lost Peter Lawford, the loving friend of the President and key to Hollywood gossip. The children lost a father who adored them even as he could not reach out to them. But I lost three people when he died – a father figure, my dearest, closest friend, and, in his own perverted way, my lover. I shall miss him always.

Epilogue

Peter's funeral bill of $10,000 remained unpaid in May 1988. The estate had no money but many debts. Back taxes were owed. And my employment had been sporadic at best, never bringing in enough money needed even to pay the interest on the debts. There was no way that I could handle the bill.

Some time after his death the mortuary was sold and pressure was put on me to pay. This was perfectly valid because a mortuary is a business, and expenses were involved just in maintaining a crypt for Peter's ashes.

In May 1988 I was faced with the reality that either the bill would be paid or Peter's remains would have to be removed.

The mortuary was as cooperative as possible, being willing to write off of the debt. I was also deeply touched by the generosity of a number of people who sent me cash and cheques after reading about the problem. These sums, totalling less than $20, were forwarded to the mortuary, though it was a meaningless gesture on my part in the context of a debt of several thousand dollars.

I was becoming distraught. I tried to think objectively about Peter's last wishes. He had not cared about what happened to him, and had suggested I wrap him in a sheet and dump him in a garbage lorry after he was gone. He was half-joking about that, yet more serious about wanting to be placed in the ocean he loved.

Why hadn't I just done that at the start, I wondered. Then I realized that I had been so grief-stricken that I had done what many people do. I had arranged for the most beautiful possible resting-place. His body had been cremated, but his ashes would rest near such old friends as Marilyn Monroe. It was my wish for him, not necessarily his first desire. In fact, if I wanted to be objective about it all, I would have gone into the ocean on a surfboard, then ridden a wave while scattering the ashes to the wind. That action would have fitted his lifestyle.

So I decided to remove Peter's ashes, discovering that approximately $2,500 would have to be paid, plus the cost for arranging to have them scattered over the ocean. When I made contact with the children they decided at this point to pay the bills necessary to keep Peter in the crypt – a relief for me. The Kennedy family just wanted to be certain that I would not consider removing the ashes in the future if I agreed to let them pay the bill. So I could finally relax. Removing the ashes was a trauma I did not wish to face. I was delighted that they were coming through with this final gift for Peter, and I wept happily after I hung up the telephone.

On a Friday I received an affidavit to be signed. It stated, in effect, that once they had paid the bills I would not remove the ashes unless at least two of the children signed an agreement allowing such an action. I was annoyed at the mistrust, yet thrilled for Peter. Of course I would sign.

It was Monday before I had a chance to do anything about the affidavit, and by then it was too late. I received a telephone call from a spokesperson for the children, who said that they had changed their minds and I could do what I wished.

I was shocked and hurt. There was still that great gap between Peter and his children – even in death they had not found any form of relationship. The situation was a sad and tragic one, and I think I wept for them all. I was also livid with anger at he sudden turn-around after they had sent me the form to sign.

Finally the children sent a cheque – $430 to cover the disinterment fee. This would cover only the removal from the crypt of the urn, which would have to be kept in the mortuary office until the remainder of the bills were paid. I could remove Peter, but I was not free to take him anywhere.

I had had it with the Kennedy family. I felt emotionally manipulated, as though their actions were a personal attack against me. It was time for me to take matters into my own hands and arrange for Peter's ashes to be released into the ocean. I talked at length with the mortuary staff and found them most understanding. We finally agreed that I could have the remains to put them in the ocean, despite the outstanding fee.

What happened next remains an embarrassment to this day. It was a nightmare that made headlines throughout the world. I talked about what was happening with some friends of mine who work for the weekly *National Enquirer*, one of America's best-selling tabloids. They realized that this was a strong story and offered to help me with transportation and other costs in exchange. I agreed to let a reporter and photographer be present at the ceremony.

The *National Enquirer* had once been one of the most disreputable papers in the United States, the headlines screaming sordid tales of lust and violence. The stories, though fictitious, were told as if they were factual and fake photographs often accompanied them. But eventually the *Enquirer* was sold and its image changed. The new owner created a mix of unusual but true stories, celebrity anecdotes, consumer information and the like. The paper was no longer an embarrassment, and Hollywood people began using it because of its sudden popularity. Some stars sell stories outright, others leak them in exchange for a finder's fee, and still others, keen for publicity, provide the information free. The staff telephones sources and most subjects and reads them the pieces to ensure accuracy, tape recording the response as proof. Lawsuits have been taken out against the *Enquirer* for inaccurate reporting, but very rarely won. The staff, both writers and photographers, are kind, friendly individuals who, though aggressive when working, understand their paper's past reputation and work to show that they are different. So I decided that the *Enquirer* could have the story. I knew that it would be treated in a dignified, respectful manner, and that once it appeared I would no longer be subject to intense scrutiny by the press at large.

What I did not know was that a man who had learned of the disinterment decided to call the entire Los Angeles area news media. By the time I arrived at the mortuary there were eighty-odd reporters, photographers and television cameramen, three helicopters and countless cars. I was faced with a three-ring circus. I was suddenly terrified and devastated. Had I done the right thing? Should I go ahead with this?

My co-author, Ted Schwarz, had arranged for a private investigator named Dan Stewart, a former Los Angeles homicide detective, to act as my bodyguard. He did not think I needed protection so much as the support which came from knowing that if I had any trouble, someone would be there to help. The urn alone weighed almost seventy-five pounds, and Stewart is six feet, five inches tall. If I became too emotional or was overwhelmed with the task, he would be there to help.

My first reaction, on seeing the mob of pressmen, was to ask the driver of the hired limousine to take me home. But Stewart had seen me when I left my apartment and knew that I was an emotional wreck. He sensed that I would not be able to go ahead with the scattering of the remains if I had to consider it a second time. He knew from talking to my co-author how distraught I was, and encouraged me to stay. From what we all knew at that time, he was right. In hindsight, I regret the action.

What happened next would have been funny in a movie, but it was devastating for me. There were microphones everywhere. Some reporters had small tape recorders with built-in microphones that they jammed into my face. Others used long 'shotgun' types. In their rush, my skirt was caught and lifted by one and my blouse caught and tugged by another. Cameras were shoved towards my face, reporters leaped on my car and tried to get inside, and others tried to wedge it in so I could not get away. Notes begging for an interview were shoved into my hand. People were screaming questions. 'How does it feel, Patricia?' 'Why are you doing this, Patricia?' 'Wouldn't the Kennedys come up with the money, Mrs Lawford?' 'You can tell us, Mrs Lawford. This is really a publicity stunt, isn't it?'

I was numb. The monsignor from my church who had accompanied me, a man whom I relied upon for spiritual guidance, was weeping. I felt as though I had disgraced Peter and cheapened what we were doing. What would have been at best an uncomfortable experience was suddenly a nightmare beyond comprehension or anticipation.

Somehow the crypt was opened, the urn removed and the monsignor led me in prayer. Finally we were able to get away. Then we were on the boat, travelling across the ocean, scattering the ashes. I helped with the sails. I laughed with relief as the bodyguard cracked jokes to keep me from becoming too depressed. And at times I wept bitterly, and Stewart held me in his arms to keep me from collapsing over the side.

It ended eventually, of course. The bodyguard arranged for a decoy car so that we could elude most of the press. The security guards in my building kept reporters away from me. My answering machine handled most of the telephone calls. There were threats of physical harm and threats from crazies. Everyone was embarrassed.

There is only so much you can fight in Hollywood and Beverly Hills, two small towns where truth and reality are perpetually twisted. The newspapers and television stations were filled with stories about the disinterment. I not only made a terrible name for myself but I created a fiasco for Peter.

Had things taken place the way they originally were planned there would have been no trouble. Peter would have wanted me to use my friends from the *National Enquirer* because he felt the same way towards them. He would have been pleased with the disposal of his ashes and touched by the actions of those who had tried to help avoid the trauma. But he would have been angry about the 'zoo' that descended upon us, regarding their actions as unprofessional and without style.

Yet the end result was that people misunderstood what happened. I am ashamed to go back to the major stars, backstage personnel and others who helped with this book. I feel as though I have been disgraced for actions over which I had no control, and I am devastated by that knowledge.

I feel more alone than at any time since Peter's death, though one burden, the pressure over what to do with Peter's remains, has been lifted. And always there is the irony of the boat my friends hired to take me out to sea to scatter the ashes. They simply hired a craft that was comfortable enough, and capable of handling the job. When we left the vessel I glanced back and saw that the last boat ride Peter and I would ever share was on a vessel named *Freedom*.

Postscript

Throughout this book I have talked about my child abuse and that which Peter endured. There is also the fact that I was still an adolescent teenager when I began living with him. Yet these are only explanations for our behaviour, not excuses.

We all make choices in our lives. For Peter and me, the choices were often bad ones. Sometimes they seemed exciting, such as running off with Peter in the first place or experimenting with mood-altering drugs. Sometimes they were made in anger, such as the affairs, a childish reaction to hurt. Sometimes they were made from weakness, my not wanting to face the displeasure that would come from saying no. And always they were foolish, destructive choices that, upon mature, objective appraisal, should not have been made.

I ask for no pity in writing this book. I certainly do not want anyone to see Peter's life or my past as the inevitable result of abusive parents. Too many healthy, active, mature adults have survived similar backgrounds for my situation to be seen as inevitable.

If anything, as a survivor I must now move forward and not repeat the past. To this end I have joined support groups intended to help me understand myself and my past addictions. I am trying to be responsible, to think ahead, to plan, to do anything other than just react to life. I know, in part, that I am currently drug free because my health cannot survive the continued use of cocaine, pain killers, uppers and downers. Yet the fact that I want to live instead of retaining the 'I don't care, what will be will be' attitude that killed Peter and nearly killed me is a positive step.

I am far from perfect, of course. I still want to take the easy way out. I still would rather drink than not. I still may slip and indulge in ways that are again destructive. I still want someone else taking care of me, making decisions for me, shielding me from life.

All I can do is live one day at a time, do my best and not become obsessed with any failures. I am luckier than Peter in that I discoverd my failings earlier. With God's help I will have the maturity to mould my own future rather than let myself be manipulated by my past. I suppose it is fitting that the first man I dated after Peter's death was a politician with a reputation as a ladies' man. It was July 1985, seven months since Peter had died, and I was staying at the Dorchester Hotel. I had been invited there for a tribute to Peter during the time of the release of his last movie, *Where Is Parsifal?*

The introduction to the politician came at what, for me, was the worst possible time. It was early morning when the public relations director of the hotel called and asked me to have lunch with the president of a Hawaiian Hotel, his wife, and a member of the House of Commons she wanted me to meet. The trouble was that I had been out the night before with some friends and had had too much to eat and drink. I felt terrible, looked terrible, and would have preferred to stay in bed with aspirin and a cold compress. However, the public relations director had always been nice to me, and I had to get up for a previous appointment in any case, so I agreed to meet the group for coffee. Anything else would have been impossible.

I have always had a stereotyped image of Members of Parliament. I imagined that they were all quite tall, fat, wore custom-tailored clothing, had florid faces and were unable to express themselves very well. They would be constantly clearing their throats, their speech would be peppered with such phrases as 'Tut-tut', 'Harrumph', and similar sounds that would make them seem like pompous idiots. I was not thrilled by the idea of having to meet such a character.

I entered the dining room wearing sun glasses, trying to avoid moving too fast because I still did not feel well. Then I made my way to the party where I saw a middle-aged, tall, dashing, handsome man. He was an MP, but he shattered my stereotype.

There was an instant attraction between us. We talked, oblivious to everyone else at the table. I realized immediately that I really liked the man, an emotion I had not experienced since Peter's death.

At first the conversation was all business. He knew of Peter's work, respected him, and wanted to get him a blue plaque for his childhood home in Half Moon Street. Normally a person has to have been dead for a hundred years before they are eligible for such an honour. However, since Half Moon Street had no blue plaques at the time, no one else famous having been born there, the MP felt that he would be able to arrange for one through a special Act of Parliament. There apparently had been precedents for such an action and he saw no reason why there should be a problem. As it turned out, the plaque was not approved, though I was grateful for his efforts.

I returned to my room after talking with the MP and called a friend to tell her how impressed I had been with him. Ten minutes after I hung up, I received a call from him. He knew that I had never been to the Houses of Parliament and invited me there for dinner. I was to go through the bomb check security at St Stephen's Gate where he would meet me following the clearance. Then we would proceed to eat in the House of Commons.

The experience was incredible. I had been in the White House and in other major government build-ings, yet nothing could compare with the sense of history I felt in the Houses of Parliament. I looked at the damage from the war, I thought of Churchill walk-ing the halls, and generally was overwhelmed by it all.

That night we dined on the terrace, admiring a beautiful view overlooking the Thames. The utensils, toothpicks, champagne, and everything else were marked with statements indicating that they were approved by Parliament. Everything there had to be authorized by Parliament, a situation I found fascinating. I tried to nick every marked item I could to take home as a souvenir.

The dinner was wonderful. A woman played the harp while we watched boaters floating down the river looking in awe at the building and the other MPs who were dining there. The Lords were wearing their robes, the members of the House of Commons were dressed in suits.

My MP laughed as he watched the looks of reverence on the faces of the people floating by on the river. 'Just wait a while,' he said. 'They're going to be drinking for the next couple of hours and, when they come back, they're going to be sloshed enough for their true feelings to come out.' And sure enough, when the boaters returned, the obviously drunk passengers hooted at the building and made obscene gestures.

As the dinner was coming to an end, he excused himself and told me to order a drink. 'I have to go to a three-way whip,' he said.

What was happening, I wondered. A three-way whip sounded like something Peter would have enjoyed. I was wondering what kind of perverted sado-masochistic sex act he was going to experience when he explained that the term referred to a complex voting procedure used by Members of Parliament. He simply had to register his vote on some issue and then would return. It was apparently a routine part of the MP's day. The men were constantly running in and out when motions arose.

Later during my stay, he took me to an Indian restaurant where he was a regular customer who had even had a drink named after him. He was proud of that honour and showed me a card with a photograph of the drink, advertising its availability. 'How many men have a drink named after them?' he asked.

'How many would want one?' I replied.

He arranged for us to use the entire lower dining area that was secluded from the rest of the facility. I don't know how he did it or what he paid to keep other eaters out, but when the dinner was over, he took pillows from the seating areas, arranged them for our comfort, and proceeded to seduce me. The waiters didn't reappear until well after we were finished and dressed.

The relationship was intense but short-lived. We were together constantly, despite him being at the tail end of an affair with an actress who he described as insanely jealous as well as being in the process of getting a divorce. When I returned to the United States we talked by telephone every day for two months. Then our conversations became weekly and, finally, we had to admit that the great physical separation made the intensity impossible to retain. His work took him to Ireland and Canada, but not to Los Angeles. Still, it was so delightful, I sometimes wonder what would happen if I decided to return to England to make it my home.

All Futura Books are available at your bookshop or newsagent, or can be ordered from the following address: Futura Books, Cash Sales Department, P.O. Box 11, Falmouth, Cornwall TR10 9EN.

Please send cheque or postal order (no currency), and allow 60p for postage and packing for the first book plus 25p for the second book and 15p for each additional book ordered up to a maximum charge of £1.90 in U.K.

B.F.P.O. customers please allow 60p for the first book, 25p for the second book plus 15p per copy for the next 7 books, thereafter 9p per book

Overseas customers, including Eire, please allow £1.25 for postage and packing for the first book, 75p for the second book and 28p for each subsequent title ordered.